WHOOPS!

'Bang on the money' *Independent*

'Wickedly funny' *The New York Times*

'Terrific . . . There is no better guide to the crazy world of high finance' *GQ*

'A lively lay reader's guide to the financial crisis, written by a novelist who sought to educate himself about banking and its failures. Funny and pointed, it exposes the gulf between the two cultures of modern Britain: financial and non-financial' Ed Crooks, Summer Reads, *Financial Times*

'Beautifully written . . . Entertaining and profoundly anger-inducing . . . the most readable explanation yet' *Evening Standard*

'An elegant, witty and – virtually a miracle to my mind – comprehensible account of the credit crunch' *Sunday Telegraph*

'This is an excellent book for anyone wondering what the hell is going on. Triple A, as the credit ratings agencies might say. Only this time they would be right' *Irish Times*

'Masterly . . . its strength lies in its wit, and Lanchester's underlying outrage' *The Times*

'A thoroughly entertaining guide to the dominant concern of our times . . . it is a supremely readable, free of jargon and accessible to anyone' *Daily Express*

'Lanchester pulls no punches' *Financial Times*

'There have been books by economists, bankers and financial analysts. The great virtue of this one is that it is by none of these . . . one of the most thoughtful and incisive volumes so far on the debacle' *Scotsman*

'Like a modern Hazlitt, his prose leaps off the tramlines and crashes through the barriers of polite expression, in order to reach the truth' *New Statesman*

'John Lanchester's newfound mission: to explain the world of finance to the general public . . . The result is the perfect read for anyone still wondering what went wrong and why. Unless you'd rather they didn't know' *Bloomberg*

'Literary and profound . . . a master explainer with an excellent grasp of sophisticated finance' Christopher Caldwell, *The Daily Beast*

'A sober message lurking among Lanchester's delightful wordplay, and it deserves attention by everyone who cares to understand where we are, how we got here and who is responsible' John Lawrence Reynolds, *Globe and Mail*

'Lanchester has turned that fascination – coupled with a kind of astonished anger – into a lucid, conversational account of the crisis designed for non-financial types and helpfully leavened with jokes, swearing and interesting asides' Quentin Webb, Reuters

ABOUT THE AUTHOR

John Lanchester is a journalist, novelist and winner of the Whitbread First Novel Award. He is a regular contributor to the *London Review of Books* and the *New Yorker*, with a monthly column in *Esquire*. John's piece on our love affair with the City, 'Cityphilia', generated much response on its publication in January 2008 and indeed predicted a worldwide crash based on the misuse of financial derivatives. In October 2008 he charted the crisis as it had developed over the year in 'Cityphobia', which also attracted much attention as a piece that explained not only what had happened, but how we felt about it. John was raised in South-East Asia and now lives in London.

Whoops!

*Why Everyone Owes Everyone and
No One Can Pay*

JOHN LANCHESTER

PENGUIN BOOKS

PENGUIN BOOKS

Published by the Penguin Group
Penguin Books Ltd, 80 Strand, London WC2R ORL, England
Penguin Group (USA), Inc., 375 Hudson Street, New York, New York 10014, USA
Penguin Group (Canada), 90 Eglinton Avenue East, Suite 700, Toronto, Ontario, Canada M4P 2Y3
(a division of Pearson Penguin Canada Inc.)
Penguin Ireland, 25 St Stephen's Green, Dublin 2, Ireland (a division of Penguin Books Ltd)
Penguin Group (Australia), 250 Camberwell Road, Camberwell, Victoria 3124, Australia
(a division of Pearson Australia Group Pty Ltd)
Penguin Books India Pvt Ltd, 11 Community Centre, Panchsheel Park, New Delhi – 110 017, India
Penguin Group (NZ), 67 Apollo Drive, Rosedale, North Shore 0632, New Zealand
(a division of Pearson New Zealand Ltd)
Penguin Books (South Africa) (Pty) Ltd, 24 Sturdee Avenue, Rosebank, Johannesburg 2196, South Africa

Penguin Books Ltd, Registered Offices: 80 Strand, London WC2R ORL, England

www.penguin.com

First published by Allen Lane 2010
Published with new material in Penguin Books 2010
1

Copyright © John Lanchester, 2010

The moral right of the author has been asserted

Printed in Great Britain by Clays Ltd, St Ives plc

A CIP catalogue record for this book is available from the British Library

978-0-141-04571-9

www.greenpenguin.co.uk

Penguin Books is committed to a sustainable future
for our business, our readers and our planet.
The book in your hands is made from paper
certified by the Forest Stewardship Council.

For Miranda and Finn and Jesse

When the capital development
of a country becomes a by-product
of the activities of a casino, the
job is likely to be ill-done.

John Maynard Keynes,
*The General Theory of Employment,
Interest, and Money*

It's such a fine line between
stupid and clever.

David St Hubbins,
This is Spinal Tap

Contents

Introduction

Annie Hall is a film with many great moments, and for me the best of them is the movie's single scene with Annie's younger brother Duane Hall, played by Christopher Walken, the first of his long, brilliant career of cinema weirdos. Visiting the Hall family home, Alvy Singer – that's Woody Allen – bumps into Duane, who immediately shares a fantasy: 'Sometimes when I'm driving . . . on the road at night . . . I see two headlights coming toward me. Fast. I have this sudden impulse to turn the wheel quickly, head-on into the oncoming car. I can anticipate the explosion. The sound of shattering glass. The . . . flames rising out of the flowing gasoline.' It's Alvy's reply which makes the scene: 'Right. Well, I have to – I have to go now, Duane, because I, I'm due back on the planet Earth.'

I've never shared Duane Hall's wish to turn across the road into the oncoming headlights. I have to admit, though, that I have sometimes had a not-too-distant thought. It's a thought which never hits me in town, or in traffic, or when there's anyone else in the car, but when I'm on my own in the country, zooming down an empty road, with the radio on, and everything is moving free and clear, as it hardly ever is with today's traffic, but when it is, I sometimes have a fleeting thought, one I've never acted on and hope I never will. The thought is this: what would happen if I chose this moment to put the car into reverse?

When you ask a car buff that, the first thing they do is to give you a funny look. Then they give you another funny look. Then they explain that what would happen is that the car's engine would basically explode: bits of it would burst through other bits, rods would fly through the air, carburettors would burst into fragments, there would be incredible noise and smell and smoke and you would swerve off the road and crash with the certainty of serious injury and the high probability of death. These explanations are sufficiently convincing that I find that the thought of putting the car into reverse only flits across my mind very temporarily, for about half a second at a time, say once every two or three years. I'm sure it's something I'll never do.

For the first years of the new millennium, the whole planet was zooming along, doing the equivalent of 70 on a clear road on a sunny day. Between 2000 and 2006, public discourse in the western world was dominated by the election of George W. Bush, the horror of 9/11, the 'global war on terror' and the wars in Afghanistan and Iraq. But while all that was happening, something momentous was taking place, not quite unnoticed, but attracting bizarrely little notice: the world was almost doubling in wealth. In 2000, the total GDP of earth – the sum total of all the economic activity on the planet – was \$36 trillion.* By the end of 2006, it was \$70 trillion. In the developed world, so much attention was given to the bust in dot-com shares in 2000 – the 'greatest destruction of capital in the history of the world', as it was called at the time – that no one noticed the way the western economies bounced back. The stock market was relatively stagnant, for reasons I'll go into later, but other sectors of the economy were booming. So was the rest of the planet. An editorial in *The Economist* in 1999 pointed out that the price of oil was now down to \$10 a barrel, and issued a solemn warning: it might not stay there; there were reasons for thinking the price of oil might go to \$5 a barrel. Ha!

---

* Gross Domestic Product, or GDP, which will be mentioned quite a few times in this story, sounds complicated but isn't: it's nothing more than the value of all the goods and services produced in an economy. GDP per capita, measuring the individual piece of the country's pie, is the standard measure for prosperity.

By July of 2008 the price of oil had risen to $147.7 and as a result the oil-producing countries were awash with cash. From the Arab world to Russia to Venezuela, the treasury departments of all oil-producing countries resembled the scene in *The Simpsons* in which Monty Burns and his assistant Smithers pick up wads of cash and throw them at each other while shouting 'Money fight!' The demand for oil was so avid because large sections of the developing world, especially India and China, were undergoing unprecedented levels of economic growth. Both countries suddenly had a hugely expanding, highly consuming new middle class. China's GDP was averaging growth of 10.8 per cent a year, India's 8.9 per cent. In fifteen years, India's middle class, using a broad definition of the term meaning the section of the population who had escaped from poverty, grew from 147 million to 264 million; China's went from 174 million to 806 million – arguably the greatest economic achievement anywhere on earth, ever. Chinese personal income grew by 6.6 per cent a year from 1978 to 2004, four times as fast as the world average. Thirty million Chinese children are having piano lessons. Two-fifths of all Indian secondary school boys have regular after-school tuition. When you have two and a quarter billion people living in countries whose economies are booming in that way, you are living on a planet with a whole new economic outlook. Hundreds of millions of people are measurably richer, and have the new expectations to match. So oil is up, manufacturing is up, the price of commodities – the stuff which goes to make stuff – is up, the economy of (almost) the entire planet is booming. Who knows, optimists think, with the global economy growing at this rate, we can perhaps begin to think seriously about meeting the United Nations' Millennium Development Goals such as halving the proportions of hungry people, and of people whose income is less than $1 a day, by 2015.[1] That seemed utopian at the time the goals were set, but with the world $34 trillion richer, it suddenly looks as if this unprecedented target might be achieved.

And then, it was as if the global economy went out one day and decided it was zooming along so well, there'd never be a better moment to try that thing of putting the car into reverse. The result . . . well, out of what seemed to most people a clear blue sky, the clearest blue sky ever, there was a colossal wreck. That left an awful lot of people wondering one simple thing: what happened?

I've been following the economic crisis for more than two years now. I began working on the subject as part of the background to a novel, and soon realized that I had stumbled across the most interesting story I've ever found. While I was beginning to work on it, the bank Northern Rock blew up, and it became clear that, as I wrote at the time, 'If our laws are not extended to control the new kinds of super-powerful, super-complex, and potentially super-risky investment vehicles, they will one day cause a financial disaster of global-systemic proportions.' I also wrote, apropos the obvious bubble in property prices, that 'you would be forgiven for thinking that some sort of crash is imminent.' I was both right and too late, because all the groundwork for the crisis had already been done – though the sluggishness of the world's governments, in not preparing for the great unravelling of autumn 2008, was then and still is stupefying. But this is the first reason why I wrote this book: because what's happened is extraordinarily interesting. It is an absolutely amazing story, full of human interest and drama, one whose byways of mathematics, economics and psychology are both central to the story of the last decades and mysteriously unknown to the general public. We have heard a lot about the 'two cultures' of science and the arts – we heard a particularly large amount about it in 2009, because it was the fiftieth anniversary of the speech during which C. P. Snow first used the phrase. But I'm not sure the idea of a huge gap between science and the arts is as true as it was half a century ago – it's certainly true, for instance, that a general reader who wants to pick up an education in the fundamentals of science will find it easier than ever before. It seems to me that there is a much bigger gap between the world of finance and that of the general public, and that there is a need to narrow that gap, if members of the financial industry are not to be a kind of priesthood, administering to their own mysteries, and feared and resented by the rest of us. Many bright, literate people have no idea about all sorts of economic basics, of a type that financial insiders take as elementary facts about how the world works. I am an outsider to finance and economics, and my hope is that I can talk across that gulf.

There is a general sense of needing to understand what has happened. It's difficult to accept the reality that in a downturn this sharp, in face of an economic crisis so systemic, we are no longer in control of crucial aspects of our lives. One way to reassert a degree of control is to try to understand what's happened. It gives us back a sense of agency. My need to understand is the same as yours, whoever you are. That's one of the strangest ironies of this story: after decades in which the ideology of the western world was personally and economically individualistic we've suddenly been hit by a crisis which shows in the starkest terms that whether we like it or not – and there are large parts of it that you would have to be crazy to like – we're all in this together. The aftermath of the crisis is going to dominate the economics and politics of our societies for at least a decade to come. It's important that we try to understand it, and begin to think about what's next.

1. The Cashpoint Moment

As a child, I was frightened of cashpoint machines. Specifically, I was frightened of the first cashpoint I ever saw, the one outside the imposing headquarters of the Hongkong and Shanghai Bank, at 1 Queen's Road Central, Hong Kong. This would have been around 1970, when I was eight. My father, being an employee of the bank, was an early adopter of the cashpoint, which stood just to one side of the building's iconic bronze lions, but every time I saw him use it I panicked. What if the machine got its sums wrong and took all our money? What if the machine took someone else's money by mistake, and my father went to prison? What if the machine said it was giving him only ten Hong Kong dollars but actually took much more out of his account – some unimaginably large sum, like fifty or a hundred dollars? The freedom with which the machine coughed up its cash, and the invitation to go straight out and spend it, seemed horribly reckless. The flow of money, from our account out through the machine and then into the world, just seemed too easy. My dad would stand there grimly tapping in his PIN number while I hung on to his arm and begged him to stop.

My scaredy-cat eight-year-old self was on to something. The sheer frictionlessness with which money moves around the world is frightening; it can induce a kind of vertigo. This can happen when you are reading the financial news and suddenly feel that you have no grip on what these numbers actually mean – what those millions and billions and trillions actually represent, how to get hold of them in your mind. (Try the following thought experiment, suggested by the mathematician John

Allen Paulos in his book *Innumeracy*.[2] Without doing the calcu-
lation, guess how long a million seconds is. Now try to guess
the same for a billion seconds. Ready? A million seconds is less
than twelve days; a billion is almost thirty-two years.) Or it can
happen when you look at a bank statement and contemplate
the terrible potency of those strings of digits, their ability to
dictate everything from what you eat to where you live – the
abstract numerals whose consequences are the least abstract
thing in the world. Or it can happen when the global flow of
capital suddenly hits you personally – when your apparently
thriving employer goes out of business owing to a problem
with credit, or your mortgage loan jumps unpayably upwards
– and you think: just what is this money stuff anyway? I can
see its effects – I can thumb a banknote, flip a coin – but what
is it, actually? What do these abstract numbers stand for? What
is the thing that's being represented? Wouldn't it be reassuring
if it was more like a physical thing and less like an idea? And
then the thought fades: money is what it always was, just there,
a fundamental fact of the world, something whose coming and
going is predictable in the way that waves are predictable on a
beach: sometimes the tide is in, sometimes the tide is out, but
at least you know that the basic patterns of its movement operate under known rules.

And then something happens to change your sense of how the
world works. For Rakel Stefánsdóttir, a young Icelandic woman
studying for a Master's degree in arts and cultural management
at the University of Sussex in Brighton, it happened early in
October 2008. She stuck her card in the wall to take out some
cash and the machine told her that the funds weren't available.
Rakel thought nothing of it. 'I know it goes through the trans-
atlantic telephone line and that sometimes has problems, so I
thought it must be that.' A day or so earlier she had paid her
first term's school fees on her card; she had been working in the

theatre for a number of years before going back to do this MA degree, and she was comfortably solvent.

We've all had the experience of sticking our card in the wall and not getting any money out of the cashpoint machine, because we don't have any money in our account. But what Rakel, and thousands of other Icelanders that day, were experiencing was something much stranger and more unsettling. Her cashpoint card was blanking her not because she didn't have the money, but because the bank didn't. In fact it wasn't just that the bank didn't have enough money, it was the *Apocalypse Now* scenario: her card wasn't working because Iceland had run out of money. On 6 October the government closed the banks and froze the movement of any capital outside the country because it was on the verge of going broke. By the time Rakel's credit-card payment for her term's fees cleared, one day later, the Icelandic króna had collapsed and the amount she shelled out had increased by 40 per cent. It took three weeks for Rakel to regain access to her bank account, and by that time it had become clear that her course of studies was unaffordable. She's now back home in Reykjavik, out of work, her entire Plan A for her future abandoned. 'What angers me most about our former government here', she says now, 'is that they didn't have the decency to be ashamed.'

That's what can happen when a country's banks go bad. Some of the detail of the Icelandic case is exotic: basically, a small group of rich and powerful people sold assets back and forwards to each other and created a grotesque bubble of phoney wealth. 'Thirty or forty people did this, and the whole country is paying for it,' a Reykjavik cab driver told me – and I've yet to meet an Icelander who disagrees with the thought. But although a small group of people were ultimately responsible for the bubble, the whole country was caught up in it, as a huge wave of cheap credit lifted Iceland into a kind of economic fantasyland. The banks were at the heart of this process. Iceland's banking sector had been state owned until 2001, when the economically liberal Independent Party privatized it. The result was explosive growth – fake growth, but explosive. A country with 300,000 people – the population of Brighton – and no natural resources except thermal energy and fish stocks suddenly developed a gigantic banking sector whose assets were twelve times bigger than the whole of the economy. There should have been a warning sign in the coinage, which is based on fish: the 50 cent coin has a crab, the one króna a salmon, the ten krónur a school of capelin, the 100 krónur a plaice. Thumbing the coins, you think: these guys know a lot about fish; about banking, maybe not so much.

But no one paid any attention to that. Credit was so cheap it seemed effectively free. I spoke to Valgarður Bragason, a mason, who bought two houses and a plot of land, taking out three different mortgages to the tune of about £600,000, on the basis of conversations with the bank which never lasted more than fifteen minutes. One of the loans was denominated not in Icelandic krónur, which had high interest rates, but in a basket of five different foreign currencies. This might sound like a crazy thing to have done – but in Iceland and elsewhere, in the early years of the new century, the normal rules of personal finance had been suspended. Yes, it's true that here as elsewhere many consumers and borrowers were personally irresponsible; but then, they were encouraged to be. All across the economically liberal world, the banks treated financial irresponsibility as a valuable commodity, almost as a natural resource, to be lovingly groomed and cultivated. Cheap credit was everywhere: cold calls from lenders and letters with pre-filled credit card applications arrived near-daily, and when I phoned my own bank, Barclays, before I was offered the option to get my account details or talk to anyone, a pre-recorded message invited me to take out a new loan. Borrowers were urged to gorge on cheap credit, like geese being stuffed to create foie gras. 'I was trying to be cautious,' one friend told me, 'but my financial adviser said, it's like when the road is clear ahead of you, it's just silly not to put your foot down. So I put my foot down.' Him and millions of others.

For a while, Iceland looked like a modern economic miracle. Then reality intruded, and the Icelandic economy crashed in the same manner that Mike Campbell went broke in *The Sun Also Rises*: 'two ways, gradually then suddenly'. A slow decline in the króna in early 2008 was made much worse by the fact that so many Icelanders had those foreign-currency loans: 40,500 of them, in fact, to a total value of 115 billion krónur, about £30,000 each at the time. (Most of this money seems to have been spent on fancy cars.) Forty thousand people is a lot of people in a country with a population of only 300,000. They were grievously exposed by the decline in value of the króna, because when the króna went south, the cost of their loans went violently north. The first nine months of 2008 were a financial bad dream, one which abruptly and irrevocably became real when, on 6 October, the Prime Minister of Iceland, Geir Haarde, went on television to tell people, convolutedly and without accepting any responsibility, that his country was effectively bankrupt. The banks were closing and all Iceland's foreign reserves were frozen, except for vital needs such as food, fuel and medicine. And that's what left Rakel Stefánsdóttir and hundreds like her standing in the street, frowning at their bank cards and wondering why they seemed so suddenly to have run out of cash. It's just as well none of them yet knew the real picture. Iceland's banks had grown so big so fast that the banking system was, in a much used phrase, 'an elephant balancing on a mouse's back'. The banks' overseas assets were frozen, a process which began when the UK government used anti-terrorist legislation to prevent the movement of Icelandic banks' money out of the country. Icelanders are still cross about that: in Reykjavik I came across a t-shirt with a picture of the British Prime Minister and the slogan, 'Brown is

the colour of poo'. A bit harsh. But they're entitled to be angry
with somebody, because the implosion of Iceland's banks left
them exposed to losses of £116,000 for every man, woman and
child in the country.

How did we get here? How did we get from an economy in which
banks and credit function the way they are supposed to, to this place
we're in now, the Reykjavikization of the world economy? As I
will argue, the crisis was based on a problem, a mistake, a failure
and a culture; but before it was any of those things, it arose from a
climate – and the climate was that which followed the capitalist
world's victory over communism, and the fall of the Berlin Wall.

   This was especially apparent to me because I grew up in Hong
Kong at the time when it was the most unbridled free-market
economy in the world. Hong Kong was the economic Wild West.
There were no rules, no taxes (well, eventually there was a top-
rate tax of 15 per cent), no welfare state, no guarantee of
healthcare or schooling. Shanty-towns sprawled halfway up the
hillsides on Hong Kong island; the inhabitants of those shanties
had no electricity or running water or medicine or education for
their children. Completely unregulated sweat-shop factories were
a significant part of the colony's economy. The ugly edge of
no-rules capitalism was everywhere apparent. But the ways in
which that same capitalism created growth and wealth were everywhere apparent too – and it was impossible not to notice that this
devil-take-the-hindmost free-for-all system was something people
were risking their lives to try. Refugees from communist China
swam, crawled and smuggled themselves into Hong Kong in every
imaginable way, and they regularly died in the attempt. If they
did get across the border, the rule was that they were sent back
when caught, unless they got as far as Boundary Street in Kowloon,
at which point they had the right to remain. There was something
horribly vivid about that rule, like a grown-up version of a child's

game: get to Home and you're safe. Otherwise, back to tyranny. But there was no mistaking the way Hong Kong shone as a place of hope and opportunity to the people who were trying to get there – and the realization that what they were trying to get to wasn't the place so much as the system. The land and people were the same; only the system was different. So the system must be something of extraordinary power. Even a child could see that. You could see it mainly in the sheer speed of change. It was a regular event to go round a corner and experience the jolt of not knowing where the hell you were, because some regular landmark had disappeared. And as for communist China, prior to its opening up to travellers from 1979, it was a subject of fear and wonder and legend. It was something visitors were always taken to see, the furthest point in the New Territories, from which you could look out into China. On the Hong Kong side was a Gurkha observation post on a hill. You looked out over paddy fields, a river and not much else. Now, go and stand on the same spot, and you are looking at Shenzhen, the fastest-growing city in China, with a population of nine million – in a place where there were literally no buildings thirty years ago.

At that time, Hong Kong was like an experiment, a lab test in free-market capitalism. Circumstances of history and demographics had conspired to make it a global one-off. Britain, in particular, seemed much slower, more cautious, more regulated, warier of change. But in the three decades after I left Hong Kong, it was as if there were a kind of reverse takeover, in which Hong Kong's rules took over the rest of the world. Instead of being a special case, the unbridled and unregulated operation of the free market became the new normal. It wasn't so much that this version of capitalism won the argument as that it won by sheer force: countries which had adopted it were growing their economies faster than those that weren't. You can't accurately measure subjective changes in the texture of people's experiences, but you can measure growth in GDP, and the evidence from GDP was irrefutable. With Ronald Reagan in power in the US and Mrs Thatcher in power in the UK, a Hong Kongite version of free-market capitalism took over the world. I couldn't go home again, but in some important respects it made no difference, because home was coming to me.

The version of capitalism which spread so thoroughly around the world had its ideological underpinnings from Adam Smith, via Friedrich Hayek and Milton Friedman, and tended to act as if there were a fundamental connection between capitalism and democracy. Subsequent events, I believe, have shown that to be untrue – but that's a whole argument, a whole different book, in itself. Suffice it to say that this version of capitalism, often dubbed the Anglo-Saxon model, spread around the world.* The formula involved liberalization of markets, deregulation of the economy and especially the financial sector, privatization of state assets, low taxes and the lowest possible amount of state spending. The state's role was seen as being to get out of the way of the wealth-creating power of individuals and companies. The US and the UK were the global cheerleaders for these policies, and their success in growing GDP led to their adoption in amended forms in New Zealand, Australia, Ireland, Spain (to an extent), Iceland, Russia, Poland and elsewhere. A version of these policies is imposed by the IMF when it goes into countries which need financial assistance. Measurable growth in GDP tends to follow the adoption of these policies; so does measurable growth in inequality.

For Marxists, and for a certain kind of anti-corporatist, anti-globalizing voice on the left, this kind of capitalism 'sowed the

---

* I use the phrase 'Anglo-Saxon' in this book because it's standard terminology, but it is in fact a horribly misleading term, because so many of the people advocating and pursuing the free-market policies aren't, in point of fact, Anglo-Saxon at all. 'Anglo-American' would be slightly more accurate, but it hasn't caught on.

seeds of its own destruction'. Marx's argument in using that phrase was that as workers were increasingly brought together in factories they would have increasing opportunities to observe how they were exploited, and also to organize against that exploitation. A more modern view would be that free-market capitalism has an inherent propensity for inequality and for cycles of boom-and-bust – there's an extensive body of work studying these cycles. We can note that, in the current case, the practice fits the theory. The biggest boom in seventy years turned straight into the biggest bust. The rest of this book tells the story of how that happened, but there was one essential precursor to all the subsequent events, without which the explosion and implosion would not have occurred in the form they did: and that was the fall of the Berlin Wall, the collapse of the Soviet Union and the end of the Cold War.

Explicit arguments about the conflict between the West and the communist bloc were never especially profitable. The camps were too entrenched; the larger philosophical issues tended to be boiled off until nothing but the residue of party politics remained. On the right, it was so obvious that the communist regimes were mass-murdering prison states that there was nothing further of profit to be discussed. On the left, it was equally clear that capitalism had its own long list of crimes to its name; that it would always make a fetish of capital ahead of the interests of human beings; and that by contrast the socialist countries were at least thinking about, or acting out the possibility of, alternatives to that model, even if they were doing it wrong. But I've always felt that both schools of thought miss a critical point. The socialist-bloc countries had grave, irredeemable flaws; the western liberal democracies are the most admirable societies that have ever existed. There is no 'moral equivalence', as it used to be called, between them. However – and this is the uncomfortable move in the argument, the one which outrages both the old right and the old left

– the population of the west benefited from the existence, the policies and the example of the socialist bloc. For decades there was the equivalent of an ideological beauty contest between the capitalist west and the communist east, both of them vying to look as if they offered their citizens the better, fairer way of life. The result in the east was oppression; the result in the west was free schooling, universal healthcare, weeks of paid holiday and a consistent, across-the-board rise in opportunities and rights. In western Europe, the existence of local parties with a strong and explicit admiration for the socialist model created a powerful impetus to show that ordinary people's lives were better under capitalist democracy. In America, the equivalent pressures were far fainter – which is why American workers have, to Europeans, grotesquely limited holiday time (two weeks a year), no free healthcare and a level of life expectancy lower than that of Europe.

And then the good guys won, the beauty contest came to an end and so did the decades of western progress in relation to equality and individual rights. In the USA, the median income – the number bang in the middle of the earnings curve – has for workers stayed effectively unchanged since the 1970s, while inequality of income between the top and the bottom has risen sharply. Since 1970, the highest paid fifth of US earners have grown 60 per cent better paid. Everyone else is paid 10 per cent less.[3] In the 1970s, Americans and Europeans worked about the same amount of hours per year; now Americans work almost twice as much.[4] That's the case for the people in the middle: for the people at the top, and especially for the people at the very top, it's different: between 1980 and 2007, the richest 0.1 per cent of Americans saw their income grow 700 per cent.[5]

Here's a way of thinking about the change since the fall of the Wall. One of the most vivid consequences was the abolition of the ban on torture which had previously been a central characteristic of the democratic world's self-definition. Previously, when the west did bad things, it chose to deny having done them or to do them under the cover of darkness, or to have proxies do them on its behalf. Corrupt regimes linked to the west might commit crimes such as torture and imprisonment without due process, but when the crimes came to light, the relevant governments did everything they could to deny and cover up the charges – the crimes were considered to be shameful things. With the end of the ideological beauty contest, that changed. Consider the issue of waterboarding. At the Nuremberg tribunals it was an indictable offence: a Japanese officer, Yukio Osano, was sentenced to fifteen years' hard labour for waterboarding a US civilian. During the Vietnam war, US forces would occasionally use waterboarding – but when they were found out, there was a scandal. In January 1968 the *Washington Post* ran a photograph of an American soldier waterboarding a North Vietnamese captive: there was uproar and he was court-martialled. With the end of the Cold War and the beginning of the 'war on terror', waterboarding became an explicitly endorsed tool of US security. (And of British security too, by extension.) At a time when the democratic world was preoccupied by demonstrating its moral superiority to the communist bloc, that would never have happened.

The same goes for the way in which the financial sector was allowed to run out of control. It was a series of events which took place not in a vacuum but in a climate. That climate was one of unchallenged victory for the capitalist system, a clear ideological hegemony of a type which had never existed before: it was the first moment when capitalism was unthreatened as the world's dominant political-economic system. Under those circumstances, it could have been predicted that the financial sector, which presides over the operation of capitalism, should be in a position to begin rewarding itself with a disproportionate piece of the economic pie. There was no global antagonist to point at and jeer at the rise in the number and size of the fat cats;

there was no embarrassment about allowing the rich to get so much richer so very quickly. With the financial sector's direct ownership of capitalism, great fortunes began to be made by employees, doing nothing other than their jobs – jobs which, in the case of bankers, involve taking on risks, usually with other people's borrowed money. To make more money, and earn more bonuses (which are usually 60 per cent of an investment banker's pay), it's simple, you just take on more risk. The upside is the upside, and the downside – well, it increasingly came to seem that for the bankers themselves there wasn't one. In 'The Quiet Coup', a brilliant piece in May 2009's *Atlantic*, Simon Johnson, a former chief economist at the International Monetary Fund – where his job had involved knocking heads together in self-bankrupted kleptocracies – explained that this process was a vital part of 'how the US became a banana republic'.

The financial industry has not always enjoyed such favored treatment. But for the past 25 years or so, finance has boomed, becoming ever more powerful. The boom began with the Reagan years, and it only gained strength with the deregulatory policies of the Clinton and George W. Bush administrations. Several other factors helped fuel the financial industry's ascent. [Federal Reserve chairman] Paul Volcker's monetary policy in the 1980s, and the increased volatility in interest rates that accompanied it, made bond trading much more lucrative. The invention of securitization, interest-rate swaps, and credit-default swaps greatly increased the volume of transactions that bankers could make money on. And an aging and increasingly wealthy population invested more and more money in securities, helped by the invention of the IRA and the 401(k) plan.* Together, these developments vastly increased the profit opportunities in financial services.

* These are tax-free wrappers for stock-market investments and pensions, analogous to Britain's ISAs and personal pension plans.

Not surprisingly, Wall Street ran with these opportunities. From 1973 to 1985, the financial sector never earned more than 16 percent of domestic corporate profits. In 1986, that figure reached 19 percent. In the 1990s, it oscillated between 21 percent and 30 percent, higher than it had ever been in the postwar period. This decade, it reached 41 percent. Pay rose just as dramatically. From 1948 to 1982, average compensation in the financial sector ranged between 99 percent and 108 percent of the average for all domestic private industries. From 1983, it shot upward, reaching 181 percent in 2007.

The great wealth that the financial sector created and concentrated gave bankers enormous political weight – a weight not seen in the U.S. since the era of J. P. Morgan (the man). In that period, the banking panic of 1907 could be stopped only by coordination among private-sector bankers: no government entity was able to offer an effective response. But that first age of banking oligarchs came to an end with the passage of significant banking regulation in response to the Great Depression; the reemergence of an American financial oligarchy is quite recent.[6]

Accompanying this increase in wealth has been an increase in political muscle. The rich are always listened to more than the poor; but this was especially true because, with the end of the Cold War, there was so much less political capital in the idea of equality and fairness. The free market stopped being one way of arranging the world, subject to argument and comparison with other systems: it became an item of faith, of near-mystical belief. In that belief system, the finance industry made up the class of priests and magicians, and began to be treated as such. In the UK, that meant ideological hegemony for the City of London. The government adopted City models for behaviour, and the vocabulary to go with it – the language of targets and goals being a sign of uncritical governmental Cityphilia. David Kynaston, author of a magisterial four-volume history of the City of

London, comes in his fourth book to discuss 'City cultural supremacy', and concludes that 'in all sorts of ways (short-term performance, shareholder value, league tables) and in all sorts of areas (education, the NHS and the BBC, to name but three), bottom-line City imperatives had been transplanted wholesale into British society.'[7] Successive governments gave the City more or less everything it wanted. This process began with Mrs Thatcher's election in 1979. One of the incoming government's first actions, practically as well as symbolically important, was the abolition of exchange controls, which opened the UK up to the international flow of capital. Subsequent legislation carried on the trend, culminating in the 'Big Bang' of 1986. This was the moment in which a deregulatory process which could have taken years or decades was packed into a single act: in effect (and for the purposes of simplification), all the historic barriers and separations and rules demarcating different areas of banking and finance and participation in the stock market were simultaneously abolished. I have used the word 'banks' throughout this book to simplify the point, but in reality many modern financial intermediaries – the bodies standing between the people who wanted to borrow money and the people who wanted to lend it – aren't strictly speaking banks at all. There are home-loan specialists, credit unions, private equity funds, securitization specialists, money-market funds, hedge funds, insurance companies, all of them differently regulated, and not a few of them functioning as separate parts of the same institution. The institutions which make up this world of non-bank banks is sometimes referred to as the 'shadow banking system', and insofar as it has a capital, that capital is the City of London.

Taken together, what this led to was the City's increasing dominance of British economic life – and Wall Street's equivalent domination in the US. This, in turn, makes it all the more striking how little knowledge most people have of what goes on in the City and the Street – what it is for, what it does and how it affects everyday life for everybody else. Even very well-informed citizens tend not to realize just what a force in the world the bond market is, a fact reflected in the famous observation of James Carville, President Clinton's campaign manager, in the early years of Clinton's first administration: 'I used to think if there was reincarnation, I wanted to come back as the president or the pope or a .400 baseball hitter. But now I want to come back as the bond market. You can intimidate everybody.' But the ordinary elector knows almost nothing about how these markets work and the impact they have. David Kynaston points out that under communism, children from primary school upwards were taught the principles and practice of the system, and were thoroughly drilled in how it was supposed to work. There is nothing comparable to that in the capitalist world. The City is, in terms of its basic functioning, a far-off country of which we know little.

This climate of thinking informed all subsequent events. With the fall of the Berlin Wall, capitalism began a victory party that ran for almost two decades. Capitalism is not inherently fair: it does not, in and of itself, distribute the rewards of economic growth equitably. Instead it runs on the bases of winner takes all and to them that hath shall be given. For several decades after the second world war the western liberal democracies devoted themselves to the question of how to harness capitalism's potential for economic growth to the political imperative to provide better lives for ordinary people. The jet engine of capitalism was harnessed to the ox cart of social justice. This was the cause of much bleating from the advocates of pure capitalism, but the effect was that the western liberal democracies became the most admirable societies that the world has ever seen. Not the most admirable we can imagine, and not perfect; but the best humanity had as yet been able to achieve. Then the Wall came down, and to various extents the governments of the west began to abandon the social-justice aspect of the general post-war project. The jet engine was unhooked from the ox cart and allowed to roar off at its own speed. The result was an unprecedented boom, which had two big things wrong with it: it wasn't fair and it wasn't sustainable.

This phenomenon was especially clear in Iceland, because it privatized its banks only in 2001. The collectivist tradition in Iceland is so strong that it is more like a fact of national character than like an ideology – and this doesn't seem inappropriate in a country very aware of its isolation, its history as a Viking settlement and the always apparent inhospitability of the geography and climate. In the 1980s, however, the Independence Party, which had been more or less permanently in power since Iceland became independent from Denmark, began to adopt a more ideological turn. Its younger and more energetic politicians looked admiringly at the free-market policies being adopted by Ronald Reagan and Margaret Thatcher, and began to wonder what Iceland might be capable of if it was freed from the current model of nationalization and regulation. A long march towards the free market began, and in 2001 the banks were privatized, a policy which was a triumphant success, until it turned into a total disaster.

That's how fast, and how completely, things can go wrong for a society if its banks go bad. This is because banks are central to the operation of a developed economy; in particular, they are central to the creation of credit, and credit is as important to the modern economy as oxygen is to us. When the banks go wrong, everything goes wrong: it's a bank crisis which gives you that slamming-the-car-into-reverse feeling.

This is how it's supposed to work. A well-run bank is a machine for making money. The basic principle of banking is to pay a low rate of interest to the people who lend money, and charge a higher rate of interest to the people who borrow money. The bank borrows at 3 per cent, say, and lends at 6 per cent and as long as it keeps the two amounts in line, and ensures that it lends money only to people who will be able to pay it back, it will reliably make money for ever. And this institution, in and of itself, will generate activity in the rest of the economy. The process is explained in Philip Coggan's excellent primer on the City, *The Money Machine*. Imagine, for the purpose of keeping things simple, a country with only one bank. A customer goes into the bank and deposits £200. Now the bank has £200 to invest, so it buys some shares with the money – not the full £200, but the amount minus the percentage which it deems prudent to keep in cash, just in case any depositors come and make a withdrawal. That amount, called the 'cash ratio', is set by government: in this example let's say it's 20 per cent. So our bank buys £160 of shares from, say, You limited. Then You ltd deposits its £160 in the bank; so now the bank has £360 of deposits, of which it needs to keep only 20 per cent – £72 – in cash: so now it can buy another £128 of shares in You ltd, raising its total holding in You ltd to £288. Once again, You ltd goes and deposits the money in the bank, which goes out again and buys more shares, and so on the process goes. The only thing imposing a limit is the need to keep 20 per cent in cash, so the depositing-and-buying cycle ends when the bank has £200 in cash and £800 in You ltd shares; it also has £1,000 of customer deposits, the initial £200 plus all the money from the share transactions. The initial £200 has generated a balance sheet of £1,000 in assets and £1,000 in liabilities. This money isn't fictitious: these are real assets and real liabilities. Magic!

This aspect of how banks work is critical to the way the economy works; it's the reason banks are not just some convenient add-on to capitalism, but are at the centre of how it's supposed to function. Banks create credit, and credit makes the economy work. In a sense, credit isn't just an aspect of the economy, it is the economy – the seamless, ceaseless, frictionless ebb and flow and circulation of credit. When it works, this process is a wonder of the world.

In this system, the recording of the movement of money is indispensable, and has a history of its own. The central inventions in this history are the financial statements, of which the most important, in this story, is the balance sheet. We don't know who invented balance sheets; they seem to have been in use in Venice as early as the thirteenth century. But we do know who wrote down the method behind them, and in the process invented modern accounting, which relies on four financial statements to provide a full picture of any given business: the balance sheet, the income statement, the cash-flow statement and the statement of retained earnings. The man who wrote down the method for gathering and recording the relevant information was Luca Paci-oli, a Franciscan monk and friend of both Piero della Francesca and Leonardo da Vinci, whose assistant he was for many years. Pacioli wrote *Summa de arithmetica*, the book that laid out the method of double-entry book-keeping which is still in use in more or less every business in the world. (He also wrote about magic, in the sense of conjuring. I'd like to think he would have enjoyed the old joke about accountants: 'What's two plus two?' 'What would you like it to be?') There's something amazing about the fact that a method used in Venice in the thirteenth century and written down in Tuscany in the fifteenth should still be in daily use in every financial enterprise in the developed world.

Of the four financial statements, the balance sheet is the one which provides a glimpse into a moment of time. The others show processes, flows of money; the balance sheet is a snapshot. A balance sheet is divided into Assets on the left and Liabilities on the right. Assets are things which belong to you, liabilities are things which belong to other people. Here's what an individual's balance sheet might look like:

Assets	£
House	200,000
Deposits in bank	10,000
Car	10,000
Stuff I own	15,000
Money people owe me	5,000
Pension	40,000
Total	280,000

Liabilities	
Share of house owned by bank	130,000
Credit card debt	2,000
Car loan	2,000
Unpaid debt on stuff I own	6,000
Total	140,000
Equity	140,000
Total liabilities and equity	280,000

You'll notice there is something mysterious there called 'Equity'. This is the miracle ingredient that makes a balance sheet always balance: it is added to your liabilities so that they match your assets. The fact that it appears on the Liabilities side of the column might make equity seem sinister, but it isn't: it's a good thing. It's the amount by which you are in the clear; it's the amount by which your assets exceed your liabilities. Your equity is your safety margin; it is your net worth, it is the thing which keeps you in business.

Now imagine for a moment that you are a business: you are now You ltd. You set out to sell shares in yourself. The part of you that you sell shares in is the equity. The buyer is taking over not the assets and liabilities, but the equity. Say I bought 10 per cent of your equity, as set out in the balance sheet above, at a price of £14,000 (an accurate price, since that's exactly what it's worth

Whoops!

today). In a year's time, say you've paid back £10,000 of your mortgage, your house price has gone up by half, you're being paid better at work and so you've another £10,000 in the bank – golly, our equity is now £190,000. My one-tenth share of your equity is now worth £19,000. Cool. I could sell my share in your equity and make a nice profit, or I could just sit on it, betting that you would do even better in the future. On the other, scarier hand, you could have had a lousy year: your house price might have halved, you have been put on part-time work so your salary has halved and wiped out your savings, various of your debtors have gone bankrupt, your car has lost 30 per cent of its value, your pension pot has been wiped out by bad investments: in sum, your assets have gone down by £160,000. Your liabilities, on the other hand, are the same. There's a problem: your liabilities now exceed your assets, by a cool £20,000. In plain English, you're broke. In the language of accountancy, you are insolvent. You have met one of the two criteria for insolvency: your liabilities are greater than your assets. The other criterion is the inability to meet your debts as they fall due. In British law, meeting either criterion makes you insolvent. It is a criminal offence to trade while insolvent.

There may be a loophole, however. Are you really insolvent? I've made things clear-cut for the purposes of this example, but you could argue – and in comparable cases people do argue – that your problem is not so much insolvency as illiquidity. Liquidity is the ability to turn assets into something that can be bought or sold. With a depressed housing market, the problem with your house could easily be not so much its value as the fact that you can't sell it, because nobody is buying property at the moment. Or rather you can sell it, but you have to do so for an artificially depressed, crazy-cheap price: a 'fire sale' price. When the market returns to normal functioning, you will be able to sell your house for its true value; so you aren't really insolvent, you're just caught in a 'liquidity trap'. In practice, all you would do, in the above example – as long as you weren't really You ltd, in which case you might well be under a legal obligation to go into receivership – would be simply to ignore the question and keep going. You'd hope to be able to pay bills as they fell due, and hang on for grim life until your house price recovered. As we speak, hundreds of thousands of people across the UK – millions across the world – are doing precisely that. The current estimate for the number of people in the UK with 'negative equity' is 900,000.

A business can't have negative equity: if it does, it is insolvent. But businesses can and do have considerably different levels of equity, and it often makes their businesses look different in an instantly recognizable, at-a-glance way. At business schools, they play a game – sorry, 'undertake an exercise' – in which students are given balance sheets and asked to determine what type of business the company is in. Sums are in millions of pounds. So what's this business?

Assets	£m
Cash and balances at central banks	17,866
Treasury bills	18,229
Loans and advances	1,048,710
Derivatives	337,410
Other	478,304
Total	1,900,519

Liabilities	
Deposits by banks	312,663
Customer accounts	682,365
Other	814,065
Total	1,809,093
Equity	91,426
Total liabilities and equity	1,900,519

Our business school chums will have no trouble working this one out: from the huge levels of assets and liabilities, and the fact that the main category of liabilities is customer deposits, it will be immediately apparent that this business is a bank. If they've been swotting up, they may even be able to work out which bank it is, because a clue is in the figure for 'total assets': £1,900,519,000,000. One point nine trillion pounds. Since the entire GDP of the United Kingdom is £1.7 trillion, this is a freakishly large bank. Any guesses? OK, this is the Royal Bank of Scotland. RBS was in 2008, by the size of its assets, not just a big bank, and not just one of the biggest companies in Europe. The Royal Bank of Scotland, by asset size, was the biggest company in the world. If I had to pick a single fact which summed up the cultural gap between the City of London and the rest of the country, it would be that one. I have yet to meet a single person not employed in financial services who was aware of it; I wasn't aware of it myself. We're all well aware of it now, though, since the British taxpayer has had to bail out RBS to the tune of tens of billions of pounds: no one yet knows how much the final cost will be, but £100 billion is probably not far off the mark, and it could easily be much more.

It seems weird, at first glance and indeed at second glance, that bank balance sheets list customer deposits as liabilities, but it makes sense if you think about it, since a liability is at heart something that belongs to somebody else, and the customers' deposits belong to the customers. This was something that my father, who worked for a bank, used often to say to me: don't forget that if you have money in a bank account, you're lending the bank money. Banks themselves certainly don't forget it. Actually, that's not true. They forget it all the time in their actual dealings with their customer/creditors – us. They act as if it's their money and they are doing us a favour by letting it sit in their bank earning interest. A spectacular example of this, in modern Britain, is the question of the cheque-clearing system. If I give you a cheque today and you pay it into your bank, the funds will clear out of my account tomorrow, but won't be credited to your account until three days later – if you're lucky; it can take up to seven days. This is much too slow; but it's OK though, because a government report, commissioned by Gordon Brown, has issued stinging criticisms of the payment system and action has been promised. Great! But wait! The report was published, and the promise of decisive action was made, in 2000. Legislation and new regulatory bodies to enforce it have been repeatedly promised, but the problem has consistently been the industry's reluctance to act, since this is change which does nothing to benefit banks' profits – it only benefits customers. The banks just can't get excited about that, especially since this reform offers a pure benefit to customers, with no extra revenues to be extracted in the process. Change was supposed to have finally begun being 'rolled out' to customers in May 2008. Speaking for myself, it's had no effect at all. Ten years after the cheque-clearing system was declared a national scandal, cheques being paid into my account still take at least three days to clear. This is the reality of how the banks view their customers, in daily dealings.[8]

Take a look at the balance sheet, however, and at the page after page of corporate reports and footnotes which accompany it, and it's a different story. There, the depositors hold all the power. High levels of deposits mean high levels of liabilities; and high levels of liabilities oblige a bank to have high levels of assets. Since banks are mainly in the business of lending money, high levels of assets mean high levels of loans. That means that a bank's main assets are other people's debts. This is another distinctive feature of bank balance sheets, the fact that its principal assets are other people's debts to it.

The balance sheets of other businesses look very different. They're smaller, for a start: only banks are this bloated with assets and liabilities. That's natural, since the business model of banking, involving lots of money coming in and sitting in accounts, balanced by lots of lending, is always going to involve big sums on the balance sheet, and relatively small amounts of equity. A company with a quicker turnover will look very different. Apple Computer, for instance, in 2008 had $39.5 billion in assets, $18.5 billion in liabilities and $21 billion in equity; compare that to RBS's £1,900 billion, £1,809 billion and £91 billion. Apple's assets are a fiftieth the size of RBS's, but its equity is bigger than its liabilities. In that sense, Apple is a safer business than RBS's; it has a larger safety cushion, a proportionately bigger margin for error. Of course, it might be that it has a bigger margin for error because it is an inherently riskier business. Banking should be much more solid than computers/gadgets/music, but the fact that banks will always have elephantine balance sheets, in proportion to their equity, means they have a tendency to be a little less secure than they look at first glance. That's one of the many reasons why banks are, in their corporate body-language, so keen to look as imposing and rock-like as they possibly can.

Apple's accounts are all about how many computers and phones and songs the company will sell, since its financial health depends on that. (I say 'songs' – Apple's iTunes is the biggest music retailer in both the UK and USA.) RBS's accounts are all about its loans, since the financial health of the company depends on the quality of those loans. It follows from that that RBS's accounts are all about loan risk, since the profitability of the loans depends on how likely they are to be repaid. For that reason the nature of the assets – the loans – are all-important; and risk is not some marginal factor but the core of a bank's business. Risk is always an important issue for any company, but for banks, it isn't just important, it's their whole business. Banking does not just involve the management of risk; banking *is* the management of risk.

A big component of that risk is how big to be. In practice, that means how much bigger your liabilities are than your equity. This is known as your 'leverage', and it is usually expressed as a multiple, the amount by which you have to multiply your equity to make it equal your liabilities. In the personal finance balance sheet given above your equity is £140,000 and your liabilities are £140,000, so your leverage ratio is 1 to 1. That's nice and safe – but it's very different from the position of Britain's banks. This has turned out to be a serious problem for Britain, because our big banks aren't just big, they're huge: the four biggest each has a capital value of more than a trillion pounds. They are highly leveraged, too. The ratio of Barclays' assets to its equity at its 2008 peak was 61.3 to 1. Because the liabilities match the assets plus the equities, that means that the liabilities are colossal. Imagine that for a moment translated to your own finances, so that you could stretch what you actually, unequivocally own to borrow more than sixty times the amount. (I'd have an island. What about you?) During the boom, the leverage ratios of the big European banks – the multiple by which their assets exceeded their equity – reached a point when they were the financial equivalent of bungee jumping: even though everyone tells you it's supposed to be safe, you still have to be an adrenaline addict to risk it. These were the ratios for the big European banks on 30 June 2008, just when the financial tsunami was about to hit: UBS 46.9 to 1, ING Group 48.8, HSBC Holding 20.1, Barclays Bank 61.3, Deutsche Bank 52.5, Fortis 33.3, Lloyd's TSB 34.1, RBS 18.8, Crédit Agricole 40.5, BNP Paribas 36.1, Credit Suisse 33.4.[9]

The figures for the big American banks aren't quite as bad, but they're bad enough: what they boil down to are median leverage ratios of 35 to 1 in the US and 45 to 1 in Europe. Another way of looking at these ratios is to say that they represent the amount of the bank's assets which have to go bad for the bank to be insolvent. In the US, on average, if 1/35th of the bank's assets went bad, the bank is bust; in the EU, 1/45th of bad assets would have the same effect. This is, obviously, a highly precarious position. It was also no accident, because those risks were also the reason why the banks had a boom period. The banks were incredibly profitable not because they were doing anything better, but simply because they were making bigger, riskier bets – plonking down more money on the roulette wheel. This isn't just a metaphor, it's the actual conclusion of an academic study made by Andrew Haldane, the Bank of England's executive in charge of financial stability. Between 1986 and 2006, the average annual return on banking shares rocketed from its historical norm of 2 per cent to 16 per cent. Why? Because the banks were making bigger bets. There was no skill, efficiency, intelligence or judgement involved: just riskier bets. In Haldane's exact words, 'Since 2000, rising leverage fully accounts for movements in UK banks' ROE [return on equity] – both the rise to around 24% in 2007 and the subsequent fall into negative territory in 2008.'[10] This is astounding stuff. Haldane, a senior figure in the Bank of England, is in effect saying that most of those bankers paying themselves monster bonuses were doing so simply as a result of taking bigger punts – and as it turned out, it was we the taxpayers who, unwittingly and unwillingly, were bankrolling their ever riskier wagers. This wasn't just looking for trouble, it was sending trouble a 'save the date' card, followed by a formal invitation, followed by nagging emails and phone calls just to make absolutely sure.

What links all the banks which have hit the skids – and all the other companies and institutions around the world which have been felled by the credit crunch – is that these bets went bad. Gigantic holes have appeared on the left-hand side of their balance sheets, where 'Assets' are listed. That suddenly and immediately means they are at risk of having their liabilities exceed their assets – that is, being insolvent. Those now worthless assets are for the most part linked in one way or another to the collapse in property prices in the US and elsewhere. They are often described as 'toxic assets', or 'troubled assets', as they're euphemistically known in the US scheme to buy them from the banks: the Troubled Assets Relief Program, TARP. But the term 'toxic assets' is misleading. It makes me think of Superman, intercepting a rocket-powered canister of vileness unleashed by some villain and deflecting it into space. The assets in question don't contain some magic property of poisonous money-juice. The thing that's toxic about them is their prices. As Stephanie Flanders of the BBC has said, it would be more accurate to call them 'toxic prices' – it would at least be an aid to clearer thinking.

The definition is usually stated as follows: these are assets which can't be accurately priced, and which therefore spread uncertainty and insecurity throughout the financial system. But that isn't quite right. It's true that some of the problematic mortgage-backed assets at the moment have no price because there is no market for them, and it's a moot point whether or not there ever will be a market again. But many of these assets do in fact have prices – there are buyers out there willing to acquire them. That makes sense. Considering Lloyds-HBOS, the merger of a high-street banking giant with Britain's biggest building-society-turned-bank, for instance, it's obviously not true that every mortgage sold in recent years by the Halifax building society is a dud, spreading poison through the company's balance sheet. That defies common sense. It's probably the case that the bulk of the company's mortgages, perhaps the overwhelming bulk of them, perhaps including many worrisome recent loans, are viable. People's houses might not be worth what they paid for them, but in most cases they're going to continue paying the mortgages anyway. There must be many comparable examples out there, of highly out-of-fashion mortgage-based investments which aren't as deeply in trouble as the markets currently think. It might make sense, if you were an experienced investor in those markets, to investigate the possibility of buying some of these investments at a bargain price. The problem is that these prices are, from the banks' point of view, too low. The buyers are willing to acquire them at, say, twenty or thirty cents to the dollar, so that an asset whose notional worth is $10 million – for example, a derivative tracing its value from sub-prime mortgages – might have someone willing to buy it for $2 or $3 million. For the bank, that price is too low. It isn't too low in the sense that they quite fancy the idea of a higher price; it's too low in the sense that, if they accept the valuation, they have a gigantic hole on the left-hand side of the balance sheet. Their assets aren't worth what they're supposed to be, and the bank is no longer solvent.

That problem is global, both in its consequences and in its incidence. In one form or another, balance-sheet abysses of this sort are responsible for all the collapses we've seen. Perhaps we can experience a twinge of national pride at the thought that this planet-wide problem began with Northern Rock, which in September 2007 experienced the single most dreaded event which can overtake any financial institution, not seen in Britain for over a century: a bank run. So many people turned up in person to withdraw money that the bank ended up paying out 5 per cent of its total assets, a cool £1 billion in cash. Perhaps we can also experience a twinge of nostalgia at the fact that at the time of its nationalization a few months later, the £25 billion Northern Rock bailout was the biggest sum any government anywhere in the world had ever given to a private company.

Such, such were the days . . . The really serious wave of bailouts and collapses began with the investment bank Bear Stearns in March 2008 and then went to the next level with the 'conservatorship' of Fannie Mae and Freddie Mac, the state-backed behemoths underwriting the American mortgage industry, on 7 September – the largest nationalization in the history of the world. It was followed eight days later by the largest bankruptcy in the history of the world, when the investment bank Lehman Brothers went into Chapter 11, the American form of receivership. The next day saw the biggest bailout of a private company in history, with the US government taking a 79.9 per cent share in the insurer AIG. Merrill Lynch, the bank whose symbol is the original Wall Street 'prancing bull', was taken over by the Bank of America on 14 September 2008. On 18 September came news of the biggest bank merger – carefully not denominated a takeover – in British history: Lloyds was to buy HBOS, the largest mortgage lender in the UK, with 20 per cent of the market. This deal trashed the market's opinion of Lloyds and led to its boss, Victor Blank, being forced out of his job. On 21 September, Goldman Sachs, the world's biggest investment bank, and Morgan Stanley, another investment bank giant, converted their legal status to holding banks, a change which allowed them access to help from the Federal Reserve in return for a greatly increased level of government supervision. On 28 September the Luxembourgeois, Belgian and Dutch governments nationalized the bank Fortis, the biggest private employer in Belgium, at a cost of €1.3 billion. On 29 September, the British bank Bradford and Bingley was nationalized, at a cost of £41.3 billion, and its branch network sold off to the Spanish bank Santander. The German commercial property loan giant Hypo Real Estate was bailed out on 5 October at a cost of €50 billion. The Icelandic banking system collapsed the next day. During the weekend of 11–12 October the British banking system teetered on the point of collapse – 'the only time in my career', a senior banker told me, 'when I've felt genuinely frightened'. That same weekend, RBS was in receipt of an emergency injection of government cash, to the tune of £20 billion – the first stage of its bailout.

Since then, things have calmed down, with only the occasional bailoutette to concern us, such as that of the US car industry or the Dunfermline building society. Nonetheless, I guarantee that at this very moment, somewhere in the world, somebody at one of the big banks is sitting with his head in his hands, looking at the company's balance sheet and sweating over this very problem. This might be especially the case in Europe, where banks and governments have delayed the reckoning with bad assets and bank insolvency for as long as they can. If the global economic crisis can be reduced to one single phenomenon, it is this one: the fact that nobody knows which banks are solvent. Because banks are crucial to the creation and operation of credit, a bank crisis leads directly to a credit crunch. It's also why the huge amounts of money being pumped into the banking sector by governments are tending not to do the thing they are supposed to do, that is restart lending to businesses and consumers. That's because – and here we can have that very rare thing, a brief moment of sympathy for the banksters – the banks are being given two totally incompatible goals. One is to rebuild their balance sheet and recapitalize themselves so they're no longer at risk of going broke. The second is to keep lending money. They're being told to save and to keep spending at the same time. It's not possible, and in the circumstances it's no mystery why banks are hoarding every penny they can get, and calling in every loan they can: they're doing it in order to 'deleverage' and rebuild their capital as fast as possible.

But that is cataclysmically destructive for the rest of the economy. It works like this: bank's assets shrink in value. Bank therefore loses equity, because its liabilities are worth the same but its assets are worth less. Bank therefore has to shrink its assets further and contract its lending, in order to stay solvent. But because the bank is so highly leveraged, it has to make an immense amount of lending go away in order to cover for a relatively small amount of equity loss. It's easy to see that many of the banks described above have leverage ratios of more than 30 to 1. That means that if they lose £100 million in equity they have to contract their assets and make £3 billion of lending go away, just to stay at the same leverage ratio. If they want their leverage to actually shrink – which in practice most of them both want to do and are being encouraged to do – they have to shrink their assets even faster. That means lending even less money to businesses and individuals. That, in turn, makes everything worse for the entire economy. As Charles Morris points out in his book *Trillion Dollar Meltdown*: a credit bubble is a special category of event: 'We are accustomed to thinking of bubbles and crashes in terms of specific markets – like junk bonds, commercial real estate, and tech stocks. Overpriced assets are like poison mushrooms. You eat them, you get sick, you learn to avoid them. A credit bubble is different. Credit is the air that financial markets breathe, and when the air is poisoned, there's no place to hide.'[11]

What the banks want to be able to do is what most of us would do in comparable circumstances. Indeed, it's what a good few of us, myself included, have done in the past, during previous busts in the property market. When that happens, you just wait. Perhaps some of us are in the dreaded position of having the famous 'negative equity', as described above. In that case we can sell and take a loss, if we can afford to – or we can just wait. Carry on living, and wait for prices to recover, and even if we don't we still have somewhere to live. That's what the banks would like to do about their toxic prices: wait for them to become non-toxic. If they were forced to value their assets today, for the price they could get today – a practice known as 'mark to market', which is supposedly enforced on most kinds of asset – some of them would be insolvent. Since the current valuations would irretrievably trash their balance sheets, they would prefer not to accept them.

The trouble is that banks are not households. If banks sit on their hands and wait for valuations to recover, the economy grinds to a halt. The flow of money would stop and the recession would be even more severe than it is already certain to be. That's because a situation in which banks are insolvent but stay in business means that you have 'zombie banks'. A zombie bank is a bank which is dead – insolvent – but has a horrible sort of pseudo-life because it is being allowed to keep trading by (usually) an over-indulgent government. Zombie banks are not hypothetical: it was zombie banks, created by an overcosy relationship between banks and the state, which since 1989 turned the Japanese economy from a wonder of the world to a comatose onlooker at global growth. The economy can't recover until the zombies are killed. The West was very free with brutally direct advice to the Japanese, during their slowdown: we told them to hurry up and get on with it and slay their zombies already. In the aftermath of the credit crunch, it turns out we're much, much slower to take our own advice. Even Larry Summers, one of the finger-waggers in chief when he was President Clinton's Treasury Secretary, has admitted as much: 'It is easier to be for more radical solutions when one lives thousands of miles away than when it is one's own country.'[12] Horror-film zombies are relatively easy to deal with: they don't have investors, they don't hire lobbyists, they don't donate to political parties, they can't pick up the phone and frighten senior politicians. Zombie banks have none of those constraints, and are much more of a problem: a scarily big problem. And unlike zombies, they actually exist.

2. Rocket Science

Finance, like other forms of human behaviour, underwent a change in the twentieth century, a shift equivalent to the emergence of modernism in the arts – a break with common sense, a turn towards self-referentiality and abstraction and notions that couldn't be explained in workaday English. In poetry, this moment took place with the publication of *The Waste Land*. In classical music, it was, perhaps, the premiere of *The Rite of Spring*. Dance, architecture, painting – all had comparable moments. (One of my favourites is in jazz: the moment in 'A Night in Tunisia' where Charlie Parker plays a saxophone break which is like the arrival of modernism, right there, in real time. It's said that the first time he went off on his solo, the other musicians simply put down their instruments and stared.) The moment in finance came in 1973, with the publication of a paper in the *Journal of Political Economy* entitled 'The Pricing of Options and Corporate Liabilities', by Fischer Black and Myron Scholes.

Derivatives have a bad press at the moment, but it's important to acknowledge their role in the long history of man's attempt to understand, control and make money from risk. The study of risk is a humanist project, an attempt to abolish the idea of incomprehensible fate and replace it with the rational, quantifiable study of chance.[13] Once upon a time, we were the playthings of fate, and the future was unknowable; but then, starting with philosophers and mathematicians such as Pierre de Fermat and Blaise Pascal and Christiaan Huygens, humanity began to work out ways in which the future could be measured and assessed in terms of probabilities. Just as experimental science had its roots in alchemy, so the study of probability had its roots in gambling: the first investigations into risk grew out of the curiosity of gamblers. Chance, and risk, began to be something which could be managed. An essential tool in doing so was to be the category of financial instruments called derivatives.

Derivatives themselves have been a long-standing feature of financial markets. At their simplest, a farmer would agree to a price for his next harvest a few months in advance – and the right to buy this harvest was a derivative, which could itself be sold. The name comes from the fact that a derivative's value derives from the underlying products. Today, the simplest forms of derivatives are options and futures. An option gives you the right, but not the obligation, to either buy or sell something at a specified future date for a specified price. Example: you spend £500 on an option to buy a Ferrari for £50,000 in a year's time. When the year is up, the Ferrari is on sale for £60,000 – so your option is now worth £10,000, because that's how much money you can make by exercising the option, buying the car and then selling it for its real price. Conversely, if in a year's time the Ferrari is on sale for £40,000, exercising your option would leave you out of pocket by £10,000 – so you just let it go, and your only loss is the £500 premium (as it's called). You could alternatively have bought the right to sell the Ferrari for £50,000 – in which case your preferences would be reversed, and you'd be hoping that the price had dropped. In that event you'd buy the car for £40,000 and immediately sell it for £10,000 more. Futures are the same as options, except that they bring with them the obligation to buy or sell at the specified price: with futures, you are committed to the deal. It follows that futures are much riskier than options.

Options and futures have been very important products in the history of finance, and it is no coincidence that these derivatives were first extensively developed in commodities markets, especially the Chicago Mercantile Exchange (which started life 110 years ago as the Chicago Butter and Egg Board). For years, derivatives existed as useful tools of this type. They were immensely practical but not in their basic essence too complicated. They've been around for a long time: speculation on tulip derivatives was a feature of the Dutch tulip crash in 1637. Their use has long been widespread, and their history involves some entertaining byways, for instance the fact that during the American Civil War the Confederacy funded its fight against the Union with a derivative bond to attract foreign currency.

As soon as the market in derivatives was professionalized at the Chicago exchange, it was quickly obvious that there was a huge potential market in the field of financial derivatives, which derived their value not from eggs or butter or wheat but from shares. The market, however, was hampered by one big thing: no one could work out how to price the derivatives. The interacting factors of time, risk, interest rates and price volatility were so complex that they defeated mathematicians until Fischer Black and Myron Scholes published their paper in 1973, one month after the Chicago Board Options Exchange had opened for business. The revolutionary aspect of Black and Scholes's paper was an equation enabling people to calculate the price of financial derivatives based on the value of the underlying asset. The Black–Scholes formula opened up a whole new area of derivatives trading. It was a defining moment in the mathematization of the market. Within months, traders were using equations and vocabulary straight out of Black–Scholes (as it is now universally known) and the worldwide derivatives business took off like a rocket. The total market in derivative products around the world is today counted in the hundreds of trillions of dollars. Nobody knows the exact figure, but the notional amount certainly exceeds the total value of all the world's economic output, roughly sixty-six trillion dollars, by an enormous factor – perhaps tenfold. This apparently impossible fact is explained by the difference between the underlying value of the products and the notional values wrapped up in derivatives deriving from them. Say you're a pig farmer, and you want to sell your next season's pork bellies in advance, to lock in a good price. A trader buys the bellies for £100,000 – and your part in the story of the pork bellies is done; but that doesn't mean the contract to deliver the bellies has finished its adventures in the financial system. The trader sells it to another trader, who sells it to a third dealer who's worried that he overpaid on some bellies earlier in the year and now wants to reduce the average price paid, but the person to whom he sells the contract holds on to it for a bit and then sells it on, because the price for next-season pork bellies in general is rising and your belly contract – which is what is being traded here, a pork-belly derivative contract – has gone up in value. So now the real value of the bellies has stayed at the £100,000 for which you sold it, whereas the derivatives have now been traded four times, to create £400,000 of notional action. Hence the term 'notional' – these aren't real deals for the bellies but deals for the derivative of the bellies, the contract to deliver them. Hence also the way in which the value of the notional contracts can spiral far, far away from the underlying real asset.*

Even once you've had it explained, however, it still seems wholly contrary to common sense that the market for products that derive from real things should be unimaginably vaster than the market for things themselves. With derivatives, we seem to enter a modernist world in which risk no longer means what it means in plain

---

* With all that trading at a remove from the real asset, it's tempting to wonder if people ever forget they've bought a derivatives contract and end up with a huge quantity of pork bellies or coffee being dumped on their doorstep six months after doing a derivatives deal. There is a perhaps apocryphal story that Keynes, as bursar of King's College, once forgot he'd taken a punt on wheat futures and had to accept delivery of several tons of wheat, which he then had stored in the college cellars.

English, and in which there is a profound break between the language of finance and that of common sense. It is difficult for civilians to understand a derivatives contract, or any of the whole range of closely related instruments. These are all products that were designed initially to transfer or hedge risks – to purchase some insurance against the prospect of a price going down, when your main bet was that the price would go up. The farmer selling his next season's crop might not have understood a modern financial derivative, but he would have recognized that use of it.

In an ideal world, one populated by vegetarians, Esperanto speakers and fluffy bunny wabbits, derivatives would be used for one thing only: reducing levels of risk. Because they are bought 'on margin' – that is, not for the full cost of the underlying asset, but for the advance premium, as in the hypothetical Ferrari example above – they offer a cheap and flexible form of insurance against things going wrong. Imagine, for instance, that you are convinced that the stock market is about to go up by 50 per cent in the next year. You know it in your waters – so much so that you borrow £100,000 and use it to buy shares. If the market goes up you'll be pleased with yourself, but if you're wrong, and the market plunges, you'll be badly out of pocket – unless you take out some insurance. So you buy a £10,000 option to sell shares at a lower price than you paid for them. That money is wasted if your shares go up – but you won't care much because your main position is in serious profit. But if shares go down, you have some insurance – you can cash in the option to sell shares at the lower price, and eliminate most of your losses. This is called 'hedging': you have used an option to hedge your main risk.

Alas, we don't live in that kinder, gentler world. In reality, the power of derivatives has a way of proving irresistible for those people who aren't just sure that the market is going up, but are beyond sure, are super-sure, are possessed by absolute knowledge. Financial experts are often possessed by this kind of certainty.

In that event, it's very tempting indeed to buy an option that increases your level of risk, in the knowledge that this will increase your level of reward. In the above example, instead of hedging the position with an option to sell, you could magnify it with options to buy, which will be worth a lot if you're right – sorry, *when* you're right. When you're right and the market goes up by half, your £10,000 option will be worth £50,000 (that's the £50,000 by which the shares have gone up). In fact, instead of buying £100,000 of shares and a £10,000 option to buy, why not instead buy £100,000 worth of options? This is called leverage: you have leveraged your £100,000 to buy £1,000,000 worth of exposure to the market. That way when you get your price rise, you have just made £500,000, and all with borrowed money. In fact, since you're not just confident but certain, why not skip the option and instead buy some futures, which are cheaper (because riskier) – let's say half the price. These futures, at £5,000 each, oblige you to buy twenty lots of the shares for £100,000 each in a year's time. Hooray! You're rich! Unless the market, instead of doubling, halves, and you are saddled with an obligation to buy £2 million worth of shares which are now worth only £1 million. You've just borrowed £100,000 and through the power of modern financial instruments used it to lose £1 million. Whoops.

It might seem unlikely that anyone would do anything that stupid, but in practice it happens all the time. The list of individual traders who have lost more than a billion dollars at a time betting on derivatives is not short: Robert Citron of Orange County, Toshihide Iguchi at Daiwa, Yasuo Hamanaka at Sumitomo, Nick Leeson of Barings, and now, most recently and spectacularly of all, Jérôme Kerviel of Société Générale. These are the traders who have each single-handedly managed to lose more than a billion dollars of their employers' money. Hamanaka used to be the poster boy – he lost $2.6 billion betting on copper in 1996. But Kerviel's $7.2 billion loss betting on European stock markets made that figure look a little dated and nineties, especially since, according to his bank, he only began accumulating the losses the same month he was caught. ¡Olé! In Leeson's case, it was a huge unauthorized position in futures on the Nikkei 225 (the main Japanese stock exchange) which destroyed Barings in 1995. Leeson had been doubling and redoubling his bets in the belief/hope that the index would rise, and hiding the resulting open position – a gigantic open-ended bet – in a secret account. (Incidentally, Leeson's big bet was on the Nikkei holding its level above 19,000. At the time of writing, fourteen years later, the index sits at 9,287 – proof, if it were needed, that when prices go down they can stay that way for a long time.) The loss eventually amounted to £880 million, and destroyed Barings, Britain's oldest merchant bank. The year before it went broke, the Chairman of the company, Peter Baring, urbanely told the Governor of the Bank of England that 'it is not actually all that difficult to make money in the securities business.'

The power of derivatives is one of the main things about them – their ability to hedge risk, but also, and much more alarmingly, to magnify it. The second main thing about them is their complexity. We are a long, long way away from a single quote for next season's wheat crop. The contemporary derivative is likely to involve a mix of options and futures and currencies and debt, structured and priced in ways which are the closest extant thing to rocket science. Maths PhDs are all over the place in this business. Some of the derivatives involved are actively designed to conceal the real nature of the assets involved – bearing in mind that the assets involved are themselves often debts, repackaged and sold on in 'black box' structures designed to hide the entities within. The products thus created are far over the heads of civilians and sometimes, it seems, over the heads of most of the people who buy and sell them. 'We invented this stuff, so we know how it works,' my friend Tony told me, referring to the fact that his bank was one of the first players in the derivatives market. 'But I get the feeling that a lot of the banks are doing it just because other people are doing it – they don't really know what they're doing.'

This is one point at which we have to face a fact of modern banking: its take-over by advanced mathematics. Things used to be different. My father, as I've already said, worked for a bank. He arrived in London for the first time in 1948 with a degree from the University of Melbourne and, thanks to his time in the Australian army, fluent Japanese. As a result he ended up getting a job with the Hongkong and Shanghai Bank and spending almost all his working life in Asia. The bank he worked for was then a conservative institution, heavily watermarked with its colonial origins, but also a well-run company which was beginning to grow: it's now a global giant, the twenty-first biggest company in the world. In 1948 it was a fairly typical bank in many respects, including the following: in my father's generation of newly hired managers, he was the only person with a degree. The fact that he had been to university made him stand out as a semi-intellectual. Half a century later, HSBC liked to hire only people with first-class degrees from Oxbridge, and preferably in mathematics and the physical sciences. That's one effect of the mathematicization of banking, which hit hard and apparently irrevocably in the nineties, as bankers began to use new tools and techniques derived from super-complex maths. In his brilliant book about risk, *Fooled by Randomness*, Nassim Taleb describes these as the days when 'every plane from Moscow had at least its back row full of Russian mathematical physicists en route to Wall Street.'[14] One of the consequences of this new turn in banking was that there could be significant gaps inside banks between senior managers and the 'quants', as mathematicians are called inside banking. (A friend of mine who did an MBA at Stanford told me that on his course students had to identify themselves as being either 'quants' or 'poets'.) The managers liked what the quants could do, but they didn't always understand it – with consequences which now, alas, are becoming clear. A very senior Treasury figure reports that a bank board member came up to him at a social function and said he had some good news: 'we're no longer going to get involved in things we don't understand.' The Treasury official added: 'We now own his bank.'

Derivatives are a central part of this new mathematical complexity. One of their main uses is in arbitrage. That's the name of investments which effectively bet both ways on the market, exploiting small differences in price to make what should be risk-free profits. (It's what Nick Leeson was supposed to be doing, exploiting tiny differences in the price of Nikkei 225 futures between the Osaka exchange, where trading was electronic, and the Singapore exchange, where it wasn't. The gap in price would last only for a couple of seconds, and in that gap Barings would buy low and sell high – a guaranteed, risk-free profit.) The complexity of the mathematics involved in derivatives can't be exaggerated. This was the reason John Meriwether, a famous bond trader, employed Myron Scholes – he of the Black–Scholes equation – and Robert Merton, the man with whom he shared the 1997 Nobel Prize in Economics, to be directors and co-founders of his new hedge fund Long-Term Capital Management.* The idea was to use these big brains to create a

---

* I don't talk much about hedge funds because they don't feature centrally in the story of the credit crunch. The main question people ask about hedge funds is a simple one: what are they? And the simple answer is, they are largely unregulated pools of investment capital. The whole point of them is to evade the rules around other sorts of publicly traded pooled capital such as investment trusts. The name is misleading, verging on useless. It refers to the idea that some funds 'hedge' their investments and aim to create structures which make money irrespective of whether the market goes up or down, and with lower levels of risk than the stock market. This is often done using large amounts of borrowed money, our old buddy leverage.

highly leveraged, arbitraged, no-risk investment portfolio designed to profit whatever happened, whether the market went up, down, sideways or popped out for a cheese sandwich. LTCM quadrupled in value in its first four years, then imploded in the chaos that followed Russia's default on its foreign-debt obligations in 1998. The fund had equity of $4.72 billion, which would have been pretty healthy, if it were not for the fact that it was exposed, thanks to the miracles of borrowing, leverage and derivatives, to $1.25 trillion of risk. So if it went broke, LTCM would leave a $1.25 trillion hole in the global financial system. The big brains had made a classic mistake: they had treated a very unlikely thing (the default and its consequences) as if it were impossible. As Keynes once observed – he who made himself and his college rich by spending half an hour a day in bed playing the stock market – there is nothing so disastrous as a rational policy in an irrational world. Keynes was preoccupied by the difference between risk in the sense of the mathematical calculation of probabilities – which is what we're discussing here – and uncertainty, the more profound unknowabilities of life and history. You can manage risk, in the sense that you can calculate probabilities and allow for them, but you can't really manage uncertainty, not in that precisely calculable way. Confuse risk with uncertainty, and you have dug a tank-trap for yourself. That's what happened with LTCM. They were caught in the gap between mathematically assessable risks, such as those embodied in their beautiful models, and a nasty piece of real-world uncertainty, which took the form – as uncertainty tends to do – of something nobody expected: the Russian default.

It couldn't have happened without derivatives, which in their modern form are the most powerful and most complicated financial instruments ever devised. And they are everywhere. More than $1,000,000,000,000 of derivatives are bought and sold every day – many of them in London. Every single thing which can be traded through derivatives, is. In the words of Warren Buffett, the greatest living stock-market investor: 'The range of derivatives contracts is limited only by the imagination of man (or sometimes, so it seems, madmen). At Enron, for example, newsprint and broadband derivatives, due to be settled many years in the future, were put on the books. Or say you want to write a contract speculating on the number of twins to be born in Nebraska in 2020. No problem – at a price, you will easily find an obliging counterparty.' Many companies which look as if their business is to do other things, are in reality in the derivatives business, Enron being the best-known example. Buffett is a derivative-phobe, not least because he prefers to know what's going on in the companies he invests in, and derivatives make that effectively impossible. He also, with a prescience so pure it verges on the spooky, said in 2002:

The derivatives genie is now well out of the bottle, and these instruments will almost certainly multiply in variety and number until some event makes their toxicity clear. Knowledge of how dangerous they are has already permeated the electricity and gas businesses, in which the eruption of major troubles caused the use of derivatives to diminish dramatically. Elsewhere, however, the derivatives business continues to expand unchecked. Central banks and governments have so far found no effective way to control, or even monitor, the risks posed by these contracts.

Buffett was horribly right about the risks. The irony is that he wasn't even talking here about the category of derivative which turned out to be the most destructive of all, the credit default swap or CDS. I am going to arraign a number of culprits for the crash: derivatives are prominent in the line-up, but among derivatives it was CDSs which were the chief baddy, the gang leader, the Mafia don, the most destructive of the WMD. As with some other culprits in the crisis, credit default swaps were a new thing, invented by bankers seeking newer, sexier ways of making newer, sexier profits.

When I first began to study the world of the City, I found it hard to come to grips with the idea that financial instruments are 'invented', cooked up in the same way as works of art or scientific theories – but the fact is that they are. Credit default swaps are complicated, but they were based on an old idea, that of a more straightforward kind of swap. Say you're in the grocery business and feel gloomy about its prospects. Your immediate neighbour is in the stationery business and he feels gloomy about his prospects, but less so about yours. You fall to discussing this, and one of you hits on a brilliant idea: why not just swap revenues? You take his profits for the year, and he takes yours. You continue to do what you're doing, and so does he – but you agree to swap your takings. The actual business doesn't change hands, thus making the swap, in banking terminology, 'synthetic'. Another example: your mortgage has five years to run and is on a fixed rate, and you're deeply pissed off about that, because you think interest rates are going to fall and you are paying more than you should. You fall to moaning about this with your next-door neighbour, but instead of commiserating he starts to sing the blues about his own variable-rate mortgage, which he is certain is about to get more expensive, because he disagrees with you and thinks interest rates are about to go up. Aha! The two of you have a Eureka! moment. Why don't you just swap, and pay each other's mortgages? That way you take the position you want to on interest rates, without doing anything complicated like selling your house or remortgaging. Again, this is a 'synthetic' deal, because the underlying assets – the houses – haven't changed hands.

Swaps first arrived in the corporate world in 1981. The first of them featured IBM exchanging surplus Swiss francs and Deutschmarks for dollars held by the World Bank: the two institutions exchanged their bond earnings and their obligations to bondholders without actually exchanging the bonds. They needed to hedge their currency risks and increase their holdings in other currencies and chose to do so through a swap rather than go through the expense, and the risk, of issuing new bond instruments, or making new currency investments, of their own.

A word here about bonds. In business, companies regularly need to raise money – to raise capital. They need to build new factories, or to expand into new markets, or to make a big push on advertising spending, or to take over a competitor, or whatever: for some reason or another, they need to raise money. There are three primary ways of doing that. The first is to borrow from a bank. The second is to sell some of their equity – in plain English, to sell shares – as in the example in the previous chapter, where You ltd sells a 10 per cent share of itself. This can be hard, psychologically, to get used to. In fact one of my former employers, Conrad Black, the one-time proprietor of the *Telegraph* newspapers, is currently in prison in Florida, apparently for failing to grasp this point. He took his company Hollinger public and then complained about the fuss and bother that his new shareholders made, saying that they had failed to understand the whole point of going public, which was that it enabled him to make 'relatively cheap use of other people's capital'. Black was subsequently tried on charges of taking that idea a little too literally. But in any case, just from a theoretical and ideological point of view, he was completely wrong. People who own your business's equity own your business, and are not in general inclined to forget the fact.

That's one of several reasons why companies that need capital often prefer to go down the third route for raising money. That is to sell bonds: in other words, to borrow money from the markets. Debt is therefore a fundamental fact of how capital works; and it's important to understand that a lot of the time, in the corporate

world, debt is a good thing. This is one way in which examples
from personal finances – where, if we're sensible, we try to avoid
debt – are misleading. In business, debt is a useful, even an indispensable, tool. Example: you have a business making cakes. You
invest £100,000 in your own business and it makes a profit of 10
per cent, so at the end of the year you are £10,000 ahead, meaning
you've put your capital to work and it's earned you a return of 10
per cent: not bad. But see what happens if you decide to expand
your business by borrowing money. You go to the bank and get a
loan of £200,000 to invest in your business, at an interest rate of
4 per cent. You now make £300,000 of cakes. Given that you're
still making 10 per cent, that's £30,000 gross profit. You pay your
4 per cent back to the bank at a cost of £8,000, and look what's
happened: by borrowing money, you increased your profit from
£10,000 to £22,000, a 120 per cent increase, achieved through the
benign miracle of debt. This is sometimes called 'leverage', confus-
ingly since the same name is given to the difference between equity
and liabilities described in the previous chapter, but the underlying
idea is similar, that of using other people's money to make your
own money work harder.

During the credit bubble, levels of this sort of leverage reached
astonishing heights. The extent and importance of debt and
leverage are one of the class of things which seem natural to
financial insiders but are hard for civilians to grasp fully. Talking
to insiders about debt can make you feel like a bit of a country
mouse. Chatting with Tony one day, I wondered aloud why a
particular entrepreneur had gone into the restaurant and club
business, which isn't famous for generating lavish profits. His
reply was instant: 'It'll have a good cash stream, and he'll just
leverage it up. Say the restaurants are losing a million a year, but
have ten million in cash coming in. He levers it twenty times,
suddenly he's got two hundred million to play with, and the
million quid a year he's losing is nothing.' Don't try this at home

. . . Well, I say that, but in fact home may be exactly where you are trying it. The commonest form of large-scale leverage in most people's lives is the mortgage: you leverage your income by a factor of three or four to make a single big long-term highly illiquid investment, in the form of a property. There seems to be something of a conspiracy to discourage us from thinking of mortgages quite as baldly and bluntly as that. Ads for share investments are obliged to warn people that values go down as well as up, but there's no such reminder about our biggest and least liquid investments of all. Instead, the reminders come in the form of brutal reality checks, such as the current downturn.

Government debt is different from business debt, and instead is a little more like personal debt – which basically involves borrowing from your future earnings in order to spend money in the present day. In order to do that, governments issue bonds, in the same way that companies do. At the moment, the British government is selling £225 billion of these bonds in 2009, in order to raise the money it needs to pay for all its spending. These numbers are scarily big, but then the whole bond market is scarily big. This is a huge, huge part of the global economy, absolutely central to its functioning. Although the stock market gets more attention and has more name-recognition among the general public, bonds are arguably even more important to the operation of the money world. It adds up to a lot of money: the total value of the global bond market is in the region of $50 trillion. Bonds are, for governments and for many corporations, the single most fundamental way of raising money. A bond repays an agreed rate of interest until it matures, and all of these things are fixed: the price of the bond, the rate of interest it pays and the date when it matures. In the case of You ltd, you might raise the £10,000 you need selling a bond for £10,000 which repays, say, 5 per cent interest every year for five years – that's £500 a year. At the end of that time, you promise to buy back the bond for its face value, £10,000.

Is that a good deal? Maybe yes, maybe no. It depends on a lot of things, such as how likely you are to be able to keep up the payments – so if you seem like a bad risk, you'll have to pay more interest for the money you want to borrow. The safety, or non-safety, of your debt is rated by a number of agencies who have a tremendously important role in the running of credit markets. The best known of these agencies are Moody's and Standard and Poor – names which, it has to be admitted, have a slightly ironic edge in current times, given how badly some of their debt ratings have malfunctioned, and given also that moody is a synonym for, in the words of Jonathon Green's great *Dictionary of Slang*, 'illicit, uncertain, false'. The highest-rated debt in the world is AAA, the same status as US government Treasury bills; the ratings thereafter go down through AA and then A down through BBB, BB, B, CCC and then R, which means the cops have been called.* Any debt of BBB and above is known as 'investment grade'; below BBB is known as a 'junk bond', on the basis that its level of risk is high – but that shouldn't make it sound as if junk bonds are a marginal or unrespectable form of finance. (You may well feel that that distinction between investment and speculation is a little blurry and subjective; and you would be right. There is a character in one of Anthony Powell's early novels, a retired major who has gone stone-broke and is living in a boarding house, owing to 'having squandered all his money in judicious investments'.) Because they have to pay high rates of interest, junk bonds can be very useful for investors; and if they didn't exist, then only super-safe companies would be able to raise money, and all sorts of inventions and investments and growth would be impossible. The important thing is that everybody involved should be well aware of what they're getting into.

---

* The two companies use a slightly different lettering system; this is the S and P version.

If You ltd's bond is given a high rating by the agencies, it will pay out a lower rate of interest – its debt is safer and therefore pays less well. If it's given a lower rating, it will have to pay out more. In time, as interest rates in the wider economy go up and down, the You ltd five-year bond will be more or less attractive to investors. If interest rates drop to 2 per cent, that 5 per cent suddenly looks tasty, and the person who bought the bond might well be tempted to sell it on at a profit, to someone else in need of a nice earner; conversely, if interest rates zoom up, and it's easy to get 7 per cent rates of interest, the 5 per cent will look less appealing, and the price of the You ltd bond will drop. It will also drop as it comes closer to maturity. This is the point when You ltd will buy it back, in return for the cash value stated on the bond; obviously, the closer in time the bond is to the point when it will be worth exactly £10,000, the more the price will converge on that figure. All these factors coincide to make the global bond market a huge, complicated, multiply overlapping and profoundly interwoven thing, with a colossal number of working parts and, therefore, immense opportunities for the kind of swapping and trading and exchanging of revenue streams.

This is where, in 1981, swaps entered into the story.[15] Swaps began life as a way of exchanging revenue between different types of bonds. The first deal, brokered by Salomon Brothers, was worth $210 million for ten years and kickstarted a whole new field of finance. Companies would swap bonds and equivalent products, and in this way gain access to each other's line of business: it was a way for firms to spread their economic tentacles while not actually diverging from their own core business. In particular, the swaps took off as a way of playing around with other firms' interest rates and exposure to different currencies. By the summer of 1994, swaps had become a roaringly successful feature of the banking world: the volume of interest-rate and currency derivatives was worth \$12 trillion, more than the entire US economy.

One of the main players in this market was the bank J. P. Morgan. Banks have different characters, based on their different histories and institutional personalities – this is true not just for banks but for most companies and indeed most institutions. The bank J. P. Morgan is named after its founder, John Pierpont Morgan, a financier of legendary power, wealth and status, and an extraordinary collector of art. In the world of money, Morgan is famous for having rescued the entire US banking system from collapse not once but twice, during the panics of 1893 (when he directly lent the US Treasury millions of dollars to buy gold) and 1907 (when he held a vital series of meetings with senior bankers at his house and bullied them into joint action to keep the system solvent). This amount of power, and his considerable physical presence, combined to give a sinister aura to Morgan, one magnificently captured in E. L. Doctorow's novel *Ragtime*, where the financier's interest in occult practices and secret knowledge causes him to spend a night in the innermost chamber of the Great Pyramid, in the pursuit of who knows what secret wisdom . . . which makes it odder that in photographs he looks chubby and bland, an unpenetrating walrus of a man with a bulbous nose and heroic moustache.

The bank J. P. Morgan was more like the man's photograph than like his reputation: it was a super-respectable old-school Wall Street firm, with a long list of similarly respectable clients. It was also one of two firms to carry on J. P.'s legacy: the other was the financial services company Morgan Stanley. The first incarnation of J. P. Morgan was broken into two in 1935 by the Glass–Steagall Act, passed during the Great Depression, which forced retail banks, that is the ordinary sort of bank with which we're all familiar, to split from investment banks, the sort which issue complex financial instruments, trade on capital markets and run mergers and acquisitions. I call the two types the piggybank and the casino: the idea behind Glass–Steagall was that the casino activities shouldn't be allowed to endanger the banks which look after the deposits of the general public.

By the nineties, J. P. Morgan was deeply involved in the swaps market. That market had boomed since the IBM–World Bank swap; but the trouble was that it had boomed too much. Everyone was now executing swaps, which was driving down margins and making them less profitable. So in 1994, the J. P. Morgan swaps team went on an off-site weekend to Boca Raton, Florida, to come up with a new, and therefore newly lucrative, product to sell. Now, the world of banking operates according to different norms from the rest of the corporate and business world. The off-site corporate weekend is one example. Normal behaviour on these occasions consists of punishing the minibar and nursing consequent hangovers, hitting on long-fancied colleagues and putting embarrassing items, ideally pornographic films, on each other's hotel bills. For form's sake, a few new ideas are cooked up and then gradually allowed to die a natural death when everyone is back at work and liver-function levels have returned to normal. Bankers, however, are different. On their off-site weekend, J. P. Morgan's team conformed to normative behaviour in certain respects. Binge drinking occurred; a senior colleague's nose was broken; a trashed jetski and many cheeseburgers were charged to somebody else's account. All standard behaviour. But the J. P. Morgan team broke with tradition by coming up with a real idea – an idea that changed the entire nature of modern banking, with consequences that are currently rocking the economy of the entire planet.

The idea that the J. P. Morgan team had was for an innovative kind of swap. Translated into the terms of personal finance, this is how it worked. Say your neighbours the Smiths approach you and ask to borrow some money – say, to pay for a loft conversion.

You happen to have a spare £100,000 in cash, which is the amount they want to borrow, and they're promising to pay you a good rate of interest, say £1,000 a month (just to keep the numbers simple), and then to pay back the principal at the end of the year. So you make the loan and then you fall to wondering what happens if the Smiths can't make their loan payments, on which you are relying for handy extra income. At which point you ask your other neighbours, the Joneses, if they are interested in making a little bit of cash on the side. They say yes, and so you swap with them: they take on the risk that the Smiths will miss their payments – in other words, if the Smiths default, the Joneses will make up the money – and in return you pay them a fee, say £50 a month. In effect, what you've done is taken out a form of insurance. So the Smiths get their £100,000; you get your £1,000 a month; the Joneses get their £50 a month. If the Smiths stop being able to pay you, you collect from the Joneses instead.

Notice that there is one enormous benefit from this deal: you have managed to lend money, at a good rate of interest, at *no risk*. You've insured the risk away. It's a basic law of money that risk is correlated to reward – the amount of money you can make is determined by the amount of risk you are willing to take on. But you've just engineered that out of existence. If the Smiths stop being able to pay you, you collect the money from the Joneses instead. That, when you fall to thinking about it, opens up all sorts of potential.

This, translated into the corporate world of bonds and loans, was the new idea: to swap the risk of default. In effect, it was to sell the risk that a borrower won't be able to pay back his debt. This had enormous potential in the world of banking. Since banking is based on making loans to customers, the risk of default by those customers is an extremely important part of the business. So a product which made it possible to reduce that risk – to reduce it by selling it to somebody else – had the potential to create a gigantic new market. The new idea was a product which would resemble a kind of insurance, with the product insured being the risk of default on a specific debt. The first such deal involved the oil company Exxon, which needed to open a line of credit to cover potential damages of $5 billion resulting from the oil spillage from the *Exxon Valdez* in 1989. Exxon was an old client of J. P. Morgan, which was therefore reluctant to turn it down, even though the deal would take up a lot of capital which the bank could use more profitably elsewhere. Banks had rules about the amount of capital they needed to keep against the eventuality of loans going bad. The Basel rules, named after the city in Switzerland where they were formulated, are the internationally accepted code of practice for banking. These rules required that the banks held 8 per cent of their capital in reserve against the risk of outstanding loans. For the bankers, that was a drag. It limited the amount of lending they could make, the amount of risk they could take on and therefore the level of profit they could achieve. If they lent the money to Exxon, they would have to keep an amount equivalent to 8 per cent of it in reserve, just sitting there, instead of going out into the markets and making more money.

At which thought, a light bulb went on. Blythe Masters, one of the Boca Raton swaps team, came up with the idea of selling the credit line to the European Bank of Reconstruction and Development, in return for a fee. So if Exxon asked for the money, the EBRD would cough it up – and in return, it would pocket a fee from J. P. Morgan for taking on the risk. Exxon would get its credit line, J. P. Morgan would get to honour its client relationship but also to keep its capital reserves intact for sexier activities, and EBRD would get the fees. The deal was so new it didn't even have a name: eventually the one settled on was 'credit default swap'. If the risk of the loans could be sold, however, it logically followed that the loans were now risk-free;

and if that was the case, surely it made sense that the capital involved – since it wasn't at risk – was free to be relent, without counting against the reserve requirements of the Basel rules. No harm, no foul; no risk, no need to suck up useful capital. After months of work and haggling about the rules, the deal was allowed through by the regulators, who accepted the idea that the selling of risk in this way was a good thing, because it spread that risk out through the financial system rather than concentrating it in one place.

So far so good for J. P. Morgan. But the deal had been laborious and time consuming, and the bank wouldn't be able to make real money out of credit default swaps until the process became streamlined and industrialized. In the above personal-finance example, the personal nature of the deal is part of the point: you know your neighbours and can take a view on how likely they are to pay you back, and therefore on how safe your investment is. To make real money out of these deals, however, it would be so much more lucrative if one could just skip past that stage – if there were a way of bypassing the tedious, case-by-case, look-them-in-the-eye stage of assessing the risk of default.

The invention which allowed all this to happen was securitization. The issue with credit default swaps was the underlying issue with all banking, everywhere and always: the risk that the person to whom you're lending money won't be able to pay you back. Every loan is a specific case which needs assessing on its merits; and it's hard to industrialize the process of deciding case by case. The EBRD–Exxon deal, for instance, took months of intense work to arrange (and the first commercial swap, the IBM–World Bank arrangement, had taken a full two years). What securitization did was bundle together a package of these loans and then rely on safety in numbers and the law of averages: even if some loans did default, the others wouldn't, and would keep the stream of revenue going, and thus the risk of default would be spread and minimized. So there would be two sources of revenue, as well as of fees: one from the sale of the loans and another from the steady flow of repayments. And then someone had another idea: that the securities could be divided up into different levels of risk and sold off accordingly, into riskier and less risky tranches of debt, all paying different rates of interest in return for differing levels of risk. This was called 'tranching'. Some customers would want the high-paying debt, which it went without saying was higher risk; others would like the safer but less lucrative flavour. Customers would be able to buy exactly the degree of risk they wanted, tailor-made to their needs. All these ideas were knocking around the banking world. Bill Demchak at J. P. Morgan put them together to create securitized bundles of credit default swaps – bundles of insurance against default – and sold them to investors. The investors would get the streams of revenue, according to the level of risk-and-reward they chose; the bank would get insurance against its loans, and fees for setting up the deal.

And there was one final component to the J. P. Morgan team's invention. They set up an offshore shell company, called a special-purpose vehicle (SPV), to fulfil the role supplied by the EBRD in the first credit default swap. The shell company would assume $9.7 billion of J. P. Morgan's risk; then it would sell off that risk to investors, in the form of securities paying differing rates of interest. So the risk of default had been sold to the special-purpose vehicle, then pooled, made into a range of securities and sold on to investors. Why did banks bother to set up SPVs? Two reasons. The first was to remove the swap from the bank's balance sheet. The more assets banks have on their balance sheet, in proportion to their equity, the more leveraged they are: if the assets didn't appear on the balance sheet, the bank would look less leveraged, therefore safer. What regulators and investors didn't know couldn't hurt them. In addition, the SPVs were located offshore, in places such as the Caymans, Bermuda, the Bahamas or the British Virgin Islands, for the simple purpose of avoiding taxes. In this case, the really beautiful part was that, according to J. P. Morgan's calculations, the underlying loans were so safe that they needed to sell only $700 million of insurance to cover $9.7 billion of debt. The credit agency Moody's hummed and hahed for a while before agreeing with that view, and behold: a whole new era in banking had dawned. J. P. Morgan had found a way to shift risk off its books, while simultaneously generating income from that risk, and freeing up capital to lend elsewhere. It was poetry. The only thing wrong with it was the name, BISTRO – standing for Broad Index Secured Trust Offering, but making the new rocket-science financial instrument sound like a place you went to for a plate of steak-frites. The market came to prefer a different term: 'synthetic collateralized debt obligations'.

Just to keep track of where we have got to with these new financial instruments, let's translate it back into personal-finance terms. Remember your arrangement to lend money to the Smiths for their loft – the one you got your other neighbours, the Joneses, to insure. That was a straightforward swap of risk. The deal went fine, and you fell to thinking about how it might be improved if another neighbour were to approach you. You've started to be a little bit annoyed by the way in which that loan tied up the full £100,000 of spare capital that you have at your disposal. When another neighbour, the Wilsons, hear that you lent the Smiths money and ask you to make them a similar loan, you're in a position to come up with something a little bit more creative. For one thing, you know that the money you're lending is totally safe. Because the Smiths are doing up their house, the capital you've lent is adding to the value of their house, which means that in your view it's not at risk. So what you now do is re-lend your £100,000 to the Wilsons. As for where you get the money from

– does it matter, since you're on to a surefire winner? House prices are zooming up in your area, so there's nothing to worry about from the capital point of view. The £100,000 simply isn't at risk. What's the worst that could happen? The Smiths or Wilsons might have a cash crisis and, OK, say it all goes wrong and they can't pay you back and eventually have to sell their house. You'll definitely get back your £100,000, so the only thing you're at risk of losing is the £12,000 of interest they owe you – and you sell that risk to the Joneses, again, so again, you've engineered away the risk. But wait! Now some more neighbours, the Millers, approach, also wanting to do the same sort of deal. They're up for it, you're up for it, the Joneses are up for it, the only trouble is that you've run out of capital because you've already lent your £100,000 to the Wilsons. But since that money is in your view completely safe, you should feel free to lend it again. So what you do is create a company, ideally based offshore where it pays no UK tax, and extend to it the credit to buy the loan from you. You lend it a virtual £100,000, it buys the Wilsons' debt from you and recredits you with the £100,000, so you're back in the black. (In practice, the personal-finance example breaks down here, because you can't lend money to yourself and create credit in quite this way. But large financial institutions can and do.) Now your company, Lofts ltd, sells the default risk on the Wilsons' debt – the credit default swap – to the Joneses. And then when another neighbour comes to you and again asks to borrow your £100,000, you do the same thing, and then again, and again, up to, let's say for the sake of this example, ten times. The cash is pouring in and everybody wins: the neighbours get their loft money, you get your stream of repayment fees paid to your offshore company, the Joneses get their stream of insurance payments, and the beauty of it is that there's no risk for you, because you've insured it away. You can stop caring about whether or not your neighbours actually can pay you back. If they can't, so what? The Joneses will pick up the tab.

The beauties of this, from a financial-engineering point of view, are almost too numerous. The new CDS instruments are a magnificently efficient way of spreading, and therefore minimizing, risk – at least, they are if used as their initial inventors intended. Financial crashes and implosions are often linked to over-concentration of risk: placing too big bets in one place. At the time of the invention of the CDS, the most recent large-scale bust in the US was the Savings and Loan debacle of the 1980s, in which overconcentration of risk on the part of the Savings and Loan associations played a prominent role. One of the reasons why regulators were minded to look favourably on CDSs was that they saw them as useful devices to disperse and therefore diminish risk. No one foresaw the possibility that they might spread unmanageable and near-undetectable amounts of risk throughout the financial system. A second attractive aspect: the new instruments offered a whole new way of participating in somebody else's business. Remember that there are two basic ways of investing in companies, which are also two basic ways for companies to raise capital: stocks, in which you buy a piece of a company, and bonds, in which you lend the company money. The genius thing about CDSs was that they offered a third way. You got a string of regular payments (as with a bond) and you exposed yourself to the risk of the other party defaulting (as in a bond), but it was sexier than a bond, because your capital wasn't fully tied up in the process. You didn't need to draw on it unless the counterparty defaulted. Add a bit of financial ingenuity, and you could use your capital very effectively over and over again, because you only ever needed to post part of the capital as collateral against the risk of default. In terms of the above example, say the Joneses were covering £100,000 of risk; the rules might dictate that they needed to have only £10,000 on hand against that. If they were sitting on £100,000 of cash, they could guarantee up to ten times that amount of risk: so their £100,000 will earn them £1,000,000 of CDS business. That's sexy indeed. So the miracle of credit default swaps has enabled you to take £100,000 and lend it ten times, and then sell the CDS ten times to another person with £100,000. The CDS has done an amazing job of putting your capital to work.

These new financial instruments were very, very clever, but they had an unfortunate side-effect: they broke banking. They did so because banking at its heart is, or should be, a simple business. Customers deposit money at a bank, in return for interest; the bank lends that money to other people, at a higher rate of interest. This isn't glamorous or interesting, but then banking is not supposed to resemble base jumping or hip-hop. Instead it is a guaranteed way of making steady money for ever (and, not incidentally, of creating credit in the economy), as long as one all-important rule is followed: the bank has to be careful about whom it lends money to. The quality of the loan is critical, because those loans are the bank's earning assets. This isn't some incidental or marginal issue, it's the very core of what banking is. The trouble with the model of packaging plus securitization was that it broke with that fundamental principle that a bank had individually to assess and monitor every loan. The new instruments made that impossible. The mathematics of valuation models – horrendously complex equations to assess probabilities and correlations, cooked up in best mad-scientist style by the firms' maths quants – took the burden of assessing statistical risk. The whole idea that a banker looks a borrower in the eye and takes a view on whether he can trust him came to seem laughably nineteenth-century. As for the risks, well, as Lawrence Summers said when he was Deputy Secretary to the Treasury, 'the parties to these kinds of contract are largely sophisticated financial institutions that would appear to be eminently capable of protecting themselves from fraud and counterparty insolvencies.' That turned out to be total rubbish. It was the taxpayer who ended up picking up that bill for counterparty insolvencies, and the sums involved were and are vast.

As chance would have it, it was insurance against those very counterparty insolvencies which was to destroy AIG. This is a gigantic insurance company, worth $200 billion at its peak and definitively Too Big To Fail. It was AIG which was, in effect, the Joneses. It underwrote all the insurance: it was the single biggest player in the CDS market. Entertainingly for fans of financial acronyms, AIG was done in by CDSs on CDOs. That's to say, it took part in credit default swaps on collateralized debt obligations, the pools of sub-prime mortgages whose dramatic collapse in value in 2008 was the proximate cause of the financial crisis. When the investment bank Lehman Brothers imploded in September that year, done in by its exposure to bad assets, there was a generalized panicked scramble to see who else was carrying similar risk. When it turned out that AIG was, and, worse, that it was valuing those assets at much higher prices than Lehmans had, investors freaked out and the company's credit rating collapsed. That meant that it had to post more collateral to cover its share of risks. In terms of the above example, the Joneses suddenly looked like a less safe risk, so the neighbours asked them to post more than the £10,000 of collateral against the loans – they were contractually allowed to insist that the Joneses now put up £20,000 for each £100,000 of risk they were covering. If the Joneses don't have that kind of money immediately at hand, they will have to borrow it. If they can't borrow it, they're toast.

And that's exactly what happened to AIG. When it had to increase its collateral cover, it couldn't, because credit markets had tightened up. For the Joneses, that would be End of Story:

they're bankrupt. But because AIG was Too Big To Fail, the US government stepped in with a bailout on 16 September, worth $85 billion, in return for 79.9 per cent of the company. (The bailout – they come in different varieties – was in the form of a twenty-four-month credit facility. To adopt an analogy with personal finances, this meant AIG could draw on the government's bank account.) On 9 October, AIG was given another $37.8 billion in credit. Enough already? No. On 10 November the US Treasury pumped another $40 billion into the company by buying freshly issued stock created for the purpose (this being yet another variety of bailout – somebody should write a Bankster Bailout Cookbook). Finally enough already? Don't be silly. On 1 March 2009 the Treasury gave the company another $30 billion and restructured the terms of its loan to make repayments of government money less arduous. The next day the company announced a loss for the quarter – not the year, the quarter – of $62 billion, the worst corporate results in history. Finally enough already already? Not necessarily. According to the US Treasury statement accompanying the fourth bailout: 'Given the systemic risk AIG continues to pose and the fragility of markets today, the potential cost to the economy and the taxpayer of government inaction would be extremely high.' To stabilize AIG would 'take time and possibly further government support'. That's what Too Big To Fail means. You could put it like this: AIG+CDS+CDO+TBTF= $173,000,000,000.

In the UK, after the collapse of RBS, we had our entertaining but essentially distracting row over Sir Fred 'Knighted for Services to Banking' Goodwin's pension; in the US they had their equivalent row over bonuses paid to senior AIG executives after the bailouts. The bonuses totalled $165 million and it doesn't take a PR professional to see that March 2009, after the fourth AIG bailout, wasn't the ideal time to have announced them. Everyone on both sides of American politics from Obama

downwards joined in the storm of outrage, which was followed
by predictable bleating from the banksters. A Republican
congressman invited the AIG executives to follow the 'Japanese
approach' and either apologize or commit suicide. (More authen-
tic to do both, surely?) A Democratic senator threatened to tax
the bonuses at 100 per cent. The *New York Times* published an
AIG executive's open letter to his boss, which said he was resign-
ing because he hadn't been a derivatives trader and his feelings
were hurt. He seemed to be expecting applause because he was
repaying his own bonus of $742,006.40. Good fun all round. But
the story was a distraction from the real scandal about AIG,
which is what was happening to the other 99 per cent of the
money the government was pumping into the company. Since
AIG wrote CDSs, which are effectively insurance against losses,
and since those losses had occurred, why then, the money was
going to companies which had lost money in the credit crunch:
companies such as Société Générale, which received $11.9 billion,
Goldman Sachs $12.9 billion, Merrill Lynch $6.8 billion, Deutsche Bank $11.8 billion, Barclays $7 billion, BNP Paribas $4.9
billion. Nothing could better illustrate the way in which this
has become a systemic international crisis than the fact that the
US Treasury is transferring these gigantic sums to foreign banks,
because they feel they have no choice if they're to keep the
financial system functioning. But it's a hell of a pill for the US
taxpayer to have to swallow – one made much worse by the fact
that Goldman Sachs went on, mere months later, to declare
record profits and pay record bonuses. AIG is broke, essentially
because it got its sums wrong about the level of risk represented
by CDSs. So it can't pay its counterparties (that's the other side
of the insurance deal, the insurees). But the counterparties made
the same mistake, since they took out insurance with an insurer
who, in the event of a structural crisis, wouldn't be able to afford
to pay them. So why are the insurees walking away whistling

with pockets full of US Treasury cash, while the US taxpayer sits on a gigantic loss? Note that AIG's market capitalization – the total value of all its shares – is no more than $2 billion. Saving the company has cost eighty-five times more than buying it would have. Why therefore has the Treasury saved it? Because AIG is Too Big To Fail. The implosion of Lehmans in September 2008 took what was already a crisis and very nearly turned it into the total collapse of the global economic system: that was the point at which, in President Bush's immortal words, 'this sucker could go down.' (Or, as *The Onion* put it: 'Bush calls for panic.') The lesson of Lehmans was, to politicians, crystal clear: it was that no financial institution of comparable size could ever again be allowed to collapse. AIG was bailed out because it had the entire economic system over a barrel.

Buffett was doubly right to compare the new financial products to 'weapons of mass destruction' – first, because they are lethal and, second, because no one knows how to track them down. If the invention of derivatives was the financial world's modernist dawn, the current crisis is unsettlingly like the birth of postmodernism. For anyone who studied literature in college in the past few decades, there is a weird familiarity about the current crisis: value, in the realm of finance capital, parallels the elusive nature of meaning in deconstructionism. According to Jacques Derrida, the doyen of the school, meaning can never be precisely located; instead, it is always 'deferred', moved elsewhere, located in other meanings, which refer and defer to other meanings – a snake permanently and necessarily eating its own tail. This process is fluid and constant, but at moments the perpetual process of deferral stalls and collapses in on itself. Derrida called this moment an 'aporia', from a Greek term meaning 'impasse'. There is something both amusing and appalling about seeing his theories acted out in the world markets to such cataclysmic effect. It was CDSs which were the crucial instrument in making that happen, spreading risk throughout the financial system, not least because most of them are trading 'over the counter', as it's called in the City – between one institution and another, with no intermediary. That means there is no central register of CDSs, and no body capable of assessing and managing market-wide risks.

As a direct corollary of that, there is no responsible body to check whether counterparties are actually in a position to pay the sums for which they are on the hook, should the insurance be called in. The principle is that of caveat emptor, buyer beware – except, actually, the buyer didn't need to beware, because the taxpayer was going to bail him out. So it emerged that the policy in fact was not so much 'buyer beware' as 'buyer, dude, don't bother bewaring, we've got this covered.' Further compounding the potential problems was the fact that many of the risks were sold on and resold without the knowledge of the initial counterparty – which meant that a deal could end up being reinsured with the same banks more than once. As for the scale of those risks, well, they became huge. By June 2008, the International Swaps and Derivatives Association or ISDA – the association of companies dealing in this stuff – was estimating the total size of the market as $54 trillion, $54,000,000,000,000, close to the total GDP of the planet and many times more valuable than the total number of all the stocks and shares traded in the world. The underlying value of the risks being insured was much lower than the notional value, of course – but the lesson of Long-Term Capital Management was that when these deals blow up, they leave giant holes in the markets, because of the sheer number of counterparties holding contracts with notional exposure to the risk. It's like a game of pass-the-parcel, in which nobody knows who's actually holding the parcel, much less what's going to be found inside it when it's unwrapped.

That was the reason why, when the crisis began, banks suddenly became reluctant to lend money to each other, and liquidity dried up, and financial institutions began to collapse. The problem was that CDSs and related financial instruments had been around and sold from bank to bank in an entirely untransparent way, in a gigantic game of pass-the-parcel. The complexities are such that even when the parcel is unwrapped and opened, people still don't know the full details of what's in it. So this tool, the CDS, which had been invented as a way of making lending safer, turned out to magnify and spread risks throughout the global financial system. It's as if people used the invention of seatbelts as an opportunity to take up drunk-driving.

3. Boom and Bust

American urban desolation has a unique quality to it, once seen, never forgotten. My first encounter with it was in inner-city Detroit in 1996, and my main impression was of the crushing, oppressive emptiness of the streets. This wasn't just the ground-level vacancy that all high-rise buildings impose around them, this was another level of abandonment, desertion, flight – a science-fiction landscape, like *I Am Legend*. The bleakness derives not just from Detroit's present but also from its history, and not just because of the way that history is blighted by urban and racial politics gone horribly wrong, but also because of the straight-forward way in which the history is one of descent and decline. Once, Detroit was prosperous; now it isn't. Once it was a pleas-ant place to live; now it is dystopian. It's a model of what can go wrong with a city. Even amid decades of general prosperity and rising GDP, it is possible for a place to go as badly wrong, as far off the rails, as Detroit. It might sound perverse, but the place it reminded me most of is Rome, in the long centuries after the ancient city's fall. It must have been a curious feeling, to look not just at extraordinary things like the Colosseum, but at the ordinary infrastructure of buildings and bridges and aqueducts, and accept that these were ruins of things which people had lost the ability to build. Detroit, especially its big buildings which once testified to civic optimism and aspiration, is like that.

I suppose it's partly because America is so rich that its poverty seems so bleak, so demoralized and demoralizing. But it's also that so many of the areas afflicted by modern poverty, and so many of the properties caught up in it, seen from another perspective, could be so pleasant to live in. There is a style of low-built row houses which feature in American cities, and which look from one point of view like ideal urban low-cost housing, built to a human scale, and simply begging to be part of an idealized, mixed, diverse, complicated, modern way of living – it's as if the ideas of Jane Jacobs, the great American theorist of urban diversity, about the patterns of neighbourhood use and city life, were built into these streets from their inception. And it's that which makes them look so terrible when they go wrong. Because the houses are built to a pattern, small differences in upkeep, in the attention which all homes need, are magnified. Big differences are glaring. A house with a front porch that's falling down, or boarded-up windows, has the effect of dragging down the homes around it – and this isn't just a matter of aesthetics, but of a now-proven pattern in sociology and urban development. The 'broken windows', as they're called, drag down standards of behaviour around them. When the houses are completely unoccupied and can be broken into, they are an immediate magnet for vandals, crack smokers, fire bugs, you name it; sometimes the power is cut off, sometimes the water, and sometimes one but not the other, leading to a simple and easy and devastating form of havoc for happy vandals – just turn on a tap and walk away.

I came to Baltimore because it is the subject of the only sustained work of art I've seen attempting to describe the lives led in this urban desolation: David Simon's HBO series *The Wire*. From the point of view of writing about the housing crisis, it was almost an arbitrary choice. All across America a boom turned into a bust; foreclosures on housing loans are a pandemic. (Difference between a pandemic and an epidemic: it's everywhere at the same time.) This is one form of 'deleveraging': the withdrawal of credit from people who often weren't in a position to repay it in the first place. It hit everywhere: rustbelt cities which had been struggling against population decline and associated problems for decades; sunbelt areas, which had experienced sharp population growth in the new millennium, much of it from new migrants (the highest rate of repossession filings in the USA in the first six months of 2009 was in Nevada); exurbs sprawling out beyond the suburbs of towns and cities all over the country; traditional boom—bust hotspots such as Florida. Some bizarre phenomena have been thrown up by the foreclosure crisis. One of the main players in the field is Deutsche Bank, which has been acting as trustee for the companies which own loans: this has led to a situation in which a German bank owns 10 per cent of all the properties in Cleveland, Ohio. Deutsche Bank has been a major player in Baltimore, too, though the sub-prime crisis is here not just an event in itself but the latest instalment in a long-running and apparently endless series of misfortunes, some of them self-inflicted by the city and its inhabitants and some of them, like this one, not. So David Simon and his colleagues made a five-part, sixty-episode work of art – in effect a huge televised novel, which as many observers have remarked is Balzacian in its scope and achievement – and still managed to miss out on one of the worst disasters to affect Baltimoreans in decades. The credit crunch has cost 33,000 householders in Baltimore their properties, victims of the wave of mortgage foreclosures. This in a city where the population has in recent decades fallen from around a million to about 300,000 fewer, and where 50,000 homes were already lying unoccupied. As you drive around past block after block of abandoned properties, boarded up, some of them mere shells, some of them – some of the saddest – leaving one or two occupied houses behind in their wake, clinging bravely or desperately to what used once to be a decent place to live – it's hard not to think that this city looks like it lost a war. It looked like that already before the credit crunch, but this city needed 33,000 home repossessions about as much as London during the second world war needed the Luftwaffe.

The foreclosed now won't talk on the record about what's happened to them: too much litigation is under way, some of it directed by the city against the lenders behind the ensuing crisis. But you can talk to them off the record, and you can also go and look at some of the homes they've lost, such as 3803 Bonner Road in West Baltimore, a foreclosed loan from Wells Fargo that is now boarded up and covered in warning notices, but would once have been a family home of proportions which aren't just generous but, by European standards, palatial. I wandered around outside, motivated by a curiosity which quickly gave way to sadness: there's just something so not-right about a big house, built for a big family, lying empty and abandoned and hauling the surrounding area slightly further downwards as it sinks further and further into disrepair. And as for what happens to the former inhabitants of this and the other 30,000 properties, that's even sadder. 'I don't know, to be honest with you,' Anthony DePastina, an attorney with the Baltimore Civil Justice, a non-profit legal organization involved in fighting for the foreclosed, told me.* 'These 30,000 essentially lost their homes because they can't make their mortgage payments. The reality is that they have little to no money. As a consequence of the mortgage-foreclosure process their credit is ruined, so oftentimes rental companies aren't willing to rent to them because their credit is shot. So they either wind up moving in with other people that they know, a relative or friend. Or if they're lucky they can rent a place on their own, either through a private landlord or a company that doesn't require a credit check. If they're very very unlucky they wind up on the street.'

I said, it's pretty bleak, that people just disappear off the grid like that.

'Yes,' he said. 'The short answer is, nobody knows where they

---

* Tony is also, we quickly and surprisedly worked out when we started discussing our Irish mothers, my third cousin.

go. There is no safety net for these people. The social system is so strained at this time that it's very difficult to find appropriate housing in the same amount of time that you're being put out of your other house. I had a gentleman this morning, he's being put out of his home because he can't make his mortgage payments. We're anticipating that he'll be out of his home within ninety days. But he can't get on the waiting list to get assistance – the lady told him it could be up to a year, a year and a half. What does he do? He can't afford anything more than 500 dollars a month and he's the sole support of two children. There are thousands like him. I had another gentleman who was injured as a result of what's going to be a contested workplace injury. He was unable to work for a period, fell behind on his mortgage, lost his home. I personally spoke to three or four churches trying to get him help and several state agencies, but we couldn't raise him enough money to even get him into the most remedial apartment. He lived in his car for three or four months. He has no family and currently he lives in what I would consider an abandoned trailer. He's trying to save his money so that he can get an apartment but it takes time to get on his feet, it's probably going to take him another month or two. He's not looking to live in the Taj Mahal, he just wants a one-room apartment. So that's it. If they're lucky they get taken in by relatives, or they find a cash job and a renter who'll take them in for cash. But mainly, nobody knows.'

And that's where the dream of owning your own home, combined with innovative new financial derivatives, has brought us. This is the other end of the causal chain behind the bank collapses and the seizing-up of credit.

It's easy to lose money in the housing market. I've done it myself.

One of my most vivid memories of the late 1980s property bubble was how insanely boring it made so much conversation. There were dinner parties at which people spoke about literally nothing else, apart from the need to 'get on the property ladder', about the inexorable rise in prices, about the fascinating new developments such as the exciting new go-go financial product, the endowment mortgage. (This was a much touted product in which the borrower repaid only the interest of the loan directly to the mortgage company; the principal was repaid via investment in a guaranteed-to-succeed investment product, set to mature when the principal was due to be paid back. These products were the focus of a huge scandal when it turned out that – surprise! – they grew more slowly than predicted and failed to cover the principal amounts owed.) Mrs Thatcher had promised to create a 'property-owning democracy', and by God she was fulfilling her promise: during her time in office home-ownership in the UK rose from 54 to 65 per cent. In the process she proved Oscar Wilde wrong. He once said that the most frightening words in the English language were 'I had a very interesting dream last night.' Not true. In fact the most frightening words in the language are 'Did you hear how much they got for that house down the road?'

The single best thing about the bubble bursting in the late eighties was that all this went away. Half a million people lost their homes, which was horrible for them, but the good news was that for about a decade and a half nobody talked about property prices any more. That caused me to have a misanthropic, or unpatriotic, reflection: maybe one reason the British love talking about property prices so much is because it's one of the only times it's socially permissible to boast about how rich we are. For sure, and thank God, you hear a lot less about the value of people's houses when they're on the way down.

Why are we so obsessed? Take a step back, and there's nothing inherently interesting about the British property market. Say you bought your house in 1970, and paid the then national average price for it: £4,378. At the peak of the current spike in prices, that same average house would have been worth £184,431. Congratulations! You've multiplied your money by forty-three times. You're rich, do you hear me? Rich! Except you aren't really. Strip out the effect of inflation, and that spectacular-sounding 4,300 per cent price rise works out as 2.4 per cent a year in real terms. This is close, in other words, to the historic long-term average for investments regarded as being more or less without any risk at all. That's where the expression 'safe as houses' comes from. Pick slightly different starting and finishing points, and the conclusions are pretty much the same. From 1973 to 2007, for instance, when inflation rates were different, and prices were higher at the start and lower at the end: the result is 2.6 per cent annual growth. That's more or less exactly the rate at which the whole British economy grew over the equivalent period. In other words house prices performed exactly the same as the economy. So there's nothing interesting to say about them.

Life, however, isn't quite as simple as that. Yes, from a historical distance, the house market is a dead-safe, dead-boring thing. Look at the graph of house prices, though, and it isn't like that. The overview shows steady, predictable progress; the close-ups show that house prices go up and down like a bride's nightie. When Gordon Brown promised us 'an end to boom and bust', he was promising something no British politician has ever achieved. All markets over-correct: they go too far on the way up, and then they go too far on the way down, which provides the momentum for them to go too far up again next time. With houses, for various reasons we'll get to in a moment, the ups and downs are worse.

I know – I've been there and done that. I bought my first flat in the autumn of 1987, egged on by the fact that everybody I knew was scraping every penny they had together to 'get on the property ladder'. The area was a bit of a dump, opposite King's

Cross station, but I could walk to work and to pretty much anywhere else in London I wanted to go. The flat too was a bit of a dump, not least because it was so small. The shape of it was weird: already narrow to start with – for most of its length, I could reach both walls by stretching out my fingertips – it narrowed more at both ends. The American writer Madison Smart Bell stayed downstairs at one point, and used the flat as the basis of a novel about a man who goes mad, partly because his flat is such a strange shape.

The flat cost £59,000. Half of the money was money left to me when my father died, and the other half was borrowed from the Halifax. I repaid the interest and was advised to repay the principal using that miraculous new product, the endowment mortgage. Prices were rocketing. What could possibly go wrong?

I had many adventures in and around that flat. A period when I got on well with my landlord, writing letters to his son's school for him, giving him unqualified advice about his insomnia, was followed by a falling out in which he almost sued me, and we didn't speak for three years. The man downstairs fell out with the landlord so badly he took an axe to the cupboard where the gas meter was, went to court to fight the service charge, lost, and sub-let his flat to two prostitutes. They fitted in well with the rest of the area, which went downhill in the second Tory recession of the early nineties, and filled up with drug-dealers, prostitutes, pimps – and, worse, their customers. I learnt a lot about a lot of things through owning that flat.

What I didn't do was make any money. When I sold the flat, a decade later, it was for exactly what I had paid for it. That in real terms represented a loss of about 35 per cent. It wasn't a surprise, because the property bubble had burst, and flats around King's Cross were not an easy sell; when I asked estate agents, which I did about every two years, they would sound shifty, ask what I'd paid for it, and then say that's about what they would expect to get. This wasn't true – what they meant was, you would be an idiot to sell. So I didn't.

And that was the most important thing I learnt from my first flat. Property prices go up and down, but the main thing is not to pay them a blind bit of notice, unless and until you have a good reason to move. I learnt that a rising price will not rise for ever; that when prices stop rising, it will be difficult to sell your flat, because the reason the price has stopped rising is because the climate has changed. The money you have in your house is not liquid money; it's not money which can easily be converted into something else other than your house. It's stupid to feel richer because the value of your house has gone up, since the resulting rise almost always isn't money you can use or spend. If you're going to move, you still need somewhere to live, and the cost of that place too will have gone up, so there will be no net gain from the increase in your property's value.

I also learnt that although I hadn't made money, I hadn't lost too much of it. That's because if you own a house, it effectively pays you an income – the money you would have spent in rent. My mortgage was a lot less than I would have spent in rent, so my flat was doing me economic favours, even while its value was freefalling. Finally, thanks to that endowment mortgage, I learnt not to put too much trust in anything I was told by the economic services industry. (Because I was mis-sold the policy so early, I'm not covered by the compensation scheme that the industry was belatedly and grudgingly forced to bring in from 1989.)

The fact is that for many people, the ups and downs on the charts, the spikes and troughs, each represent a manic–depressive roller coaster. The ups are the bubbles, and the downs are the crashes, and it is the recurrence of these which makes the UK housing market so distinctive; which in turn brings us back again to the question, why? Why are we so obsessed with our properties and their price?

*

That question has a short answer and a long one. The long one concerns the fundamental structural differences of the UK property market. So many of us own our own houses: 70 per cent of the British population live in their own homes. The number has continued to go up since Mrs Thatcher, as successive governments have continued her pro-ownership policies. This is a much higher figure than in comparable economies in Europe: for instance, only 40 per cent of Germans own their own home. Many, many things flow from that fact.

The first is to do with that small word 'own'. In practice, most of us own our homes through mortgages, which means that we don't own our home at all. Back in the days of my first flat, you didn't even hold the property deeds of your own property if you had a mortgage: the bank held the deeds. There was something brutal about that, but at least the point was stark: if you have a mortgage, you don't own your own home, and it's a good idea to remember the fact.

If you have a mortgage, though, your life is in thrall to a number: the interest rate. In continental Europe, policy wonks and bankers care what the interest rate is, but no one else does. Here, the interest rate has the potential to dominate your life. This is the single biggest reason why the UK has not joined the euro – because the British economy has cycles which aren't exactly in phase with Europe, and because the interest rate has such a directly personal effect on people's finances here. If we had joined the euro and our mortgages were tied to those groovily low euro interest rates, money would have been even cheaper, and credit even more easily available, so the housing bubble would have been even bigger, and the crash correspondingly crashier. (Two examples of countries where that happened: Ireland and Spain.) The credit crunch has exposed significant problems with the running of the European Central Bank, the body which oversees the euro. The ECB has a Europe-wide theatre in which to operate, and there are sure to be times when the concerns of its member countries will vary sharply. The range of competing needs to be juggled by the ECB is diverse; sceptics would say unmanageably diverse. That isn't necessarily true, but it was certain that, in a crisis, the setting of a continent-wide interest-rate policy was always going to be a challenge. The demands of a car manufacturer in Düsseldorf who is worried about wage inflation can't be squared with those of a Latvian restaurateur who needs to borrow capital, or a Spanish financier worried about economic overheating. This is a process in which there are bound to be losers. Ireland and Spain desperately needed a spike in interest rates to pop their respective bubbles, but that was just too bad – the needs of other countries prevailed. The result, for them, was the grotesque bubble and the horrific crash which inevitably ensued.

Britain can't join the euro because its mortgage market, and therefore its interest rates, are just too politically important. The first thing that's different about British mortgages is that there are more of them. Second, they are bigger: the size of the loan is proportionately bigger, in relation to the value of the house. German banks, for instance, will lend only a maximum of 60 per cent of a property's value. In France, it's even more strict. For a start, our model of the mortgage, in which the loan is keyed to the value of the house being bought, doesn't apply. In France, it's the other way around. The critical figure is not the value of your property but the size of your income. Banks will lend only the money you can reasonably afford to pay back out of your monthly paypacket. In practice, that figure has been assessed as being a third of your gross income. So a bank will lend only a third of what you're earning – and if the bank stretches the rules and you get into trouble paying it back, the bank can be sued for reckless lending. It's the bank which bears the responsibility for your not borrowing stupid amounts of money.

Linked to this is the fact that attitudes to debt are different. For instance, there are no cheque-guarantee cards in France, and if that sounds as if it implies a happy-go-lucky, carefree attitude to money, the exact opposite is true: there are no cheque-guarantee cards because it is a criminal offence to write a cheque for more money than you have in your account. (It's a bit like French libel law. The sums awarded in French libel cases are tiny – not because the French don't care about their reputations, but because they do. The point of honour is sufficient in itself. Contrast this with Britain, with our ridiculously crook-friendly libel law and lavish cash awards – if anybody cared about the point of alleged honour, the cash wouldn't be necessary.) Add this together and you get an entirely different culture of money and borrowing and debt, one which means that the French have dramatically lower levels of household debt than the Anglo-Saxon economies. In Britain going into the credit crunch, the typical household owed more than 160 per cent of its average income – an alarmingly high figure, and one which reflects our high levels of mortgage debt and our general willingness to borrow, borrow, borrow in order to spend, spend, spend. In France the equivalent figure was 60 per cent. Individually and collectively, French households are much less stretched and much less at risk from a downturn. Economists attribute to this the fact that Germany and France were the first countries to emerge officially from the current recession.

Back in the days of my first mortgage, British loans were like European ones, in that the bank preferred not to lend you more than half, or at the most three-quarters, of the value of the property. They also preferred not to lend you more than two-and-a-half times your annual income; if two of you were buying a property together, you could stretch to three times your joint income. Back in those days it was very hard, verging on impossible, for people who do what I do now – write for a living

– to get a mortgage, because we couldn't produce the relevant payslips and employment history.*

All those rules have long since gone from the UK property market. A banker involved in picking over the corpse of Northern Rock told me that 'most of the loans were sound, but one or two of their books had blown up, and one of the worst of them was the hundred and twenty per cent mortgages.' I asked why anyone would want to borrow 120 per cent of the value of the thing they were buying, and he just shrugged. That product only makes sense if you are absolutely certain that the value of the property you're buying will go significantly up: and there is no reason to be absolutely certain of that. We have these crazily risky, heavily leveraged mortgages, and Europeans don't. Also, they borrow for shorter periods, a decade or twenty years at most, as opposed to the twenty-five or thirty years standard in Britain. It is also much harder for Europeans to remortgage. All these reasons, taken together, are why Europeans are more likely to rent than to own. In turn, it means that we are borrowing much more money, for longer, at much greater risk.

Another feature of the UK mortgage market adds to that risk: the fact that we prefer to pay our mortgages at variable rates. The US has a similar home-ownership rate to the UK: more mortgages, for a higher proportion of the property value, and with

* These days it's different – or was until the credit crunch – and writers can get mortgages, the same as everyone else. But some areas are still harder and/ or more expensive for writers, and one of them is car insurance. Writers' premiums are significantly higher than for regular citizens. I asked a mortgage broker why this is: is it because novelists are supposed to be drunk all the time and prone to crashing into things? His reply: 'Yeah, partly, but it's more that you'll write a book, and it'll be a big success, like Bridget Jones or something, and then they'll make it into a film and you'll meet Renée Zellweger and then you'll be driving around with her and have an accident and she'll go through the windscreen of your car and the insurance company will have to compensate her for loss of earnings. That's what they're really worried about.'

longer repayment periods. In the US, though, far more of the loans are at fixed interest rates. British householders are allergic to fixed interest rates; we prefer variable loans. No one quite knows why, since fixed interest rates often make good sense, and have the effect of transferring some of the risk of the loan to the banks. If you have a variable-rate mortgage, and the central bank interest rate goes up, you feel it in your pocket; if you have a fixed rate, and the same thing happens, the bank feels it. In the USA the two institutions designed to help the banking system to bear the risk of this fixed-rate lending are Fannie Mae and Freddie Mac; and the reason they went under was precisely because they were swamped by the cost of these risks.

The lack of these products in other countries reflects the historic differences in attitudes to property. I have a theory about why we are like this: our longing is connected to the sense of dislocation which spread throughout British society during the industrial revolution. If we for a moment ignore what we already know about property, and imagine what property markets in different countries might be like – if we think counterfactually – then it might seem logical for things to be the other way around. Countries with the go-go attitude to the free market, countries which pride themselves on their openness to competition, willingness to take a chance, lack of feather-bedding and protection from the laws of the jungle, might be expected to have a property market in which people were easy-going about renting and reluctant to tie up all their money in a single illiquid asset. On the other hand countries with more traditional, less capitalistic attitudes, less open to the cold winds of the markets and more willing to protect their citizens from market realities, might well have a conservative appetite for bricks-and-mortar. Instead it's the other way around. Why? Well, perhaps that's exactly why. It's precisely the most free-market, go-go countries which show this overpowering appetite for people to own their own homes.

The less security there is in the workplace, the more exposed the rest of life is to the pressures of competition and uncertainty, the more people want to feel secure within their own four walls, at the beginning and end of the harsh working day. Britain was the first country to experience the transforming impact of industrial life, and the associated disconnections between land and labour and place. Just as the industrial revolution broke the food culture of Britain, it also created a new emphasis on the distinction between the industrialized workplace and the private space of home. The huge expansion in British home-ownership began during the 1840s, when the effects of the industrial revolution had spread sufficiently to create a new middle class with the economic means to buy their own homes. Because we were alienated and insecure at work, we felt an increased need to own the walls we live in, to feel safe and in possession of our own property. It was the psychic trade-off for the other losses of industrialization.

All those factors taken together add up to the reason why the UK housing market is different. They are the long answer to the question 'why?' But the short answer is different. If you try to ask why these factors arose – why it is that our mortgages and hence our market are different – you end up with this answer: nobody knows. The investment products which allow people to own homes in Britain are different than elsewhere because they grew up to answer a need that is different: our obsessive need to own our own homes. Our risky, long-term, innovative (sometimes recklessly so) mortgages came into existence because the market set out to find ways to let us fulfil our heart's deepest desire, to own our own property. The appetite created the products, not the other way around.

The broad distinction is that in some countries home-ownership is regarded as a good thing, but not an essential. If you can afford it and if you prefer owning to renting, then by all means own your own home. If you can't afford it or temperamentally don't want to be tied down by a long-term, highly leveraged, highly illiquid investment, then so what, you rent. In other countries, however, home-ownership is an unquestioned primary good. It implies safety, prosperity, full participation in society. Owning your own home could almost be seen as a fundamental right. It follows that in these countries governments will pursue policies designed to increase home-ownership. The UK and USA are two of those countries.

This isn't exclusively, or even primarily, a preoccupation of the political left. In Britain, it was Mrs Thatcher who spoke of a vision of a 'property-owning democracy', and who, more energetically than any other modern politician, pursued policies designed to increase the level of home-ownership, extending mortgage tax relief and introducing a new right for council-house tenants to buy their own homes. There was a strong political tinge to these ideas, involving the belief that home-owners were – to put it bluntly – more likely to be both small-c and big-C conservative. In America, it was the unlikely figure of Herbert Hoover who began the drive to create government policies favouring home-ownership.[16] Hoover was later to be a model of complacent conservatism at its sleepiest, which is why it's all the odder that he saw home-ownership as such a crusade. He was apparently motivated by the 1920 census, which showed a tiny drop in the percentage of home-owning from 45.9 to 45.6 per cent since 1910. This, thought Hoover, was a disaster. 'Nothing is worse than increased tenancy and landlordism,' he argued. The parallel with Mrs Thatcher's views about the virtues of home-ownership, over half a century later, are clear, though Hoover expressed his opinions more fruitily. 'The home-owner has a constructive aim in life . . . He works harder outside his home, he spends his leisure hours more profitably, and he and his family live a finer life and enjoy more of the comforts and

cultivating influences of our modern civilization.' At the other
end of the political spectrum, they would have put it differently,
but they basically agreed. In the words of the *New York Times*,
on the decline in home-ownership revealed by the 1920 census:
'The nation's stability [is] being undermined . . . The masses [are]
losing their struggle for a better life.'

The result was a decades-long emphasis on policies designed
to increase home-ownership, beginning with Hoover's Own
Your Own Home campaign, and continuing through the Home
Owners' Loan Corporation which bailed out troubled mortgage-
borrowers during the Great Depression, and the creation of
Fannie Mae and Freddie Mac. With home-ownership established
as a political good, and a government mechanism created to
extend home ownership through the decades of prosperity which
followed the second world war – decades which had their ups
and downs, but which nonetheless saw a general upward movement in living and working conditions – everything was
hunky-dory. Or almost everything. The trouble with near-
universal increases in prosperity is in that small word 'near'. From
the sixties onwards there was clear and growing evidence that
specific sectors of the community, especially ethnic minorities,
were discriminated against in the way the mortgage industry
worked, not in theory, but in practice. Behaviour such as 'redlin-
ing' – drawing a red line around certain neighbourhoods and
refusing to lend money to them – came under well-deserved
attack. Pressure grew for the government – which after all, thanks
to Fannie and Freddie, was the single biggest player in the mortgage market – to correct this inequality.

The campaign achieved some of its aims when the first President Bush signed off on legislation to force Fannie Mae and
Freddie Mac to make sure that 30 per cent of their loans went to
borrowers with low and moderate incomes. President Clinton's
Housing Secretaries, first Henry Cisneros and then Andrew

Cuomo, set out to execute policies which would extend housing-ownership among groups which had historically been excluded from it. There had been a number of changes over the previous decades, which came together to make new forms of lending possible. In 1980, the Depository Institutions Deregulation and Money Control Act, DIDMCA, made it legal to charge higher rates and fees to some borrowers, which was the very definition of a sub-prime loan. In 1982, the AMTPA or Alternative Mortgage Transaction Parity Act made it legal to charge variable interest rates and 'balloon payments' to catch up the unpaid balance at the end of a loan, and then the TRA or Tax Reform Act in 1986 allowed the tax deduction of interest on mortgage loans, immediately and dramatically increasing their appeal as a form of debt. So a new category of lending already existed, conjured into being by changes in the law under administrations and congresses of both political flavours. The Clinton administration continued in this direction of travel, giving the existing policy a strong but inexplicit racial edge: the preferred euphemism was to speak of 'underserved' communities. As for the things which could be done differently to target the previously excluded, the innovations included making it possible to borrow the full value of a house, without a deposit; de-emphasizing credit history and instead saying that if a would-be borrower was paying rent and utility bills they could be considered for a loan; allowing borrowers to claim seasonal employment and financial assistance as income; and raising the limit of mortgages which could qualify for protection from the government. Because Fannie Mae and Freddie Mac were these strange officially-private-but-really-public hybrid corporations, the government was able to get what it wanted in this area of mortgage policy – and the reason it was able to do so was that mortgage lenders began to see the new field of lending to low-income borrowers as a vast area for potential growth. Obviously these loans had to be assessed carefully, on a case-by-case basis; but, as long as that happened, the new loans were a thing of beauty. American home-ownership increased to a historic high of 68.9 per cent, and the gap between ethnic minorities and the white population (or 'non-hispanic white' as the US census data term it) narrowed: between 1994 and 2005 white home-ownership increased by 8.3 per cent, African American by 13.6 and Hispanic by 20.1. From the point of view of encouraging home-ownership, the policies were working. The borrowers wanted money to buy houses, the government wanted them to have the money, the lenders wanted to make money, and everybody could get what they wanted.

House prices go up and down and in the long run, the evidence says, don't grow any faster than the rest of the economy, plus inflation. That makes sense, if you think about it – why should they grow any faster? The whole industry of hype and bubble-building and kerfuffle around property investing is based on ignoring this boring truth. That doesn't mean that people don't make and lose fortunes in property, during the spikes and jags of the market; but in the long run and on aggregate the research is clear. The best way to make money with investments, over a long term, is through shares; or, as they are known in financial-speak, through equities. (A sometimes overlooked but essential compo-nent of this is to do with the dividends, the regular payments the company makes to its shareholders.) Compared with the effect of holding money in property or a bank account, the long-term advantages of investment in equities are obvious. At least, that's what the historical data show. But the time-scale of these data is crucial: we're talking about minimum periods of five years at a time. In the shorter run, as everybody knows, share prices go up and down like a gorilla on a pogo stick.

With bonds – which, remember, are the other main way in which companies raise money and fund themselves – it's a little different. Share prices are like the weather, choppy and variable. Bond prices are more like a sea swell, slower and more gradual and with a momentum which is impossible to ignore or contradict. The biggest single influence on them is the official interest rate: the rate at which the government is willing to lend short-term money to financial institutions to keep the economy running. This rate is set by the Federal Reserve in the USA and by the Bank of England in the UK, and it is this rate which in turn determines the rate at which banks lend money to each other, and then to businesses, and then to us. So although the Governor of the Bank of England doesn't barge into your bank manager's office and tell him how much your mortgage should cost, actually he sort of does. This interest rate is critical for the economy in all sorts of respects. In fact, in terms of how the economy is functioning, it is the single most important number, because it is the interest rate which determines how expensive money is.

This point is so familiar to the economically literate that they don't bother to explain it to the rest of us: money does not always cost the same. There are times when money is expensive: the late seventies and early eighties, for instance, when the UK interest rate peaked at 17 per cent and the American rate at 20 per cent. When money is expensive, the economy will tend to slow down, unemployment will rise, consumer spending will slow, it will be harder for businesses to raise money, it will be harder to make money on the stock market because everyone will be eyeing the attractive interest rates they can get elsewhere. Inflation – which involves money being worth less over time – will come under severe pressure from the fact that money is more expensive in the present. And as for the bond market, the main way in which companies raise money, the effect is impossible to exaggerate. If US government Treasury bills, the securest investment in the world, are paying 20 per cent, for no risk at all, then what sort of interest rates would you have to offer customers to get them to buy your company's pesky bonds? Answer: incredibly high ones. And if your bond was issued a few years before, and pays only a paltry 5 per cent, what will have happened to its price? Answer: it will be, as traders so elegantly put it, in the toilet. On the other hand, if the interest rate is low and money is cheap, then there is the risk of inflation – of money losing its value over time – but on the other hand it's easy for companies to raise money, the economy will pick up speed, and so will consumer spending. Employment will rise. It will be suddenly cheaper for companies to issue new bonds, so existing bonds with higher rates of interest will spike in value. Notice that both these states are, or should be, self-correcting. High interest rates will slow things down and gradually bring inflation down, which in turn will exert downward pressure on interest rates; low interest rates, which governments use to boost the economy, will heat things up in a way which causes inflation and leads to a rise in interest rates.

Stocks and bonds are the two biggest single fields of global investment, reaching into every corner of economic life. At the beginning of the new millennium, however, both of them were going through an odd patch. The stock market had undergone a spectacular bubble in internet and new-economy stocks. Some of what was happening seemed to be a classic hysteria equal to that of the great historical bubbles such as the Dutch tulip mania or the South Sea bubble or the nineteenth-century bubble in railway stocks. The broad rules of these bubbles and implosions are well known. They were first systematized by the economist Hyman Minsky, and their best-known popular formulation is in the classic text by Charles P. Kindleberger, *Manias, Panics and Crashes: A History of Financial Crises*. The basic pattern of these manias is that a real phenomenon comes along (overseas exploration, railways, the internet), is latched on to by investors, gets blown out of all proportion and continues surging upwards anyway so more investors pile in on the basis of what's now called 'greater fool theory'. I vividly remember the first time I heard this term, on the lips of one of the cleverest people I've ever met, explaining why he had invested heavily in what were obviously hugely overvalued technology stocks. He told me what he'd done, I said I thought he was nuts, and then he explained 'greater fool theory'. What it means is that even though everyone knows what's happening is crazy, there's still money to be made by buying stocks and selling them on a little while later to the eponymous 'greater fool'. So it doesn't matter how overvalued the stocks are, as long as there is a bigger idiot out there willing to buy them from you when you've made a nice profit. It works, until it stops working. Historically, what happens is that the bubble starts to wobble, often in response to a piece of bad news, and people begin to express doubts; then everything abruptly collapses and everybody loses an enormous amount of money. That's exactly what happened with the bubble in technology stocks. It burst in March 2000 and the Nasdaq index of tech stocks fell by 80 per cent. The dot-com crash wiped out $5 trillion of investors' money and came to be known as one of the greatest destructions of capital in history.

When there are stock-market busts, investors for a period turn cool towards equities. This is no surprise; and, historically, crashes of this sort almost always uncover frauds and malfeasances of a type which had escaped everyone's notice while prices were rising. Downturns put pressure on earnings, and companies which are less than wholly honest begin to creak at the seams; at the same time, the voices which have been warning that there is something funny about Charles Ponzi (in 1920) or Ivar Kreuger the match king (in 1931) or Bernie Ebbers (in 2003) or Bernard Madoff (in 2008) begin to earn themselves a hearing. The decline in share prices rolls over a rock, and an unsettling variety of financial beasties emerge. In the case of the millennial dot-com bust, the creature which came crawling out from underneath the rock was a fraud so spectacular and so systematic and so magnificently, reekingly wrong that it was in its way almost a thing of beauty: Enron.

To understand fully the impact that Enron had, you have to appreciate just how admired the company was in its pomp. *Fortune* magazine has an award for the most innovative company in the USA. Enron won it in every year from 1995 to 2000. Its revenues reached $101 billion. It had interests in everything from paper and broadband to natural gas and its core business, electricity, and it traded extensively in derivatives in all these areas.* Much of its profits were registered via the company's enthusiastic adoption of 'mark to market' accounting, which – in Enron's interpretation anyway – allowed it to account as current profits deals where the revenues were due to come in some distance in the future. Thus a long-term contract to buy gas over a period of many years could be booked right now, today, as current profits.[17] In addition, Enron created an extensive array of external companies off its own balance sheets, and sold assets to those companies at artificially inflated valuations. Basically, it bought things from itself at made-up prices. All of these tricks kept the share price zooming upwards. When an analyst raised concerns about the balance sheet during a conference call, the company's chief executive Jeffrey Skilling said, 'Well, thank you very much, we appreciate that . . . asshole.' (The call was taped, and now features on lists of 'top ten CEO outbursts'.) Except the asshole

---

* If you live in the West Country, you have literally drunk Enron's water. The Texas-based fraudsters bought Wessex Water in 1998, a disastrous investment as it turned out, because the wave of deregulation in the industry caused the price of water to drop – not through competition, as free-marketeers would tell us to expect, but because the regulators insisted on bringing the price down. That caused Wessex Water to be a much less useful cash cow for Enron, and they eventually sold it at a loss of $1.1 billion.

was right: Enron's accounting was so corrupt that, when the nature of the frauds came out, the share price crashed from $90 to nothing, Skilling went to jail for twenty-four years, the auditors Arthur Andersen (one of the world's five biggest accountancy firms) were put out of business, many employees lost their life savings, and many investors' sentiments turned sharply against the stock market, since if a much admired, much analysed blue-chip investment such as Enron could turn out to be worth nothing, then whose accounts could you trust?* The economist Robert Shiller regularly sends out a questionnaire to investors, and the response in 2001, after the Enron crash, was that 'Investors told us in no uncertain terms that the accounting scandals were a major factor in their withdrawal from the stock market.'

As a result of the dot-com crash and the Enron implosion, the early years of the new millennium were a time when the money which chases the new idea, the go-go idea, had turned its attention away from the stock market.

The traditional bond market, also, was not a place to seek the new new thing. The reason was simple: interest rates were, by historical standards, unusually low. Alan Greenspan, the head honcho of US monetary policy during the Clinton years, had presided over a period of economic growth during which the US economy seemed to have achieved a highly desirable 'Goldilocks point' of being neither too hot nor too cold, so that it kept growing without causing inflation. (Economists sometimes call this period of regular, non-inflationary, non-boom-and-bust growth 'the Great Moderation'. The term was coined by Greenspan's successor, Ben Bernanke.) When the dot-com crash came, the fear was that the stock-market bust would spread into the rest of the economy and bring it grinding to a halt; so Greenspan responded by cutting interest rates. Non-American readers may

* 'Blue chip' is a term originally from poker: it is the highest-denomination chip. Hence the term's use for the biggest companies on the stock market.

wonder what this has to do with them. The answer is twofold. One, the US economy is the biggest in the world, and to a large extent it drives world output and the world economy. Two, the US dollar is what is known as the world's reserve currency: it is the currency in which a majority of other countries save money, and also the currency in which a number of global commodities such as oil and coffee (the world's number-one and number-two most traded commodities) are priced. The dollar interest rate is not the planetary interest rate, but in many respects it comes close. In May 2000, the Federal funds rate was 6.5 per cent; Greenspan cut it and kept cutting. Then 9/11 happened and for a time it seemed as if the entire world order was teetering on its axis. Translated into the language of the economy and of markets, that meant uncertainty; and if there is one thing which markets and economies hate, it is uncertainty. Greenspan surveyed this landscape, took in the imminence of war and the certainty of sharply spiking oil and commodity prices, at a time of what looked like general slowdown, and made what with the benefit of hindsight was a major mistake: he continued to cut interest rates. This process carried on until June 2003, when the rate hit 1 per cent, an exceptionally low rate by historical standards. The rate stayed at that level way into 2004.

The low interest rates meant that it was easy for businesses to raise money cheaply; and also easy for consumers to borrow money; and also easy for construction companies to raise money; and also easy for borrowers to take out mortgages. Bond prices stayed low: by historical standards, very low. I've said that this would normally be a self-correcting phenomenon. Because bonds were giving low yields, buyers would drift away from them; because buyers were drifting away, bonds would have to increase their yields to attract them back. Here, though, a new factor entered the equation. Economists are arguing about this phenomenon and how important it was – Alan Greenspan himself has

attributed the entire bubble and crash to it – but the broad outline
is apparent and can be summed up in a single word: China. The
Chinese economy had boomed and China had effectively become
the factory for the developed world, making pretty much everything. (A brief check on my immediate surroundings: my
underpants, socks, trousers and t-shirt, and the shiny Apple
laptop on which I'm typing these very words, were all made in
China.) As a result of these export earnings, China was awash
with money. And what did it do with that money? A democratic
country would have faced strong pressures to take the hundreds
of billions of yuan flowing into the country and invest them in
roads, schools, hospitals, research, infrastructure, medicine,
higher pay for state employees, higher levels of benefits, you
name it. A non-democratic country doesn't have to face the same
pressures; not in the same way. China took its unprecedented
trade surplus and invested enormously in the USA – specifically,
in US government debt. China bought US Treasury bills to the
tune of $699 billion dollars; and those are just the explicit
purchases of T-bills, rather than the numerous other investments
China made in dollar-based securities and bonds. So rather than
spend its own money, China chose to fund America's spending.
One can argue about just how much of the credit bubble can be
attributed to that, but the basic phenomenon is clear to observe.
Chinese factories held down US inflation by keeping goods cheap
at a time when prices would normally have begun to rise; Chinese
investments enabled the US government to borrow money
cheaply and spend more, at a time when that borrowing would
normally have got more expensive. The Chinese bought T-bills,
and carried on buying them, at a time when their low yield would
normally have kept investors away – which would in turn have
driven up the yield that T-bills were paying.

So low interest rates were bad for the bond market. But there
was one place where they were pure catnip: the housing market.

It was cheaper than ever to raise the money to buy yourself a first house, if you didn't already have one, or a bigger and better house if you already did. It had never been cheaper or easier to borrow money. With all this credit around, house prices began to go up. This is called 'asset-price inflation', and, simply put, it means that instead of stocks going up (which they weren't much, in the aftermath of the dot-com crash) or bonds going up (which they weren't much because interest rates were so low), other categories of assets go up in price instead. What's most people's single biggest asset? Their home. With low interest rates, the entire developed world began to experience a run-up in house prices. In the decade to 1995, US house prices went up by 57.7 per cent, British ones by 134.7 per cent, Irish by 242 per cent, Spanish by 114 per cent. That got a lot of money-men thinking about how to profit from the new boom in house prices.

4. Enter the Geniuses

This is one of those points where it helps to see capital as an agent, a force in its own right. So let's ask ourselves what at this point capital would have wanted, if it had had its own way. Assume that capital is like a virus, and its motivation is to replicate; capital wants to grow. The return on equities is at a low. The return on bonds is at a low. So capital begins to seek innovative ways of growing and replicating. If the old formulas aren't working, money will seek new formulas.

Not much is going on in stocks and bonds. (Apart from the many trillion dollars of them which change hands every day, obviously – but what I mean is, not much new or out of the ordinary.) Where things are going on is in the property market. There, prices are zooming up. An enormous amount of money is therefore piling into the mortgage market. That, from capital's point of view, is good news, because mortgages offer a steady stream of repayment money, as well as the potential to take part in the increase in house values as property prices steadily rise. Also, even when interest rates are low, mortgage rates are that little bit less low: we home-owners pay more for our borrowing than governments or companies do. At this point we can imagine capital sticking its head up, its nose twitching, sensing that it might here be on to something.

But it gets better. In this property boom, all sorts of people who have for years been sitting on the sidelines are now wanting to buy houses, to share in the dream of security and prosperity and inclusion which is represented by home-ownership. The great thing about these new entrants to the property market is that they have no history of home-ownership and not much other record of financial good citizenship; they have lousy credit ratings. Fantastic! That means they have to pay more when they borrow. Because they are assessed as bad risks, they pay over the odds to take out mortgages. That means that their debt gives a wonderfully high yield; and at a time when yields in everything else are disappointingly low, that makes them the answer to capital's whispered prayer.

Somebody had long since worked out a way of making collateralized debt obligations out of mortgages, the same way that they had out of corporate debt and bonds and suchlike. Remember, a collateralized debt obligation is a pool of debt being paid back by a group of borrowers, which is added together and then sold on as a set of bonds paying a range of different interest rates. Collateralized debt obligations began with corporate forms of debt, and had now moved into the area of mortgage holders paying off their mortgages. As always, there would be two streams of revenue, one from the fees to set up the deal and another from the repayments themselves.

Up until now, these mortgage-backed CDOs had been made up only from what was called 'conforming' mortgages. Fannie Mae and Freddie Mac had rules about who could be lent money and under what terms. Mortgages which conformed to those rules were known as 'conforming loans'. The mortgage lenders in between Fannie 'n' Freddie and the general public – remember, F and F don't lend directly to the public, but lend to the financial institutions which actually own the mortgages – had even more rules. There were restrictions based on credit history, on the percentage of the full house price lent to the borrower, and so on. Now, though, there was a huge new market in 'non-conforming' mortgages, which didn't fit Fannie and Freddie's criteria. Mortgage lending to 'underserved' communities was a principled policy which had been ingeniously executed by a careful extension of the mortgage-lending criteria to lower-income, higher-risk groups. The policy seemed to work, and it did not take mortgage lenders long to realize what that meant: that there was a new market in riskier and therefore more lucrative lending to be found among poorer and apparently less creditworthy borrowers. So mortgage lenders, first cautiously and then with increasing enthusiasm, began expanding their lending to this new class of creditors. These 'non-conforming' mortgages were also known as 'sub-prime' mortgages, a name which was confusing in one respect, because 'sub-prime' mortgages paid a higher rate of interest than prime ones. From the point of view of capital, 'sub-prime' was better because it paid out more. So if someone could work out a way of designing a CDO based on these sexy sub-prime mortgages . . .

It would be perfect. And again, the power of securitization would do its magic work. That process of securitization and selling on would free up more capital for more lending. Except for one slight problem, which is that it was impossible. The reason it was impossible was because of an apparently insuperable statistical problem. In the corporate world which underpinned the already thriving global market in CDOs, there was a massive amount of evidence and statistics and history underpinning the deals that were made. All the evidence for corporate histories of interest rates, repayments, defaults, the whole kaboodle, was publicly known. In fact it wasn't just known, it was pored over, sweated over, broken down and analysed, and the process of doing so was the whole function of some of the most important agencies in the financial world, the credit-ratings agencies, Moody's and S and P's and the rest. Assessing default rates and the security of bonds was their raison d'être, it was why they got up in the morning. The default rate was a particular crux for the credit-ratings agencies, because default rates can have such an impact on the quality of a loan: if you make ten loans and one of them goes bad, that bad loan is likely to wipe out all your profits from the other nine good bets. So there was an entire industry devoted to studying the underlying pools of debt which went into CDOs.

Regular vanilla, plain-Jane mortgages were broadly speaking similar. If you had large numbers of respectable citizens with good credit histories it wasn't too hard to model the risks involved when it came to designing CDOs. But sub-prime mortgages were different. There simply weren't the same pools of data available on how they performed, since they had popped into existence only about ten minutes ago. And another big issue was that the USA was regarded not as a single housing market, in the way that most countries' housing markets are a single entity. The USA consisted of dozens of different local markets which behaved according to local differences, local demographic patterns, local booms and busts. Some states had steady property markets. Others, such as Florida, were famous for cyclical episodes of bubbles and crashes (often linked to lurid, spectacular, only-in-Florida frauds). It was hard to be sure – because the data were local and patchy and had never been properly collected or correlated – but it seemed likely that there had never been a national property crash in the USA. That's to say, although there had been innumerable ups and downs in specific markets, the national housing market had never gone down in its entirety.

The risk assessments of lenders are based on statistics. Particular scenarios are modelled, and then the effect on loans is measured and analysed. But how was it possible to do that with so little data? How could you assess the effect of a national downturn in house prices? The problem in particular was one of correlation. This is a term in statistics which is close enough to its regular English usage to be accessible to common sense. Just how could anyone assess the risks of things – in particular house-price crashes and defaults – happening to different people at different places? Correlations were a much studied feature of the stock market, and could be used to hedge and to reduce risk. It was a considerable help to know which stocks moved together and which moved in different or opposite rhythms. If banks knew how to correlate sub-prime mortgages – how to build models to assess probabilities – they would feel much safer about building credit derivatives out of them.

And then, bingo, somebody did it. David X. Li was a maths jock from rural China. If the credit crunch had been a novel by John le Carré or Robert Ludlum, or for that matter Stendhal, he would be the central character: shadowy but determined, a true international man of mystery. He's now back in China, still – apparently – working in risk management. Li had been sent to North America on a government scholarship in the late 1990s to learn about capitalism. (That's a period detail in itself: the time can't be far away when students keen to study capitalism will be piling on planes to Shanghai.) In the process he acquired four degrees, the first in economics from Nankai, the second an MBA from Quebec, the third and fourth, both from the University of Waterloo in Ontario, a Master's in actuarial sciences and a PhD in statistics. Then he went to work, at first for the Canadian Imperial Bank of Commerce (a name which might well be what Oscar Wilde called the Royal Irish Academy, 'a triple oxymoron'). In 2000, while working at J. P. Morgan, Li managed to apply a piece of mathematics called a Gaussian copula function to the creation of CDOs. This is what the maths looks like:*

$$C_p(u, v) = \Phi_p\left(\Phi^{-1}(u), \Phi^{-1}(v)\right)$$

I have absolutely no idea what any of that means, but in plain English it is a way of modelling lots of different things happening

---

* From Wikipedia, which has its flaws but is brilliant on science.

in different ways at the same time. The formula was already much used in statistics; Li found a way of applying it to the world of CDOs, and published the result in the *Journal of Fixed Income* (which is basically *Zoo* or *Heat* for the CDO market), in a paper called 'On Default Correlation: A Copula Function Approach'. He had found the Great White Whale of the CDO market, a way to correlate the apparently uncorrelatable – and thus had opened up the whole field of sub-prime loans as a source of CDOs.

As we've already seen via the story of the Black–Scholes equation, the markets are not slow to pick up on innovations of this sort. Li's new equation could model almost anything, especially the kinds of diverse risk from diverse sources which had previously been unmodellable. It was a magic formula, a magic wand. The CDO and CDS markets were already pretty frisky, but they now went berserk. The CDO market was worth $275 million in 2000, and had grown to $4.7 trillion by 2006. Growth in the CDS market – which had just as much use for the new rocket-science equation – was even more spectacular. By the end of 2001, CDS markets were worth $920 billion. By the end of 2007, they were worth $62 trillion. That means that they were everywhere, spread throughout the global financial system, unsupervised and largely invisible to even well-informed investors.

The exciting thing about these new CDOs based on sub-prime mortgages was that they created a world in which everybody won, helped by the central inventions behind the new credit derivatives: securitization and tranching.[18] Banks and financial institutions were now able to buy job lots of mortgages and put them together into a single pool. Then they could divide that pool up into units which could be sold on to investors. That took the risk off the bank's books and freed the capital to be lent to someone else. If people had been looking at things differently, they would have seen a glaring risk in the fact that the lender – the lender actually at the coalface, the one directly making the loan to the person who wanted a mortgage – now had no need to be particularly bothered about whether or not the borrower could repay. If the borrower defaulted, so what? The lender no longer owned the risk anyway: it had been securitized and sold on. The initial lender was free to quote Bart Simpson: 'Sayonara, sucker.'

Tranching also played a starring role in the new sub-prime-backed CDOs. Remember that this is the technique for dividing paying assets into different categories of risk, the safer ones less lucrative, the riskier ones more so. In the case of sub-prime CDOs, the wonder of tranching could be used to create a range of securitized assets, the safest of them being AAA, as safe as US Treasury bills, the safest debt in the world. And then there would be other tranches of debt too, down to the 'junk' level – wonderfully, juicily high-yielding debt.

I have several times read explanations of how the CDO geniuses managed to turn poor people who struggle to make their mortgage payments into a source of funds as stable as US Treasury bills. I can understand the explanations, with at least part of my brain. The answer was that the cash pouring in went into the equivalent of a series of buckets, the top bucket being the AAA tranche of CDOs, and then when that was full spilled over into the AA, then down into the BBB and beyond. If the flow of cash slowed down, well, it would be tough luck on the people holding the lowest buckets, which would be the first to dry up – but then they were being compensated for that risk by the sexily high yield on the CDOs. The bucket at the top, of course, would never run dry. As long as any money at all was coming in, that bucket would fill up first. That was the idea and, as I've said, a part of my brain follows the explanation. But a larger part is still left reeling with incredulity at the idea that anyone could be so clever/stupid as to believe that human fallibility could be engineered into non-existence. They had forgotten Murphy's Law, an important principle of engineering – and not at all the same thing as Sod's Law, which is the facetious idea that the worst thing always happens (in French, 'le loi de l'immerdement maximum'). Murphy's Law is an engineering principle, and it states that if something can go wrong, it will. So the idea that something will go wrong has to be built into a machine – how to monitor it, how to fix it and what to have in place as a backup when it fails. The designers of the CDOs forgot Murphy's Law. That, to civilians and outsiders, is one of the things which strikes you hardest about this new type of CDO. You can follow the basic principles of swapping and securitizing debt and stay with the thought that the various inventions were all brought in with the intention of spreading risk and freeing up capital – but there's a point at which people got carried away, and the momentum behind this wave of innovative finance went too far.

The designers of the new sub-prime-backed CDOs had been given access to the models of risk used by the credit-ratings agency Moody's. This was an honourable thing to have done, because companies such as Moody's are at risk of being told that their decisions – their hugely consequential judgements about not just companies but governments – are untransparent and arbitrary. Sunlight is the best disinfectant, and the decision to make the assessment models public was a principled one, but it also gave opportunities for the designers of structured debt – this kind of parcelled and chopped-up debt – to custom-create bonds to fit Moody's criteria. That's what the designers of the new CDOs did. There was no limit to the kind of funds that you could have flowing into a CDO; they could even be flows of money from other, pre-existing CDOs. Great idea! So people began to design CDOs of CDOs, pools of pools of structured debt, chopped and sliced and then chopped and sliced again, the underlying assets beneath these super-ingenious financial instruments being people with patchy credit who were struggling to pay back their loans. The new CDOs of CDOs were known as CDO²s, or CDOs squared.

One more component was borrowed from the first of these deals. Remember the SPV, the special-purpose vehicle designed to keep the securitized debt off the bank's books (and out of the reach of the taxman)? Many of the new CDOs were set up via a similar innovation, the SIV or structured investment vehicle. These were part-independent subsidiaries of the banks which got some of the earnings from selling off the CDO assets and some from their parent companies, but they did the same thing as the SPVs: they kept assets off the banks' balance sheets and thus helped them avoid the Basel restrictions on capital reserves. The way in which they did that was sheer genius. The Basel rules applied to all credit lines which existed for a year. So the SIVs were set up to last for 364 days or fewer. Fantastic! The rules existed for a reason, of course – to help keep the banks solvent in times of trouble by maintaining the capital levels at a sensibly cautious level – but, really, who gave a damn about that? There's something almost thrilling about the pure indifference to the reasons behind the rules, the reasons why the rules were set up. The banks were certain, absolutely certain, that they knew better. Many of the biggest banks in the world piled into the new mortgage-backed CDOs as if their lives depended on it, among them UBS, RBS, Merrill Lynch and Citigroup – every one of which has now been bailed out by their respective country's taxpayers.

It should be stressed that not every financial institution did this. Critics who argue that the bankers are all as bad as each other – or who argue, like the US Federal judge Richard Posner, that the risks some banks were taking were rational under the circumstances, and that the pressures of competition meant that they had no choice – aren't giving sufficient weight to the example of banks who didn't join in.[19] Conspicuous among them was the J. P. Morgan team who had pretty much invented the entire CDS and CDO industry. They could see how profitable the new mortgage-backed versions of their CDOs were. But after a long hard look at the new business, they took a pass. They simply didn't see how the risks were being engineered down to a safe level. The other banks must be seeing some way of doing it which they couldn't work out. Blythe Masters, the woman in charge of the *Exxon Valdez* deal and of selling the very first BISTRO bonds, and thus one of the creators of the entire CDS industry, was baffled by the CDO boom. 'How are the other banks doing it?' she asked. 'How are they making so much money?'[20] According to Gillian Tett in *Fool's Gold*, 'she was so steeped in the ways of J. P. Morgan that it never occurred to her that the other banks might simply ignore all the risk controls J. P. Morgan had adhered to.'

And now the story takes an even nastier turn. If we for a moment recall the idea that money has intentions of its own, we might ask this: what would capital do next? It has found a way of making money at good rates of interest and it has ingeniously engineered away the associated risks. The only thing which stands in the way of this money-making engine is the shortage of borrowers in the relevant category; because it's important to remember that the underlying source of funds in this amazing new financial invention is still poor or poorish, or unreliable or unreliable-ish, people who are paying back their mortgage loans. They're a specific category: not secure or rich enough to be eligible for ordinary mortgages, but not so risky that they won't pay back their loans. As I've already said, mortgage borrowers who default are disastrous for a lender, because each one of them wipes out the gains from a large number of successful loans. It stands to reason that this particular section of the target market, the risky-enough-to-be-profitable, not-risky-enough-to-default sub-prime borrower, is not going to be infinite in number.

In the days when the mortgage industry rested on a lender looking a borrower in the eye and determining whether to lend her a big chunk of money to be repaid over the next twenty-five years, there would obviously come a moment when credible candidates for these loans could no longer be found. The lender would sigh regretfully, then pack up her papers and shut down new lending. But that model no longer applied. This is where we finally encounter the consequences arising from the fact that the invention of securitization broke banking, in separating lender from borrower by selling on the loan to somebody else. People wanted to find the money to buy houses, and the money in turn wanted to find a way to get to the people. The result was a giant wave of mortgage-linked financial innovation. So what now happens when the money is looking for new borrowers, and the circuit-breaker of risk assessment is no longer in place? Answer: the lending goes on regardless. A terrible change-over happens, in which the process of lending is no longer driven by the legitimate desire of poor-but-reliable people to own a house, but is instead a manufactured process driven by capital which is set loose looking for people to sign up loans. An epidemic began of what has come to be called 'predatory lending': mortgage lenders doing everything they could to sign up borrowers at higher-than-ordinary, sub-prime interest rates, so that the debt they created could then be pooled and securitized and sold on as tranches of various grades of CDO. Some of this happened in the UK, but the overwhelming bulk of activity in this area happened in the USA.

Bear in mind that this was an industry in which a lot of what went on was already of a nature designed if not exactly to stretch the rules, then to look for flexibility within them. That was the whole point. Sub-prime borrowers were usually people who had poor credit ratings, as calculated by the companies which assess the credit of every single adult, breaking down patterns of spending and credit history to produce a single number. (The three biggest credit-ratings agencies in the USA, the ones most relevant to the US sub-prime story, are Equifax, Experian and Trans-Union; the first two are also the two biggest in the UK.) In the USA, the number is called the FICO score, after the Fair Isaac Corporation which invented it, and it runs from 300, meaning you're on the FBI's most wanted list, to 850, meaning you're Warren Buffett. Actually, having said that, Buffett's credit might not be as high as you'd think, because one of the things which improves your credit is being in debt, and having a regular history of repayments. If Buffett has no mortgage, has only one credit card, has his utility bills paid by someone else and has no outstanding debts or credit lines of any sort, his credit history might conceivably be a little thin. Credit ratings are all about history, and if you don't have much credit in the form of utility bills, credit-card bills, and suchlike, your credit history can look sketchy: it's not unknown for people in impeccable financial condition to have poor credit ratings because they don't have enough history of debt. Welcome to Bizarroworld . . .

I checked my own credit rating with Experian – you can do it online in about two minutes, and if you're worried about identity fraud it's not a bad idea – and was amazed to see that it's pretty good, a point score of 900, which in the British system of scores from 0 to 999 means I'm in the top 30 per cent. The reason I'm surprised is that I'm a bit chaotic in my personal affairs and sometimes forget to pay things like utility bills, causing me to be rung up and told off by people from Bangalore as a semi-regular event. That hadn't happened recently, however, or my score would be worse. The credit-ratings report and score are all completely explicit, and tell you what you need to do to improve your rating and what the factors are dragging it down. In my case, the lowering factor is a largish amount of outstanding credit-card debt. Most of that is the as-yet-unpaid bill for the

MacBook Pro on which I am typing these very words (the same made-in-China one I mentioned last chapter). How postmodern is that? I'm looking up my credit rating on the very laptop which is dragging it down.

Under the American FICO system, 60 per cent of scores are in the range from 650 to 799, and the median score – the one with half of all scores below it and half above it – is 723. From the point of view of the mortgage market, a number over 620 identifies you as a steady-Eddie good citizen, qualifying for one of the 'conforming' mortgages sold by Fannie and Freddie. Below that you're in sub-prime territory, which runs down to about 500, beyond which no one will lend you money for a mortgage. The exact details of the number are extremely important and directly affect both the willingness of lenders to take on a borrower and the amount the borrower will have to pay.

According to Richard Bitner, an expert in the field as the owner of a sub-prime brokerage and author of a candid and very useful book about the industry, *Confessions of a Subprime Lender*, sub-prime borrowers fall into five main categories.[21] They have a history of being slow to pay; they are underqualified, because they don't have much credit history (as in the hypothetical Warren Buffett example above); they have had a bad thing happen to them, such as illness or bereavement, causing them to go off the grid for a time; they're plain unlucky and missed a series of utility payments because they were away and their housesitter forgot to open the brown envelopes; or they are on the margin between conforming and sub-prime and chose a mortgage broker who, because sub-prime pays more commission, deliberately arranged their application the wrong side of the sub-prime line.

As that last example shows, the system was chronically, structurally prone to abuse, right from the start. A system designed to bend the rules in the direction of increased flexibility and increased lending is always going to be at risk from people who want to use it to cheat and go beyond the rules. Then house prices began to go up, which they did from about 1998, making it more of a stretch for people to buy homes; and then from 2001 credit became dramatically cheaper, rendering it ever more tempting to make the stretch (especially since prices were going up, so that houses looked like a bet with lots of upside and no downside); and then new money flooded into the market, money which, because of securitization, didn't actually care how risky the loans were. Now bear in mind that by 2000 there were 250,000 mortgage brokers in the US – mortgage brokers being the people who have direct contact with the would-be borrowers, and who act as the intermediary between them and the sub-prime lender. The business, in theory regulated, was in practice the closest thing imaginable to a free-for-all. In Maryland, where I went to look at the effect of foreclosures, individual brokers did not need a licence or qualification of any kind. The companies to which they belonged needed licences, but the individuals needed no credentials. Nationally, there were hundreds of thousands of brokers and millions of new mortgages, all of them beginning with already flexible rules and stretching them as far as they could be taken. It was chaos. The whole idea of 'stated income' loans, in which the borrower simply says how much he earns and the lender takes his word for it, is a standing invitation to fraud. These are now known as 'liar loans'. Their existence led before long to the creation of what is called the ninja loan: no income, no job or assets. Why would any sane person lend money to someone with no income, job or assets? Answer: because they were selling the loan to somebody else, so they didn't care.

Bitner left the business in 2005, after a moment of clarity with a mortgage application. He had clients called the Cutters, who bought a house in 2005, but quickly fell behind on payments when Mrs Cutter became ill. She lost her job and had no health insurance, a cruel double whammy meaning that her costs rocketed upwards just as her income crashed. Bitner ran through their options and explained that their best one was to accept that they couldn't pay the loan and give up their house. They accepted that, and their home was repossessed. But it was when he went through the file afterwards that the penny dropped. The Cutters had borrowed $90,000, on a joint income of $2,800 a month. After putting down their deposit of $4,500, they had $250 left in the bank – that was the sum total of all their assets. After the mortgage payments, they had $700 left for all expenses each month. They had a lousy credit rating and a poor history of repaying debt. There was no evidence that they had ever paid rent to anyone. In the last three years, neither of them had been employed for more than nine months at a stretch. And – this is the real sting – *all of that was fine*. In Bitner's words, 'we did nothing wrong.' The Cutters met all the relevant criteria for this kind of loan. It was by the book – the sub-prime book. And that was what caused Bitner to decide that it was time to walk away.

The only thing unusual about that story is that Bitner felt ill about what was going on, quit and wrote a book about it. In Baltimore I heard many variations of the same tale, featuring loans which should never have been made to people who would never have been able to pay them back, and shading into darker practices. 'We all saw it coming, but nobody would listen,' Mary Waldrow of the Belair-Edison housing association told me. 'A lot of people in [the Maryland housing coalition] saw it coming.' Belair-Edison is a poor East Baltimore neighbourhood which has had a third of its homes foreclosed on over the last decade – and when you hear what the lenders got up to, and the extent to which they depended on the desperation and naivety of first-generation home-owners, it's no surprise. The city of Baltimore is currently suing one of the banks involved in extending loans, Wells Fargo, on the basis that it systematically targeted African Americans to be put on sub-prime loans, even in instances where the borrower qualified for better rates. The case is ongoing, but affidavits already entered into the record state that, in the words of one former employee of the bank, 'Wells Fargo mortgage had an emerging-markets unit that specifically targeted black churches, because it figured church leaders had a lot of influence and could convince congregants to take out subprime loans.'[22]

The whole market was riddled with scams and tricks. One standard move: a buyer finds a property, fixes up a loan with a mortgage broker and arrives at the settlement hearing, where the deal is to be done and the papers are signed. When there is an attorney present at the hearing – which there doesn't have to be under Maryland law, but when there is – the attorney is representing the company holding the title deeds, and not the purchaser. At the settlement, the mortgage broker says, aw shucks, I know we said we could get you a loan at 6 per cent but unfortunately we couldn't, the rate here is 12 per cent, but don't worry, if you sign now we can change it later. But that's not true. You can't change it later. In the words of Philip Robinson of the Civil Justice coalition: 'That's a common scam. Just sign and we'll fix it tomorrow. They promise 6 or 8 per cent. Then they come to the table and they offer a different rate. Another thing you can sign with these documents is you waive your right to a jury trial, go to private arbitration. Do they ever explain that to you? No. There's another document they make you sign that says: you have a right to receive a copy of the appraisal for your property but only if you ask for it in writing and then we have 90 days to give it to you. Well if you get that 90 days after settlement what good is that appraisal to you? The appraisal that you already paid for? You need to see that appraisal to know that the house is worth what you're borrowing. Also, even when you do see it, the appraisals use comparisons from blocks away and two years old – they're worthless.'

And the shocking thing – or at least the shocking thing to me, because everyone in the field has got used to it – is that this is perfectly legal. It's all legit. The principle is that of caveat emptor: the mortgage brokers are salesmen, and if you buy something from a salesman, the onus is on you not to get screwed.

In response to this, Philip Robinson and his colleagues at Civil Justice have come up with an idea which is both noble in its motivations and devastatingly, dazzlingly, breathtakingly cynical. This is the idea: how do you drive change in America? Real, non-cosmetic change? Answer: by finding ways for lawyers to make money. 'We do litigation that no one else will do, we try to teach the private bar how to do it once we've figured out how to do it successfully,' Robinson explains. 'Our theory is if you can teach the private bar how to help home-owners with these predatory real estate practices, then we can begin to drive change. We've done that pretty successfully for ten or eleven years.' So Robinson's idea is to locate a category of mortgage fraud so flagrant, and so clear in the evidentiary record, that even courts not minded to rule against Wall Street will find for his client. Then he will have a template that he can teach to private law firms, and they will start to file cases and win proper money. 'My hook is, if you can show someone how to make money, a private attorney can do the same kind of case a hundred times.' And then, because by this point it will be costing the banks real money, the banks will finally begin to change their practices.

The particular type of case Robinson is working on now is a scam called foreclosure rescue. All over the blighted parts of Baltimore I had seen signs with wording based on the theme 'Home at risk? Call us!' I felt a small flicker of hope: perhaps someone had the best interests of East Baltimore's vulnerable neighbourhoods at heart after all; perhaps their plight wasn't so bad. I should have known better. These ads are touting a complex scam. The scammers offer the endangered foreclosee a way out of her plight by signing over the deeds of her house to someone with good credit, who takes out a new mortgage on the property. The idea is that the original home-owner has a year to fix her credit and save up some money, and then takes back her home. In the meantime, the 'rescuer' charges the original home-owner a string of fees, all of them notionally helping her rebuild her credit, but in practice simply running down the victim's bank balance and asset-stripping her. The usual technique is for these fees and charges to go unmentioned when the original home-owner is being enticed into the deal; then, when she turns up at the settlement meeting, she is presented with dozens of pieces of paper to sign, without warning and without legal representation. Some of these pieces of paper assign fees to the mortgage rescuer. Most of the time, the person with good credit is a straw entity, not even a knowing party to the transaction, so none of the mortgage money is ever repaid. The first the home-owner knows about this is when the bank slaps a foreclosure notice on the house, and bang, she's lost her home. Now, the point of legal interest is to do with how much care the bank should take in extending a loan to the straw person. At what point does it have to interest itself in the fact that the whole thing is a scam? At what point does it have to bestir itself to think about the home-owner's interests?

I say 'her' not least because, in the test case Robinson is currently pursuing, the woman who lost her home is Harriette Julian, who entered into one of these foreclosure-rescue agreements with a local company. She signed the deeds of her house over to Lashawn Wilson – who wasn't present at the settlement meeting and was represented only by a purported signature on a piece of paper. The idea was that Ms Julian would rebuild her credit and then, after a period of time, buy back her house. Everyone was aware that Ms Julian was in foreclosure. Ms Wilson was buying the house for $482,000, but had no income. Not just a little income: no income. That was a routine feature of these scams. So these are the things the bank ignored. One: Ms Wilson's HUD-1 (a stand-ard form used to itemize transaction fees) had no address. Two: foreclosure scams were known to be everywhere; a new Maryland law, the Protection of Homeowners in Foreclosure Act, had been passed specifically targeting them. Three: Harriette Julian wasn't moving from the home she was signing away – another classic sign of a foreclosure scam. Four: no payments were made on the mort-gage, not one, ever – yet another classic sign. Five: during the process, Harriette Julian and Lashawn Wilson told the bank that they were the victim of a foreclosure scam – but the bank ignored all of that, and having gone ahead with the loan, then went ahead with the foreclosure. Civil Justice and Philip Robinson are trying to show that at some point in the process the onus falls on the bank actually to give a shit – and thereby create a way for lawyers to make money out of it. At which point the bank will have to start acting as if it gives a shit.

'Most of my clients who are in foreclosure,' Robinson said to me, 'they're hard working, they're making money, but they couldn't afford the loan from the beginning. Remember *It's a Wonderful Life*? It's not like that any more. They don't care about you. If they did, they wouldn't give you a $300,000 loan if you didn't have a job and had no chance of paying it back.'

From 2005 onwards, across the industry, most of the lending was reckless and some of it actively criminal. Bitner's estimate at the time he left the business was that 70 per cent of mortgage applications were erroneous or fraudulent; and that was before the very worst of the excesses. As for what the worst of it was, well, that would be deliberate fraud, of which there was much, starting with lies about employment and income. A survey from 2007 found that by 2006 some 60 per cent of sub-prime applicants were lying about their income by more than 50 per cent – so more than half of applicants were lying by exaggerating their income by more than half.[23] By this point, more than half of all applications for mortgages were either 'piggyback' loans, meaning that they were double loans taken out to buy the same property, or 'liar loans' in which applicants were invited to state their own income, or 'no doc' loans in which the borrower produced no paperwork. Gee, what could possibly go wrong? And all this is just business as usual, legitimate lending, not allowing for instances in which there was systematic, organized fraud, involving false identities and multiple applications for credit. The whole business was set up to lend, no questions asked – no real questions asked. The loans generated money for everyone, and generated huge amounts of sub-prime debt so that the banking industry could create all the CDOs it wanted. And as for the idea that these people's mortgage payments were being miraculously transmuted into AAA-grade investments . . .

5. The Mistake

And yet, the financial industry could still have got away with it. All the things described up until now could have been survived, and the resulting chaos been avoided, if it weren't for a single mistake. It was the mistake which underpinned all the other mistakes and errors of judgement; it was the mistake which brought the global economic system up to the edge of the abyss, and although in some senses it is not a single mistake, because it was made by lots of people in lots of different places over many varied occasions, in another way it was the same mistake everywhere. That mistake can be summed up in a single word: risk. The bankers made inaccurate calculations about the mathematics of risk. That in essence was the mistake which destroyed some banks, forced others into public ownership, put taxpayers on the hook for hundreds of billions of pounds, and brought the world financial system to a juddering, panicky standstill. It led directly to the slowdown currently dominating every economy in the world.

I'm willing to make a bet. This is the bet: that somewhere near you, wherever and whoever you are, there is a killer. A killer you've never noticed as a killer, a killer you've never thought about as a real danger to you. I'm not talking about an invisible killer, like a virus or bacteria; I'm not talking about an obvious killer, like the idiot in the 4x4 roaring down the road outside, or the mugger lurking behind the wheelie bin. I'm talking about a killer who is plainly visible, whom you see every day, whom you've known your whole life, and to whom you never give a second's thought. This killer kills more than a thousand men and women in the UK every year, year in year out, and yet you've never heard a word about the dangers it represents. Bear in mind that road accidents – that's drivers, passengers, pedestrians, cyclists, every-body – cause fewer than 3,000 deaths a year. So this killer is between a third and a half as dangerous as all the road traffic in the UK.

Give up? I'm talking about stairs. That's right, humanity's friend the humble stair. If stairs were invented today, and a full analysis of their dangers was made, along with the gory statistics – the literally gory statistics – then there would be an impas-sioned, sustained and I'm pretty sure eventually successful campaign to have them banned on health and safety grounds. It's happened to much safer things than stairs. Stairs are absolutely lethal. I even myself know someone killed by his own stairs, one of the 1,000-odd deaths in a typical year.* Yet we don't perceive stairs as being risky. They're filed away in the part of our consciousness where daily objects live, not in the part of our head which attends to dangers and threats and risks-to-life. We don't see these things entirely rationally, and familiarity breeds not

---

* Although 21,648 Americans were killed by falls last year, the various types of fall are not separated out. Perhaps the feared stairs lobby has been at work suppressing the dark truth. In the UK, the government's mortality statistics for 2007 list only 620 deaths-by-stairs, perhaps because the injuries sustained falling down stairs often take a little while to finish the victim off. The govern-ment acknowledged the figure of a thousand deaths a year with a stair-awareness campaign in 2000. The victims are overwhelmingly older people: only seventy Britons under the age of forty-five were killed by stairs. A warning about the government mortality statistics: if you are of a nervous or hypochondriacal disposition, avoid them at all costs. Here are some of the categories of deaths: 'Accidental suffocation or strangling in bed' (eight deaths), 'Contact with plant thorns and spikes and sharp leaves' (one death) and 'Drowning and submersion while in bath tub' (eighteen deaths). Interestingly, only one person died after being bitten by a rat, but ten from being 'bitten or struck by other mammals'. But which mammals? Dogs? If so, why not say so? Badgers? Dolphins?

contempt but a lack of attention. Why? Well, we don't really know. Our intuitive understanding of risks and of numbers is limited. The explanations usually reached for are of the currently fashionable cod-evolutionary-psychology sort which reaches back to ancestral humanity on the African savannah. We are bad with risk because our hunter–gatherer ancestors blah blah blah. The long and the short of it is that we aren't all that good with risk.

In fact, we aren't all that good with numbers in general. We seem to be hard-wired to make certain sorts of mathematical mistakes. This is a profound challenge to the way much of the economics profession sees the world. It would be such a powerful explanatory tool if it were to turn out that we always act, from an economic point of view, rationally. If you plug assumptions of economic rationality into your view of the world, you can come up with all sorts of fascinating explanations of everything from why there are so many teenage single mothers (they were making a rational choice to marry the state), why the bankers got everything so wrong in the run-up to the credit crunch (they were responding rationally to a skewed balance of risks and rewards), and why the Dutch tulip bubble took place (it was a rational application of greater-fool theory). Most of this exemplifies what I would argue is the most common mistake of very smart people: the assumption that other people's minds work in the same way that theirs do. To non-economists, the mathematically based models and assumptions of rational conduct which permeate the field often have the appearance at best of toys, entertaining but by definition of limited utility; at worst, they can seem wilful delusions, determinedly ignoring reality. The general reader needs no persuading about the influence of non-rational, non-economic forces on economic thinking. The economic profession, however, is split between economic rationalists in the Milton Friedman tradition and economic liberals in the tradition of Keynes, and the subject of strict rationality is the occasion of a permanent pitched battle. The fact that non-economists see the general assumption of rationality as self-evidently ridiculous has no effect on economists. What has had an effect, however, is the work of two Israeli psychologist–economists, Daniel Kahneman and Amos Tversky, who have produced a body of work studying 'the susceptibility to erroneous intuitions of intelligent, sophisticated, and perceptive individuals', in the words of the fascinating autobiography written by Kahneman on the occasion of winning the Nobel Prize in Economics in 2002.

I have a confession to make about Kahneman and Tversky. I'd never heard of them until Kahneman won the Nobel,* and when I first read about their work it seemed to me to consist of things which were surprising only to economists. One of their interests was 'hindsight bias', the way in which a random sequence of events is given structure and narrative by the false perspective of looking back over it from its outcome. Another was 'loss aversion', the fact that people place a higher value on not losing money than on gaining it; another was on 'the law of small numbers', referring to people's tendency to draw over-confident conclusions from small amounts of evidence. Their particular interest was in 'heuristics', or the patterns of thinking people use to interpret data, and the strong conclusion they reached was that people's heuristics are often wrong: we are much less accurate and less rational in our thinking than we believe ourselves to be. My initial reaction to this was to think, so what: everybody except economists knows this anyway.

Then I had a look at their work first-hand, and soon came to

---

* Tversky would have won it too if it hadn't been for his too-early death in 1996. The prize is actually the Sveriges Riksbank Prize in Economic Sciences in Honour of Alfred Nobel – people refer to it as the Nobel Prize in Economics, but strictly speaking it isn't a Nobel prize since it wasn't one of the five prizes Nobel himself set up: Physiology or Medicine, Chemistry, Physics, Literature and Peace.

realize that I was missing the point. Kahneman and Tversky directly take on the central shibboleth of contemporary academic economics. The assumptions of rationality permeate modern economics, and are one of the reasons the field has sharply contracted in its practical usefulness. Instead of being concerned with what actually happens in practice – this is left to a sub-field within micro-economics, which is, broadly speaking, the study of people's behaviour and decisions – the field is increasingly preoccupied with developing pseudo-mathematical formulas. These provide models of behaviour which never quite fit what actually happens, in a way which resembles the physical sciences gone wrong: instead of equations describing reality, economics produces equations describing ideal conditions and theoretical clarity of a type which never occurs in practice. Many disciplines suffer badly from envy of the physical sciences, of a world in which f = mv means exactly what it says; academic economics has a particularly bad case of physics-envy. Assumptions of rationally modelled behaviour are a big part of this wrong turn in the field, and that is why Kahneman and Tversky's work is so important: because it *proves* – not asserts, *proves* – ways in which our thinking, our heuristics, have built-in mistakes. This, from the point of view of the economists' received wisdoms, is revolutionary. The impact of their work on economics has been big and is only going to get bigger (and it's readable too, which is not something you can often say about academic economics).

Kahneman tells three great stories in his official Nobel autobiography (even that is unusually readable and interesting), the first about how he became interested in psychology, while living as a small child of about eight under the Nazi occupation of France.

In one experience I remember vividly, there was a rich range of shades. It must have been late 1941 or early 1942. Jews were required to wear the Star of David and to obey a 6 p.m. curfew. I had gone to play with a Christian friend and had stayed too late. I turned my brown sweater inside out to walk the few blocks home. As I was walking down an empty street, I saw a German soldier approaching. He was wearing the black uniform that I had been told to fear more than others – the one worn by specially recruited SS soldiers. As I came closer to him, trying to walk fast, I noticed that he was looking at me intently. Then he beckoned me over, picked me up, and hugged me. I was terrified that he would notice the star inside my sweater. He was speaking to me with great emotion, in German. When he put me down, he opened his wallet, showed me a picture of a boy, and gave me some money. I went home more certain than ever that my mother was right: people were endlessly complicated and interesting.[24]

The next story came from Kahneman's time in the Israeli army, where he devised the questionnaire used to test recruits' suitability for various kinds of operation. The need to do this came from his encounter with existing methods which, in his view, simply didn't work:

We used methods that had been developed by the British Army in the Second World War. One test involved a leaderless group challenge, in which eight candidates, with all insignia of rank removed and only numbers to identify them, were asked to lift a telephone pole from the ground and were then led to an obstacle, such as a 2.5-meter wall, where they were told to get to the other side of the wall without the pole touching either the ground or the wall, and without any of them touching the wall.* If one of these things happened, they had to declare it and start again.

Two of us would watch the exercise, which often took half an hour or more. We were looking for manifestations of the candidates' characters, and we saw plenty: true leaders, loyal followers, empty boasters,

* As far as I know, the British army's officer-selection process still uses a version of this test.

wimps – there were all kinds. Under the stress of the event, we felt, the soldiers' true nature would reveal itself, and we would be able to tell who would be a good leader and who would not. But the trouble was that, in fact, we could not tell. Every month or so we had a 'statistics day', during which we would get feedback from the officer-training school, indicating the accuracy of our ratings of candidates' potential. The story was always the same: our ability to predict performance at the school was negligible. But the next day, there would be another batch of candidates to be taken to the obstacle field, where we would face them with the wall and see their true natures revealed. I was so impressed by the complete lack of connection between the statistical information and the compelling experience of insight that I coined a term for it: 'the illusion of validity'.

And then a final, shaping experience came in 1958 at the Austen Riggs Center in Stockbridge, Massachusetts, a psychotherapeutic community. There was a weekly case conference on Friday.

Those attending would have received and read, the night before, a folder with detailed notes from every department about the person in question. There would be a lively exchange of impressions among the staff, which included the fabled Erik Erikson. Then the patient would come in for a group interview, which was followed by a brilliant discussion. On one of those Fridays, the meeting took place and was conducted as usual, despite the fact that the patient had committed suicide during the night. It was a remarkably honest and open discussion, marked by the contradiction between the powerful retrospective sense of the inevitability of the event and the obvious fact that the event had not been foreseen. This was another cognitive illusion to be understood.

The study of these 'cognitive illusions' and the effect of Kahneman and Tversky's work is going to resonate for many years to come, because it forces economists to acknowledge the ways in which human beings don't and perhaps can't make accurate assessments of perceptions and probabilities. One simple and now-famous-to-economists example: people will judge the probability of a deadly flood in North America to be lower than that of a deadly flood in California. Naming the specific place – with, perhaps, subliminal associations of earthquakes and fires – triggers something in the brain which makes disaster seem more likely. Another famous example, not from Kahneman and Tversky but similar to their work in its gist: if a test for some disease is 95 per cent accurate, and the disease affects one person in a thousand, and you go for a test and it comes back positive, what's the probability that you have the disease? Most respondents say, well the test is accurate, so the probability is 95 per cent. The correct answer is 2 per cent, because if you test 1,000 people, the test will give fifty positives, whereas only one of the population actually has the illness. But the real sting in the story lies in the fact that the respondents who were answering this question were doctors. Our hard-wired difficulties with probability and risk go very deep.[25]

Kahneman and his colleagues have created an important body of work, with a single big takeaway for the non-expert reader: they proved that we humans, even expert humans, are chronically prone to make certain sorts of cognitive mistakes. We have a particular propensity to errors in relation to risk. Given that, it was perhaps not surprising that it was a mistake involving risk that lay behind the credit crunch. It was this which Alan Greenspan was talking about when he appeared before the US Congress's House committee of oversight and reform on 23 October 2008 and spoke about 'a once-in-a-century credit tsunami' based on a 'whole intellectual edifice' which had now collapsed. That's an amazing admission for Greenspan to have made, given that he more than anyone else was in charge of the monetary policies behind both the long boom and the abrupt bust. He had

charge of the Federal Reserve under four presidents, from Ronald
Reagan who appointed him in 1987 to the second President Bush
whom he served until his retirement in 2006, and during that
time Greenspan oversaw the response to several crises, from the
crash of October 1987 (during which shares fell 20 per cent in a
single day) through the recession of 1991, the implosion of LTCM
in 1998 and the dot-com bust of 2000. For most of this time,
Greenspan's militant advocacy of deregulation and laissez-faire
capitalism seemed to be an effective intellectual underpinning to
his policies. Greenspan was a close friend and disciple of Ayn
Rand, the Russian-born philosopher who advocated a philosophy
she called 'Objectivism' (she wanted to call it 'Existentialism', but
some pesky Euros had already bagged that name).* Objectivism
is undergoing a vogue on the internet at the moment, perhaps
because its libertarian ideology is appealing to a certain type of
computer nerd. Rand's central ideas focused on her belief that
society must get out of the way of great men. Man is 'a heroic
being, with his own happiness as the moral purpose of his life', and
the only good society is capitalism, which Rand glossed as follows:
'When I say "capitalism", I mean a full, pure, uncontrolled, unregulated laissez-faire capitalism.'[26] Objectivism seems a sophomoric
belief system today, whose main truth lies in its unexpressed but
profound longing for the world to be a much simpler place than
it is. Still, there's no denying Objectivism's impact on the world,
thanks to its direct influence on the most economically powerful
man alive, Alan Greenspan. His emphasis throughout all his years
in office was on the belief – the mystical belief – that markets
could be entirely trusted to regulate themselves. That was why

---

* Rand was also a huge fan of *Charlie's Angels*. 'It's the only romantic television show today. It's not realistic. It's not about the gutter, it's not about the
half-wit retarded children and all the other kind of shows today. It's about
three attractive girls doing impossible things, and because they're impossible,
that's what makes it interesting.' It sounds even better in her accent.

it was such an explosive admission when he went before the House committee and said: 'those of us who have looked to the self-interest of lending institutions to protect shareholder's equity (myself especially) are in a state of shocked disbelief.' In response to questioning, he said that he had found 'a flaw in the model that I perceived is the critical functioning structure that defines how the world works'.[27]

It's worth dwelling on that phrase: 'the critical functioning structure that defines how the world works'. That's a hell of a big thing for a man like Greenspan to find a flaw in. That flaw was to do with risk. To understand what happened, we have first to get a grip on the financial understanding of risk.

Moneymen don't see risk in the same way that civilians do. To most of us, risk is for the most part a bad thing; at best, it's something we seek out under specific circumstances, to generate a feeling that things are just-dangerous-enough-to-be-exciting. In the world of money, risk is different: it's desirable. That's because, in investments, risks are correlated with rewards. Anyone can invest their money entirely risk-free: all you do is buy a US Treasury bill, and hold it to maturity, and then you know, for sure, exactly what your return will be. Note that buying bonds with a view to trading them – selling them if the price goes up – is not risk-free, because the price of the bond could go down. It's also the case that inflation could overtake the interest rate paid by the bond, and you could end up making a net loss in inflation-adjusted terms. From both those points of view, it's apparent that something being risk-free can nonetheless involve you losing some money. But the fact remains, if you buy a T-bill and hold it to maturity, you get exactly what you paid for, guaranteed.

So why not do that? Well, at the time of writing, a T-bill that you hold for a year will yield 0.41 of a per cent. You pay quite a high price for complete safety. Historically, the rate of completely risk-free investment, taking out the effect of inflation, has been about 3 per cent. Three per cent isn't nothing; in twenty-four years' time, 3 per cent compounded will double your money, which isn't bad going for no risk at all. On the other hand, 6 per cent will double your money in twelve years, and 12 per cent will double your money in six; so if you invest £10,000 at 3 per cent, a quarter of a century later you'll have £20,000, whereas your more aggressive chum who invests it at 12 per cent will have £160,000. Compound interest, plus increased risk, is a powerful formula for making a lot more money than you can make in complete safety.

For this reason, the world of money is all about risk: seeking it, and seeking to master it, to understand the risks being taken and to adjust one's thinking accordingly. A borrower will always try to get the lowest possible rate for his loan, and a lender will always try to get the highest, and the perennially shifting dance between them is determined by the balance of risk, a constantly moving assessment of risk and probability which gives a role to all sort of factors to do with external circumstances, business conditions, interest rates, actuarial tables and many phenomena which are ultimately to do with mood – with what Keynes called 'animal spirits'.★ The dance between lenders and borrowers – a cross between a dance and a fight, like caipoera perhaps – doesn't always lead to accurate prices for risk, because over time one side can do much better than the other at the agreed rate; but it

---

★ In fact Keynes seemed to use the term to refer to the basic optimistic will-to-act which underlies much investment. 'Most, probably, of our decisions to do something positive, the full consequences of which will be drawn out over many days to come, can only be taken as the result of animal spirits – a spontaneous urge to action rather than inaction, and not as the outcome of a weighted average of quantitative benefits multiplied by quantitative probabilities.' In their book *Animal Spirits*, George Akerlof and Robert Shiller appropriated the term to apply to the whole area of emotion and confidence in economics, and it's in that spirit that I'm using the term here.

does lead to prices which perfectly summarize the balance of views about risk at any given moment. My mortgage loan cost me 7.25 per cent when it was taken out: on the one hand, that price represented the sum of what the mortgage market thought of the risk it was taking in lending to me and the most cash it could squeeze out of me, and on the other hand from my point of view it represented the cheapest access to capital I could find at the time. (Just to show how the balance of these things changes, I thought that the interest rate was a bit higher than I'd like when I took out the mortgage. But now I'm a lot happier than the bank is, because it was an adjustable-rate mortgage and is currently costing me 1 per cent. For an ordinary citizen, capital doesn't come much cheaper than that. In fact, Woolwich/ Barclays no longer issues this particular kind of mortgage. So although I was comprehensively screwed on my first endowment mortgage two decades ago, I have very, very slightly screwed – perhaps one-eighth screwed – the bank this time. That's an example of how, although the market gives a very good summary of the balance between borrower and lender at any particular moment, that balance will change over time, and one side is likely to come out ahead.) The thing to understand in the financial world is that people actively go looking for risk, because a riskier investment will be a higher-yielding investment. Then they try to master the risk. If you ever come across an investment which is less risky but yields more, take it. You have found the Philosopher's Stone.

How does the industry seek to master the risks? Through mathematics. The common-sense version of what sophisticated investors do is diversification, a technique so old it's mentioned in the Talmud, where the strategy advocated is to have a third of your assets in trade, a third in cash and a third in land. Here's a nice simple example of diversification from Wikipedia:

On a particular island the entire economy consists of two companies: one that sells umbrellas and another that sells sunscreen. If a portfolio is completely invested in the company that sells umbrellas, it will have strong performance during the rainy season, but poor performance when the weather is sunny. The reverse occurs if the portfolio is only invested in the sunscreen company, the alternative investment: the portfolio will be high performance when the sun is out, but will tank when clouds roll in. To minimize the weather-dependent risk in the example portfolio, the investment should be split between the companies. With this diversified portfolio, returns are decent no matter the weather, rather than alternating between excellent and terrible.

What the pros do is a sophisticated version of that.[28] I've mentioned Fischer Black and Myron Scholes's paper in 1973 as the moment when the derivatives market underwent its modernist revolution. In share investing, the equivalent moment was the 1952 publication in the *Journal of Finance* of a paper called 'Portfolio Selection' by Harry Markowitz, a twenty-five-year-old grad student at the University of Chicago. Markowitz had read Hume while still in high school: 'I was particularly struck by David Hume's argument that, though we release a ball a thousand times, and each time, it falls to the floor, we do not have a necessary proof that it will fall the thousand-and-first time.' By the time he was at the university, this had translated into an interest in uncertainty, and when Markowitz began to study for his PhD on the maths of share pricing, he was hit by an idea. The current theory of share prices, the 'fair value' theory of John Burr Williams, argued that the present value of a share was no more than the value of the future dividends it would make, discounted to allow for the effect of inflation. Williams, in other words, disagreed with the various thinkers who stressed the casino-like aspect of share investing, in favour of a belief that shares did in fact have an intrinsic, measurable value. Markowitz, working on his PhD, fell to reflecting on the fact that the fair-value theory made no allowance for uncertainty, for the fact that, in reality, we can have no sure idea what dividends a share will pay in the future. Because of that, investors diversify their portfolios, as in the umbrellas-and-suncream example; and Markowitz began to study the mathematics of how they diversify, and how the movement of different shares in different directions could be analysed and used to reduce the overall risk of a portfolio of shares.

Markowitz's ideas boiled down to two fundamental insights. The first was about volatility. As Nigel Molesworth would say, any fule kno that the main thing about a share price is how much it goes up, or down, over time. That much was obvious. But Markowitz saw another thing: that as well as knowing how much a share went up, it was also essential to know how much it wobbled up and down en route to its destination. That was critical, because it told you how much risk you were taking on. A share that over time made an average gain of 5 per cent a year, but in any given year stood a good chance of losing a quarter of its value, was a very different proposition from a share which made the same gain but hardly ever lost more than 10 per cent. The owner of the less volatile share will sleep much better, for a start. So now you had two principal numbers for a share, the average growth and the average volatility; both numbers, taken together, gave the investor dramatically more information than just the growth on its own.

Another idea gave the first even more power. It was to do with correlation, which is the way in which shares either do or don't move together. In our umbrellas-and-sunblock example, the share prices of the companies have negative correlation: when one goes up, the other goes down. It's easy to think of other real-world examples: shares in online gambling companies versus shares in casinos, say, or (more subtly) shares in oil companies versus shares in car manufacturers (because high oil prices will mean people buying fewer cars). Some of the correlations are between whole sectors of stocks with, for instance, technology shares having a low correlation with service-industry stocks (meaning they tend to move in opposite directions) and real estate having an even lower correlation with oil services (why? No idea). Again, correlation is something that can be measured, using historical data, and given a precise number: the maths tells you just how much specific shares have historically been correlated with each other.

Markowitz showed how important volatility-plus-correlation could be as a tool in managing a portfolio of investments. By identifying stocks which don't move in the same direction, investors could get the upside of share-price movements, while significantly reducing the up-and-down volatility of the overall portfolio. In his history of risk, *Against the Gods*, Peter Bernstein makes the point with a chart showing a portfolio of investments in thirteen emerging stock markets. Over the two-and-a-half-year period of the chart, the portfolio of a-little-bit-of-everything grew at just under 2 per cent a month – a tasty yield for any portfolio, in any language – and had less volatility than any single one of its thirteen constituent markets. Since some of those markets had a 20 per cent chance of moving by a third in any given month, the stability given by the use of negative correlation would be invaluable in preventing the investor from going nuts with anxiety. All this led to the invention of what came to be called the 'efficient' portfolio, one which maximized the possible return for any chosen level of risk: basically, an efficient portfolio is one which uses volatility and correlation to engineer away unnecessary risks.

Notice, however, that a small sideways shuffle has taken place. When you and I and the postman talk about risk, we are talking about the possibility of something bad happening – of being bitten by a dog, say, or catching swine flu. When financial types talk about risk they are usually – as in the examples above – talking about volatility. Volatility is the measure of how much prices see-saw around, which isn't at all what the rest of us mean by risk, not least because volatility embraces both upward movement, which is what we do want from shares, and downward, which is what we don't. So risk in the mathematical sense is both a good thing and a bad thing. This is confusing. Don't worry if you feel confused, because you're in good company. Warren Buffett insists on the old-school, common-sense understanding of risk, and sticks to his own view that 'risk comes from not knowing what you're doing'. That, as the current crisis has shown, is no more than the plain truth; but it's also a philosophical position directly at odds with the current trend in banking.

This approach to risk was one of the things which put mathematicians at the heart of modern banking. It was one new invention in particular which put them there. The new model was first adopted by the US company Bankers Trust in the late seventies, under the chairmanship of Charles Sanford. In his view, 'successful people understand that risk, properly conceived, is often highly productive rather than something to avoid. They appreciate that risk is an advantage to be used rather than a pitfall to be skirted. Such people understand that taking calculated risks is quite different from being rash.'[29] He put this into practice by encouraging Bankers Trust to develop a precisely quantified measure of risk, a system which became known as RAROC, for 'risk-adjusted return on capital'. RAROC offered a numerical analysis of risk and added to it a measure of the impact of that risk on a business's profitability; just as portfolio management gave a way of assessing and optimizing the risk of a set of shareholdings, so RAROC did the same for a company's or bank's range of businesses. In time, however, the industry came to prefer a newer model of risk, called VaR for Value at Risk. (My favourite thing about VaR is that groovily modern lower-case 'a'.) This was a statistical technique which really took off in the late eighties, as a response to the Black Monday stock-market crash of October 1987. On that occasion, many players were appalled by the speed and severity of their losses – losses which, it's now thought, were in large part caused by computer programs running 'portfolio insurance'. That was yet another invention, the brainchild of a young Californian academic called Hayne Leland, who worked out that, thanks to the Black–Scholes equation and the subsequent take-off of the options industry, options could now be used to create a form of insurance against share prices dropping, not just one by one, but across an entire investment portfolio.

Leland had his idea in 1976; by 1987, the use of portfolio insurance was widespread. There was a problem, though: the most commonly used form of insurance was against the whole index of the top 500 shares, the S and P 500. People insured their holdings against a basket of all 500 top stocks. The idea was that if prices started to go down beyond a certain point, the computer program would kick in and sell the stocks, thus preventing further losses. That way, there was insurance guaranteeing that investors would never lose more than a predetermined amount of money. The problem was that everybody's automatic program was set up the same way; and all these programs concentrated on selling a basket of the top 500 stocks. This was an accident waiting to happen, and it duly happened on Monday 19 October 1987. Stocks had been wobbling downwards, as investors' nerves grew unsteady. Over the previous weekend, a number of sell orders had built up. This meant that the market, when it opened on that Monday, started falling as the sell orders were executed; the portfolio insurance kicked in and began automatically selling shares. But because everyone's automatic programs were kicking in at the same time and trying to sell the same basket of stocks, no buyers could be found, so the stocks dropped more, and the automatic selling programs kept on trying to sell into a market with no buyers. The result was that the Dow dropped 22.6 per cent in one day, worse than anything that had happened in the Great Crash of 1929.

That left many bankers saying, Never again. In retrospect, Black Monday looks more like a speed bump in the general upward movement of markets from 1982: nonetheless, it also showed how the increasingly interlinked nature of markets and computer-assisted trading could make bad things happen with great speed. Black Monday came out of the blue and cost a lot of people a lot of money. It left them wanting to know just what risks they were running, at any given moment. It had started to become obvious that, now that financial institutions were so big and complicated, different parts of the same firm would, without realizing it, be making very similar bets, thus unwittingly magnifying certain risks. VaR was the statistical tool which promised to let managers get a grip on this. It was first adopted by Dennis Weatherstone, the chief executive of J. P. Morgan. In 1989 he initiated something called the 4.15 report, a piece of paper which landed on his desk every day at 4.15 p.m., a quarter of an hour after the markets closed, carrying a VaR number which summed up the risk the bank was taking that day. VaR has three components: a time frame, usually in the one-day to two-week range; a number stating the amount of money at risk; and a fixed probability, usually either 1 or 5 per cent, expressing the chance that that money will be lost. So you might have a VaR of one day, £1,000,000 and 5 per cent. That means that there is a 5 per cent chance that you will lose £1,000,000 within the next twenty-four hours. Put more cheerfully, there is a 95 per cent chance that you won't lose £1,000,000. The way to think of VaR is as a worst-case scenario, a statement of how much you can lose within – that is the hugely important proviso, *within* – the given range of probabilities. Outside that range, all bets are off. This is a vital fact, and one of the dangers with VaR is that, in the dialogue between the quants and the managers, the meaning of the figures can be mislaid. The percentage sets the 'VaR break', as it's called, the point at which all bets are off and you can lose not just your house but your shirt.

It was easy, though, for people to hear a VaR of one-day, 1 per cent and £1,000,000 as telling them that the worst that can happen is that they will lose a million quid – which isn't what the figures are telling them, not at all. (And by the way, that 1-per-cent-per-day outcome is likely to happen a couple of times a year.) Still, VaR brought a degree of certainty where none had previously existed, and that alone felt like a breakthrough. The increasing prevalence of derivatives in the financial system also added to the popularity of VaR, because it provided a way for managers (and investors, regulators and everybody else) who didn't understand derivatives to put a figure on the risks that were being run. In 1997, the Securities and Exchange Commission required corporations fooling around with derivatives to give quantitative statements of their activities; lots of firms chose to do so by publishing VaR figures. VaR became the industry standard, so much so that it was used as the preferred measure of market risk in the Basel II accords (the ones whose rules about capital requirements and suchlike the bankers were busily circumventing).

But there were and are problems with VaR, and the system has never been without vociferous critics. The first problem is the same as with all probabilistic and computer-based systems, in more or less every field of human activity: the system is only as good as its data. It's one of the most important maxims in computing: GIGO, meaning garbage in, garbage out. There were areas in which there were plenty of data – to do with corporate bonds and risks of default and suchlike – and other areas where the data were much thinner. The apparent precision of the VaR number had an inbuilt propensity to be misleading, because it didn't admit that it could only ever be as good as the data on which it was based.

The other problem was even deeper and more consequential. The probabilities in the VaR models were based on the bell curve. Everybody knows the bell curve, and for a good reason, because an enormous number of phenomena fit into it, including most things about people which can be measured – heights, weights, IQs. The bell curve, known in mathematics as the normal distribution curve, fits all phenomena which tend to cluster around a mean or average. The further away from that mean, the less likely phenomena are to occur. The normative distribution underlies all sorts of mathematics and it is central to the study of probability.

The problem with using the bell curve here is simply put. How do we know that the normative distribution applies to events in the financial markets? The way in which people move and jostle around a room might be plotted and mapped with statistical tools and shown to resemble something like a normative distribution – sometimes people are over here, sometimes they're over there, but most of the time they're somewhere in the middle. But shout 'Fire!' and the movement of people in the room will look very different – it will feature a stampede towards the exits. There's nothing bell-curvey about that. How do we know that financial markets, under stress, will stick to the probability distributions plugged into the VaR models? Well, we don't. In the words of Nassim Taleb, the first and most vociferous critic of VaR, in the course of a famous debate about the value of the models in 1997: 'You're worse off relying on misleading information than on not having any information at all. If you give a pilot an altimeter that is sometimes defective he will crash the plane. Give him nothing and he will look out the window. Technology is only safe if it is flawless.'[30] Taleb's disagreement with the whole idea of 'engineering' risk was, and still is, profound, his disagreement with VaR especially so:

VAR has made us replace about 2,500 years of market experience with a co-variance matrix that is still in its infancy. We made a tabula rasa of years of market lore that was picked up from trader to trader and crammed everything into a co-variance matrix. Why? So a management consultant or an unemployed electrical engineer can understand financial market risks.

To me, VAR is charlatanism because it tries to estimate something that is not scientifically possible to estimate, namely the risks of rare events. It gives people misleading precision that could lead to the buildup of positions by hedgers. It lulls people to sleep.

The most lulling thing about it is the false confidence offered by the precise statements of probability: the 95 per cent chance of a measurable loss, which was also the 5 per cent chance of what could be total disaster. The point about VaR should have been what it couldn't tell you, the terribleness of the catastrophes which awaited just outside its confidence levels. If you have a 95 per cent chance of losing less than £1,000 today, and a 5 per cent chance of being taken hostage, tortured, then being covered in honey and eaten alive by ants, are you likely to say, 'A thousand pounds? That doesn't sound so bad!' I doubt it. But that's what many of the banks did.

The most thoughtful advocates of VaR at times sound oddly like its critics. Philippe Jorion is a California-based French economist who took part in a famous-to-quants exchange with Nassim Taleb in April 1997. Jorion made a number of measured points about the usefulness of VaR, and then disagreed with Taleb about some specific issues to do with how well VaR predicted unusual and non-bell-curvey phenomena. A wobbly speedometer, Jorion said, was more useful than no speedometer at all. And then he came to this moderate and sensible-sounding conclusion:

It seems premature to describe VaR as 'charlatanism'. In spite of naysayers, VaR is an essential component of sound risk management systems.

VaR gives an estimate of potential losses given market risks. In the end, the greatest benefit of VaR lies in the imposition of a structured methodology for critically thinking about risk. Institutions that go through the process of computing their VaR are forced to confront their exposure to financial risks and to set up a proper risk management function. Thus the process of getting to VaR may be as important as the number itself.

So what VaR boils down to is that it forces people to think properly about risk. We're back to where we started: to the fact that we as a species are rubbish at thinking about risk.

By the early years of the new millennium, everybody and his dog was using the new technique for assessing risk. What you thought of that depended on whether you believed critics of VaR, advocates of VaR or managers who didn't know what they were doing. These would have told you, in order, that the financial world was sleepwalking over the edge of the Grand Canyon; that it was navigating by a rough-and-ready compass which was preferable to no compass at all; or that everything was fine and the bankers knew very well where they were going. Crucially, though, the idea had taken hold that the new techniques provided a way of quantifying and assessing risk, and therefore of managing it. Risk could be arranged so that everything boiled down to a number.

This was why David X. Li's application of the Gaussian copula function to CDOs hit so hard.[31] Up until now the whole problem with mortgage-backed CDOs had been that they couldn't be reduced to a number. To recap, there was no national housing market in the USA; there had never been a national downturn in house prices; there were only patchy data for housing; and the new sub-prime mortgages were so new that there was no chance of having a historical accumulation of data, because there was no history. Li's formula came along as a wizard's wand to wave away all these troubles and magically solve them, thanks to its novel way of calculating correlation.

This, remember, is at the heart of the modern quanty way of investing. The power of correlation was what Harry Markowitz had taught the investing world: how you needed to understand the way prices moved, together or separately, to design a portfolio with the lowest possible level of unnecessary risk. In trying to correlate mortgage data, what was being calculated was all the diverse risks and life histories of the various US sub-prime borrowers – a stoner dude with dodgy credit in Seattle, an immigrant family with no credit history in Arizona, a young couple with a history of maxed-out cards and non-payment in Michigan. How do you make a mathematical model of that, and show what's likely to happen to them and what they're likely to do under a range of different circumstances? Bearing in mind that the kind of loan they have didn't exist until about five minutes ago?

Easy – the new formula ignored the history altogether. There was one number, gamma, plugged into the formula to represent correlation, and that number was taken not from the historical analysis of mortgages but from the price of credit default swaps on those mortgages. That was Li's big idea, or one of them: instead of trying to access the underlying raw material of data on mortgage payments – which nobody could say with a straight face that they had done – quants could just ignore them and look at the way the relevant CDS prices moved. If your insurance has just got more expensive, but your neighbour's has just got cheaper, well then, your insurance and his insurance are negatively correlated. If his goes up, but less than yours, then there's a small positive correlation. If his goes up even more than yours, then you're positively correlated, but his is more volatile. You don't (the advocates of the new formula argued) need to know all the detail of exactly what's influencing the price of your two different insurance policies. Maybe you occasionally leave the door open while he's a ragingly house-proud neat freak; maybe you go away for six months and let the house to students who trash the place. Who cares? It doesn't matter, since all the relevant information is in the price. The way your insurance price moves in relation to his tells you all you need to know about how your risks and his are correlated. Since CDS is at base a form of insurance, the principle is the same. You didn't need to know the specifics of mortgage history to work out the correlations; all you needed to do was look at how the prices were correlated – and all you had to do to find the prices was look them up. Just plug those data you have into the Gaussian copula formula, and it will give you back a number which quantifies the level of risk you're taking.

It was beautiful. The Gaussian copula formula used historical CDS correlation data to create accurate – theoretically accurate – assessments of risk and thereby unlocked the whole new market of sub-prime CDOs. There was only one problem, and it's not just a problem apparent in hindsight, since many people warned about it at the time. The problem was that the correlation data were rubbish. Sub-prime mortgages were new and had never been through a severe period of market difficulty. There was simply no way of knowing what would happen if they did. Of course, there was a common-sense way of guessing what would happen, based on the permanent truth that what goes up must come down, and that the housing market was an obvious bubble that was going to burst. If that happened, lots of risky new borrowers would fail to pay back their mortgages and would go into default, and since there were so many of them, there would be a precipitate crash in the housing market and an especially precipitate one in the group of people who had taken out the risky and high-yielding new loans. Since this group's mortgage payments were what underpinned a whole new category of CDOs, that category was in for a very, very bumpy ride. That's what common sense would have suggested. But the ninja-level quantitative models used in the CDOs were precisely not based on common sense; they were based on data which were simply inadequate. Using the Gaussian copula formula and the modern edifice of risk engineering, the figure the quants came up with for the current market implosion – based on a 20 per cent decline in house prices, feeding through into the CDO industry – was that it was likely to happen only in a time-frame many, many trillions of years longer than the history of the universe.

You have to ask yourself how intelligent people could ever have come to persuade themselves of that. I'm only forty-seven, but this is the second time in my adult lifetime – the second time in my lifetime as a mortgage-paying property owner – that property prices have fallen by more than 20 per cent. It seems wilful and bizarre and well over the fine line between clever and stupid for entire banks to have persuaded themselves that such a drop in US house prices was not just unlikely but trillions-and-trillions-to-one unlikely. And what makes this even less excusable is that equally unlikely events had happened before – and yet the models of risk and probability had been allowed to remain intact.

A brief word on statistics: the measure of unlikelihood in any given distribution – that's the picture made by the graph, the best known of which is our friend the bell curve – is called the standard distribution. This is a mathematically determined amount which tells you how much volatility, how much up-and-down and side-to-side movement, there is in the statistics. A school with an average IQ of 100 but a high standard deviation has some very high-IQ kids and some very low ones; a school with the same average IQ but a smaller standard distribution has more kids in the middle and fewer outliers. One standard deviation on either side of the average includes about 68 per cent, just over two-thirds, of all the data; two standard deviations includes about 95 per cent. Three standard deviations is 99.7 per cent. Standard deviation often appears in equations as the Greek letter Σ, sigma. It's a useful measure of how spread any data are, and it's also a useful measure of probability. A 'three-sigma event' is something supposed to happen only 0.3 per cent of the time, that is about once every three thousand times something is measured.

Quants use these measures of probability all the time. According to the models in use by the quants, the Black Monday crash of 1987 was a ten-sigma event. Translated into English, that meant that, in the words of Roger Lowenstein's book *When Genius Failed*: 'Economists later figured that, on the basis of the market's historical volatility, had the market been open every day since the creation of the Universe, the odds would still have been against its falling that much in a single day. In fact, had the life of the Universe been repeated one billion times, such a crash would still have been theoretically "unlikely".'[32] The defiance of common sense here is flagrant. If your mathematical model tells you that something is impossible – which is what, in practice, that degree of improbability implies – and then that thing happens, then you know with certainty that your mathematical model is wrong. It doesn't make sufficient allowance for reality. In this case, the unacknowledged reality was to do with portfolio insurance, but it doesn't in fact matter what the unacknowledged thing was: it just matters that your model doesn't work, because when unexpected things happen – and as every grown-up in the world knows, unexpected things happen all the time – the historically based mathematical model can't cope with it. If the Black Monday crash wasn't adequate to make that point, then it could equally have been made by the Russian bond default of 1998 and the market panic which accompanied that. (That incident destroyed Long-Term Capital Management, the genius-only hedge fund mentioned earlier.) The 1998 default was a seven-sigma event. That means it should statistically have happened only once every three billion years. And it wasn't the only one. The last decades have seen numerous five-, six- and seven-sigma events. Those are supposed to happen, respectively, one day in every 13,932 years, one day in every 4,039,906 years, and one day in every 3,105,395,365 years. And yet no one concluded from this that the statistical models in use were wrong.

The mathematical models simply didn't work in a crisis. They worked when they worked, which was most of the time; but then the whole point of them was to assess risks, and some risks by definition happen at the edges of known likelihoods. The strange thing is that this is strongly hinted at in the VaR model, as propounded by its more philosophically minded defenders such as Philippe Jorion: it marks the boundaries of the known world, up to the VaR break, and then writes 'Here be Dragons'. But nobody paid enough attention to the Dragons and other beasties which lay outwith the boundaries of the VaR model. What they relied on instead was historical data. The great problem with historical data is in the name: it is historical. By definition they don't include new phenomena. They aren't like actuarial tables, or charts of how tall people are, in which you can reliably accumulate and measure and draw conclusions. Financial markets aren't like that: the impact of uncertainties are just too high. In financial markets, the lesson of history is paradoxical but clear: the lesson of history is that you can't rely on historical data.

The ultimate absurdities were reached during the early days of the credit crunch. Remember the basic reality underlying that: people with bad credit histories, who for the most part lied to get loans, not being able to pay back their mortgages. Consider the case of Lashawn Wilson in Baltimore, with no job and no income, supposedly making mortgage payments to the trustee which was the ultimate owner of her mortgage, Citigroup Mortgage Loan Trust Inc. How likely is a problem with that and similar mortgages? Not too unlikely, one would have thought. But by the time the market had finished with its packaging and securitization and CDOs and CDSs and VaR and Gaussian copula formulas, that turned into events which the CEO of Goldman Sachs, David Viniar, described like this: 'We were seeing things that were 25-standard deviation moves, several days in a row.' It is almost impossible to put into words how big a number twenty-five sigma is, expressed as odds-to-one. Twenty sigma is ten times the number of all the particles in the known universe; twenty-five sigma is the same but with the decimal point moved fifty-two places to the right. It's equivalent to winning the UK national lottery twenty-one times in a row. That's the probability of a single twenty-five-sigma event. Goldman was claiming to experience them several days in a row. That is so wrong you can't put it into words. It shouldn't be humanly possible to be that wrong.[33]

Remember, what we're talking about here is a drop in house prices which caused people with bad credit to have trouble paying their mortgages. That was turned into something that was literally the most unlikely thing to have happened in the history of the universe.

When Alan Greenspan spoke about 'a flaw in the model that I perceived is the critical functioning structure that defines how the world works', that was what he was talking about. He was talking about the fact that he felt certain, as an article of faith, that markets could be relied on accurately to price and manage risk. (Pricing risk correctly is more or less the same as managing it correctly: it implies that you've got your sums right.) This was Greenspan's testimony to the House committee on oversight and reform, the account of the crisis in the words of the most important central banker in the world, with my commentary – and my hope is that by this point in the book, you'll now be able to understand him.[34]

What went wrong with global economic policies that had worked so effectively for nearly four decades? [Well, that's one way of putting it. But it ignores the increasing inequality since the end of the Cold War and also the increasing power of the financial industry, and how it secured from willing politicians the right to deregulate itself and become more casino-like. It also ignores the near-disasters such as Black Monday and the Russian debt/Long Term Capital Management crisis, and all the other occasions which should have shown the inadequacy of mathematical models of correlation and risk.] The breakdown has been most apparent in the securitization of home mortgages. The evidence strongly suggests that without the excess demand from securitizers, subprime mortgage originations (undeniably the original source of crisis) would have been far smaller and defaults accordingly far fewer. [All true.] But subprime mortgages pooled and sold as securities became subject to explosive demand from investors around the world. These mortgage backed securities being 'subprime' were originally offered at what appeared to be exceptionally high risk-adjusted market interest rates. But with U.S. home prices still rising, delinquency and foreclosure rates were deceptively modest. Losses were minimal. To the most sophisticated investors in the world, they were wrongly viewed as a 'steal'.

The consequent surge in global demand for U.S. subprime securities by banks, hedge, and pension funds supported by unrealistically positive rating designations by credit agencies was, in my judgment, the core of the problem. [Yes.] Demand became so aggressive that too many securitizers and lenders believed they were able to create and sell mortgage backed securities so quickly that they never put their shareholders' capital at risk and hence did not have the incentive to evaluate the credit quality of what they were selling. [True.] Pressures on lenders to supply more 'paper' collapsed subprime underwriting standards from 2005 forward. Uncritical acceptance of credit ratings by purchasers of these toxic assets has led to huge losses. [True.]

It was the failure to properly price such risky assets that precipitated the crisis. In recent decades, a vast risk management and pricing system has evolved, combining the best insights of mathematicians and finance experts supported by major advances in computer and communications technology. A Nobel Prize was awarded for the discovery of the pricing model that underpins much of the advance in derivates markets. This modern risk management paradigm held sway for decades. [All true so far.] The whole intellectual edifice, however, collapsed in the summer of last year because the data inputted into the risk management models generally covered only the past two decades, a period of euphoria. Had instead the models been fitted more appropriately to historic periods of stress, capital requirements would have been much higher and the financial world would be in far better shape today, in my judgment. [True, but he's missing the point: it's not that the data didn't have enough history – though they didn't – it's that the whole idea of relying on historical data is inadequate. The unforeseen event is the unforeseen event, by definition: if these things fitted into models, the models would work; but they demonstrably don't work, when faced with the unexpected. They are, in the words of the hedge-fund manager David Einhorn, 'like an airbag which works all the time except when you get into a crash'.]

So we can quibble with the precise details of Greenspan's hindsight view. In essence, though, he was right: the mistake all came down to risk. He was much, much too late, but he was right. Banking is all about the management of risk; and in this central respect the bankers massively failed. They did so by relying on inaccurate mathematical models which they themselves didn't fully understand. (Mervyn King, Governor of the Bank of England: CDOs 'have a distribution of returns which is highly sensitive to small changes in the correlations of underlying returns which we do not understand with any great precision'.)[35] The result was that they failed as utterly and completely as it is possible to fail. They weren't just wrong-in-practice, the way you are wrong if you call heads and the coin lands tails; they were philosophically wrong. They were exposed as doing something which was contrary to the nature of reality.

6. Funny Smells

The credit crunch was based on a climate, a problem and a mistake. It was also based on a failure, that of the regulators and politicians and central bankers whose job it was to look out for the signs of economic danger. Part of this was to do with ignoring warning signs, in the form of too-good-to-be-true data, economic overheating and funny smells.

Financial crashes, implosions and scandals are always accompanied by funny smells. An example: in 2007 I went to the Cúirt festival in Galway city. The previous time I'd been there was in 1999, for the annual Mass a year after my mother's death. That occasion happened to be during a solar eclipse, so the first thing that guests were given on arrival at the hotel was a set of instructions about how you were to be sure not to look at the sun. Cut to eight years later and the same hotel: and this time, no sooner had you crossed the threshold than you were given a set of instructions about how you weren't supposed to drink the water. The water in Galway was contaminated by an outbreak of cryptosporidium, a single-cell protozoa which causes symptoms of gastroenteritis including, says the medical dictionary, 'profuse, foul smelling, watery diarrhoea, vomiting (especially in children)', and lasts for one to three weeks. There is no treatment. Nice. At the time I was mainly amused by the coincidence, and also fell to wondering what would happen next time I was in town: don't look at the sky, don't drink the water – what next, don't breathe? A plague of locusts? I didn't pay nearly enough attention to the meaning of the cryptosporidium outbreak. It's grotesque that a place with a hinterland as rural as Galway, and as copious a supply of fresh rainfall, should have no drinkable water. The reason why it didn't was because the whole area had grown so fast, and with so little planning and attention to sustainability, that the infrastructure had broken down – in this case, the water-treatment infrastructure. That should have been a glaring indicator of the crisis which was about to engulf the 'Celtic Tiger', thanks to the carelessness with which its politicians had mismanaged the good years. To some of us who know and love Ireland, it was always a bad sign that the Irish economic miracle was named after an animal which doesn't exist. Only a few months on from that, and Ireland was in the worst economic contraction of any developed country since the Great Depression. Ireland, joked *The Economist* in February 2008 (or maybe that should be semi-joked), is at risk of being 'Reykjavik-on-Liffey', and it quoted a local witticism: 'What's the difference between Ireland and Iceland? Six months and one letter.' Just over a month later, economic figures came out showing that the annualized rate of decline in the economy was 25.5 per cent. The Irish have had two of the worst things you can have in the current climate, a housing bubble and a credit bubble, all on the back of a decade-long economic boom. Now the country is in one of the worst recessions to hit a developed economy in modern times, and one which is likely to get worse: if 25 per cent of your gross domestic product and 13 per cent of your employment comes from house building, and house building stops, then it's time to switch metaphors: Celtic Dodo? Celtic Zeppelin? Celtic Zombie? Celtic Car Crash? The undrinkable Galway water was a classic funny smell.

In fact it's noticeable how often people who speak of or report these things refer to things smelling off or funny. The exact phrase was used to me by a man who turned down an invitation from Bernard Madoff to participate in his hedge fund. This man worked for a big investment bank, which offered clients the chance to participate in a fund-of-funds service: in other words they offered a fund which consisted of investments in several different hedge funds. For the banker, this should have been a win–win, because he had clients who were clamouring to join in Madoff's funds – which were famous for their consistency, returning a steady 10 to 12 per cent in all years and all weathers – and the inflow of money would in turn generate a steady income in fees. And Madoff was known for being choosy about his clients. (We now know the reason why: he didn't want any investors who were likely to ask the wrong sort of questions.) So there was nothing not to like . . . except that this man didn't like it. The steadiness of Madoff's returns seemed wrong. He turned down the opportunity to participate in Madoff's fund, a decision which cost him a good deal of political capital at his bank, until Madoff was exposed as a fraudster (and the banker who turned him down was promoted). Why did he turn down Madoff? 'Because it just didn't smell right.'

Funny smells come in a variety of types. The funny smells surrounding the credit crunch were not for the most part to do with fraud – though, having said that, a CDO investor who had had a long look at the way mortgages were being originated would have been gagging on fraud-related stench. Mainly, they were funny smells to do with things which were just too good to be true. That is a critically important category of funny smells, and it is the kind which is most relevant in the story of the credit crunch. It is a category of funny smell which involves an element of the wilful, or of wishful thinking; or perhaps just of ignoring what's in front of your nose. To adopt a metaphor I heard used by the Chancellor of the Exchequer, Alistair Darling, it's a bit like putting flowers in the hallway as a solution to the problem of dry rot.

There are people whose job it is to sniff out these funny smells, to think about them and what they mean, and to make plans about them on our behalf. They are the central bankers. There is a passage in Norman Mailer's novel *Harlot's Ghost* in which the narrator rhapsodizes about the CIA being 'the mind of America'. Central bankers are a little like that. Their job is to notice everything and think about everything – everything economic – and then to act on it via one tool and one tool only: the interest rate.*

This determines, or anyway influences, the level of borrowing, the level of credit, the level of economic activity, the level of inflation, the level of unemployment, the speed of growth, the exchange rate, the whole kaboodle, but it is also a fairly crude tool: it's as if the central banker were sitting at a desk console with thousands of flashing lights and digital read-outs and heads-up visual displays, all pouring in overwhelming quantities of data, and in response to it the banker can only move one lever, in a straight line backwards or forwards, and preferably only a very little at a time.

That's the job of central banking. I've already said that the most influential central banker in the world, in the lead-up to the credit crunch, was Alan Greenspan, and I've mentioned the dogmatic laissez-faire ideology (underpinned by Ayn Rand's Objectivism) for which he is famous. I haven't mentioned that one of his traits was an extraordinary nose for and attention to detail. During his tenure at the Fed, Greenspan was legendary for his ability to hoover up gigantic amounts of raw data and bring them to bear in his assessment of the desired movements in interest rates. The account I've given of him so far might make

---

* This is an oversimplification, because, as the current crisis has shown, central banks can also print money, and do so via a number of mechanisms such as the new favourite 'quantitative easing'. This is essentially buying its own debt instruments without issuing anything to back it up; it's not literally the same thing as printing money but it's as good as. It is a measure that's resorted to when interest rates have been cut so much or so fast that there's nowhere else to go with them. All this is a response to a desperate crisis, and is a sign that all normal measures have failed. Under normal circumstances, the interest rate is the whole ballgame.

him sound like a man committed to abstractions, but it must be stressed that Greenspan's attention to practical detail and to what the facts were telling him was at the heart of what he did. Funny smells were what he was all about.

As for the specific risks of a bubble in house prices, Greenspan was well aware of the dangers. Or at least, there had been a time when that was true. Talking to American estate agents in 1995, he said that 'It is hard to overestimate the importance of house price trends for consumer psyches and behaviour . . . Consumers view their home equity as a cushion or security blanket against the possibility of future hard times.'[36] That seems unequivocal: the importance of house prices is 'hard to overestimate'. But this raises the question of why he went on to ignore them so hard for so long. It was the bubble in house prices which both caused people to pile into the housing market and then to lose their shirts when it popped. That bubble was based on low interest rates, and the man responsible for setting those low rates was Greenspan. I've mentioned the chronology already: the years of the 'Goldilocks economy' and 'Great Moderation', growing neither too hot nor too cold, during which interest rates never moved by more than 0.25 of a per cent at any time.

During these years the markets came up with the phrase 'the Greenspan put' to describe the Fed Chairman's apparent determination to protect share prices. A 'put' is an option to sell shares if prices drop, so the 'Greenspan put' implied that Greenspan would always be there to bail out the market if it fell – which was a little paradoxical, because he had famously warned, as early as 1996, about 'irrational exuberance' in the stock market. But he seemed to say one thing and do another, because if he wanted to chill that exuberance, a couple of sharp jolts to the interest rate, combined with a scary speech or two, would do the trick. It's almost impossible to exaggerate the prestige and influence Greenspan had in markets during these years. In the words of

Richard Posner's book *A Failure of Capitalism*: 'Greenspan's tremendous prestige gave him a largely free hand, which he did not use, to choke off the housing bubble by raising interest rates and to rein in risky lending by exercising more assertively the control that the Federal Reserve has over commercial banks. He thought he could avoid political controversy by waiting for bubbles to form and pop and clearing up afterwards by lowering interest rates.'[37] There was an element of mutual admiration in all this: Greenspan loved the doctrinally pure free markets, and the doctrinally pure free markets loved him. That, in turn, was the reason why he was and would continue to be reluctant to burst any bubbles: who was he to interfere in the operation of the market, which by definition was wiser about itself than any individual could be? The free market was She Who Must Be Obeyed, and if the market wanted to have a bubble, a bubble it must have.

Then came the dot-com crash, followed by the implosion of Enron. And this is the point at which hindsight sees Greenspan as having gone off the rails. On 3 January 2001 he broke with his policy of slow-and-steady movements in the interest rates and cut them by half a per cent in one go, down to 6 per cent, and followed in the subsequent months with further rate cuts – this being an example of the Greenspan put in its most flagrant form. After all, if markets were irrationally exuberant in 1996 and had kept going up, why wouldn't a crash, even one leading to a small recession, be desirable? The best analogy is with the management of forestry in a dry, hot country. The landscape needs fires – preferably small ones at regular and not too frequent intervals. If it doesn't get them, the undergrowth builds up, and offers a dangerously copious supply of fuel for the big fire when it eventually and inevitably comes. Had Greenspan fallen a little in love with his own publicity, as the all-knowing seer whose superbly judged nudges on the levers of interest rates had never been equalled? Or perhaps he had come to believe the hype about the new financial instruments, as he seemed to indicate in a speech a year after his comments on 'irrational exuberance', when he said that we were witnessing the dawn of 'a new paradigm of active credit management'. In either case, he seemed to have forgotten the old principle, much quoted by my father, that 'all you need to be an investment genius is a short memory and a rising market'. We won't know what Greenspan was really thinking and he certainly wouldn't say; whatever it was, commentators were beginning to wonder whether interest rates had been cut too far too fast. By 2003 the rate was 1 per cent, and stayed there for a year, even after the economy started growing at an annualized rate of 7.5 per cent.[38] Is it any wonder a bubble built up? For the reasons already given, it was a bubble not in stocks or bonds, but in assets.

The 'asset-price bubble' is economist-speak for the housing bubble. During the years of the build-up, while interest rates were low and debt was cheap, people borrowed cheap money and poured it into houses; or they drew money out of their houses by taking out loans against the increased value of those houses, treating them as if they were giant cashpoint machines. They then spent this on whatever they spent it on, as described by Greenspan in 1995. The point to bear in mind here is that the credit bubble, the debt bubble, the asset-price bubble and the housing bubble were all basically the same phenomenon.

In Greenspan's account of the causes of the crisis quoted at the end of the last chapter, he doesn't mention low interest rates and the house-price bubble; they are conspicuously absent as contributing factors from all the self-justification he's given since the crisis. When he does blame someone for the bubble, he tends to blame China. His argument is that interest rates stayed low not because he (and other central bankers) kept them low, but because the Chinese were buying up so many T-bills that there was no reason for the prices to rise. History will, I believe, judge this view to be mainly incorrect, and will say that the blame for the asset-price bubble was about 90 per cent to do with central bankers ignoring the dangers of low interest rates for too long. This was the first of the crucial funny smells ignored by Greenspan. He was far from alone, though. Chinese saving can't take either the credit or the blame for the interest-rate/asset-bubble phenomena which happened in the UK or the EU: China's savings were overwhelmingly in the US. Niall Ferguson has called the resulting economic hybrid 'Chimerica'.[39] I don't think there's any historical parallel for this new transnational economic entity, and the look of it, frankly, gives me the willies: there's something profoundly unnatural about such a skewed trans-Pacific balance of saving and spending. The Chinese would, I suspect, dearly love to dump a significant proportion of the T-bills and diversify into other areas of savings, but they can't, because it would be an act of economic Mutually Assured Destruction: the dollar would crash, which would wipe out (a) American consumption and (b) Chinese savings, with consequences roughly equal to a smallish world war.

But the EU had no equivalent phenomenon, and therefore no China to blame; and as Greenspan points out in that piece, it also had historically low interest rates. It had a doozy of a bubble, too, though it was one which was concentrated on specific countries such as Spain and Ireland. Lovely though it would be to blame the Chinese, we can't. As for the UK, our interest rates were higher than those of either the US or the EU during the relevant years. We nonetheless had an absolute corker of a housing bubble. What could the government, or the Bank of England, have done about that? Well, the government could have pursued a set of policies designed to cool things off: allowing councils to build more homes; loosening the planning system to make it easier to build new accommodation; abolishing mortgage relief

on buy-to-let properties, and thus putting the brakes on one of
the main areas of speculative activity; uttering dark threats about
the introduction of property-based taxes. But the housing bubble
translated so directly into consumer spending, and the consumer
spending translated so directly into a growing economy, and the
growing economy (even if it was growing unsustainably) translated so directly into a paradise of raised government spending
and relatively unraised taxes, that the government – which in
this case means Gordon Brown, Chancellor and de-facto head
of domestic policy during the boom – found it unincumbent on
him to act. It is easy to be critical, and correct to be critical,
though it should also be admitted that very few Chancellors in
his position would have refused such a lavish free lunch. About
the only person who could possibly have exerted any serious
pressure on Brown to do otherwise was the Governor of the
Bank of England – 'Steady Eddie' George up to 2003, and then
Mervyn King.

The trouble was that the Governor's remit to act was crucially,
and in retrospect fatally, flawed. In 1997, immediately on coming
into office, the new Labour government had given the Bank of
England complete independence over the management of inflation and the setting of interest rates. Inflation was to be 2 per
cent, with a permitted margin of error of 1 per cent in either
direction, and if it wasn't, well then, the head of the Bank would
have to . . . would have to . . . would have to *jolly well write a letter*
to the Chancellor to explain why it wasn't. (I love the idea of
having to write a letter when you'd prefer not to as the ultimate
sanction.) The body which sets the interest rates is called the
Monetary Policy Committee, and the process of voting on the
interest rates is transparent, with the voting made public a few
weeks after it takes place, so the markets can see the Committee's
balance of thinking – thus helping to avoid nasty surprises with
subsequent rate changes. It's an interesting sidelight on how

government in Britain works: when something really does have important consequences – like interest rates – it's too important to faff about with the usual layers of needless secrecy. The new economic structure was announced on Tuesday 6 May 1997, despite not having been mentioned, or even implied or hinted at, in the Labour Party's manifesto for the general election which took place on Thursday 1 May: the most important economic initiative ever to have been imposed on the British public without any democratic consultation.

The power to set interest rates had been something of a Holy Grail for those economists who argued that the management of inflation was too important a matter to be left to politicians. I've been writing about interest rates and inflation and these subjects in the way that economists usually do, as if they were matters of technical management of the economy, but another way of thinking of them is in terms of whom they directly benefit, and whom they directly punish. For people on fixed incomes, inflation is a disaster, whereas for government employees and others with incomes protected against inflation it is much more neutral; for middle-class savers, it can be catastrophic; for people in debt, it can bring either ruin or – if their debt is of a fixed amount, one whose real value will go down as inflation eats it up – it can be a godsend. In a country with a minimum wage, inflation doesn't hurt the poor nearly as badly as in a country without; in fact it can even help them, if they have debts, by making those debts worth less in real terms. Similarly, the indebted middle-class home-owner can benefit from inflation, because it makes the value of her mortgage smaller; on the other hand, if the same middle-class home-owner is in the unfortunate position of having lent other people money, she has a problem, because when that amount is paid back it will be worth less than it was when it was lent.

These aren't abstract issues. Individual lives get easier or harder as interest rates and inflation do their dance: they take away from some and give to others. The classic example – every economist's favourite horror story – is that of Germany and the hyperinflation that overtook it after the first world war. By the early 1920s, the German economy, damaged by defeat, had become crippled by the attempt to pay the reparations demanded by the victorious European Allies and simultaneously develop a social-welfare state. The government printed as much money as it could, and inflation was running out of control. In 1914, the German mark had stood at 4.2 to the dollar; by 1922, it was 190 to the dollar; by the end of that year, it was 7,600. By November 1923, a dollar was worth 630 billion marks, a loaf of bread cost 140 billion marks, and Germany was disintegrating under the strain – which was a significant contributor, perhaps even the main contributor, to the rise of the Nazis.

The giving up of control over interest rates was therefore an epochal moment for the government and for the Bank of England. But in return for becoming so powerful in that respect, the Bank had to offer something back, and that was its direct supervisory role over banks and financial institutions. That was now the responsibility of the Financial Services Authority, the FSA. This was a body born after the collapse of Barings Bank, when it was felt self-evident that the banking industry's attempts at self-regulation weren't working and some external supervision was needed. As so often happens in public life, the body set up to supervise the business consisted largely of insiders (in this case, from the financial services industry) and civil servants, with representatives of the public absent. The institution carried the watermark of its origins, as institutions tend to do: it wasn't proactive in its view of the industry and didn't see itself as looking at the operation of the business from the outside. Regulatory bodies should have access to the perspective of outsiders, looking in at the industry from its periphery and prepared to ask obvious, which sometimes means obviously unpopular, questions. The

FSA wasn't like that: it didn't have somebody saying 'I don't understand, please explain.' It was dedicated to what was often called the principle of 'light touch' regulation. As Adair Turner, head of the FSA, said in his post-crash report:

An underlying assumption of financial regulation in the US, the UK and across the world, has been that financial innovation is by definition beneficial, since market discipline will winnow out any unnecessary or value destructive innovations. As a result, regulators have not considered it their role to judge the value of different financial products, and they have in general avoided direct product regulation, certainly in wholesale markets with sophisticated investors.[40]

This didn't mean that nobody at the FSA or the Bank or the Treasury – the third pillar of the 'tripartite' regulatory system supposed to run the British financial system – had a clue what was happening. Many individuals thought that debt and leverage were running at dangerously high levels. But the trouble was that nobody felt a need to own the problem. The Bank had had responsibility for this kind of thing directly taken away from it; the FSA was basically an industry body, which thought that market discipline would keep the industry on track, with the occasional quiet word and gentle nudge on the tiller; the Treasury was in the hands of political masters who were the principal beneficiaries of the boom and who had no incentive to go around raining on parades, bursting bubbles and telling the permanent and permanently unwelcome truth that what goes up must come down. It wasn't that everybody was asleep at the wheel; it was that no one wanted the responsibility of grabbing the wheel and changing course.

Regulation, and the lack of it, and the slack enforcement of it, was central to the crunch. In fact many students of the crunch think this is the central issue in the crisis. Accounts of the banking-and-credit crisis tend to focus their explanations, which usually also means their blame, on one or more of the following four factors: greed, stupidity, government or the banks. The process resembles a children's game in which you spin an arrow and it lands on a word. You can spin more than once. Many people who play the game land on government. When they do that, the issue they're focusing on is that of regulation. Their argument, put forcefully by Richard Posner, is that 'We are learning from [the crisis] that we need a more active and intelligent government to keep our model of a capitalist economy from running off the rails. The movement to deregulate the financial industry went too far by exaggerating the resilience – the self-healing powers – of laissez-faire capitalism.'[41]

The financial industry caused the crisis, but it could not have happened without the help of the governments which spent decades committed to a pure idea of laissez-faire capitalism. What that ideology did, in practice, was essentially to allow bankers to write their own rules – or their lack of rules. We had a decades-long process of deregulation and opening up, of stripping out all measures designed to second-guess the financial world's ability to regulate itself via 'market discipline'. This played out in a number of ways. One of these took the form of unregulation. That's what happens when a new product comes along and the industry lobbies for the new product to be set loose in the markets without much (or ideally any) regulatory supervision. One of the critical examples of this is to do with the new derivatives. CDSs and CDOs were not inscribed on stone tablets and handed down from on high, they were invented, and their function in the marketplace was something for which the banks that created them fought hard, in the face of initial scepticism from regulators and occasional anxious noises from politicians. The first set of Basel accords had been drafted before derivatives expanded to their new importance. The banks saw in that fact both the threat that governments might step in to legislate the huge new market and an opportunity, to step in first and write their own rulebook. The result was the creation in 1985 of the International Swaps and Derivatives Association, a trade body set up by the big international banks. Over subsequent years the ISDA fought and won a series of battles with various regulators, and won the right to regulate itself.

It helped that derivatives had a swooningly ardent admirer as head of the Federal Reserve. Step forward Alan Greenspan. 'By far the most significant invention in finance during the past decade has been the extraordinary development and expansion of financial derivatives,' Greenspan said in a 1999 speech given in the very Boca Raton hotel where the J. P. Morgan team had got plastered and invented the CDS. 'The fact that the OTC [that's over-the-counter] markets function quite effectively without the benefits of [regulation] provides a strong argument for development of a less burdensome regime for exchange-traded financial derivatives . . . These new financial instruments . . . enhance the ability to differentiate risk and allocate it to those investors most able and willing to take it.'[42] Admittedly, this is the sort of thing that a computer program written to impersonate Alan Greenspan would have said: free-market good. Trust free market. More free market. As so often with the ideologically committed free-marketeer, there is no sense that he's actually thinking about what he's saying: he's merely adumbrating arguments towards a conclusion he had reached in advance.

A big advantage held by the banks here was that legislators had next to no idea what derivatives were or how they worked; there was something lulling and seductive about the idea that the banks should be allowed to police themselves, thanks to self-regulation and, of course, 'market discipline'. So the banks' lobbying had an attentive, even a grateful, audience. The campaign was so effective that it didn't just succeed in persuading legislators not to legislate; the derivatives lobby went one better than that. They managed to get Congress to pass a law actually *banning* legislation. In 2000, it passed the Commodity Futures Modernization Act, which among other things asserted that CDSs were not futures or options and were therefore exempt from regulation; it also added provisos protecting the trade of derivatives over the counter, that is from one party to another rather than through an exchange. The great disadvantage of over-the-counter trades is that they are unmonitored, and no one knows what the risks are and where they are being spread – but they were much quicker and more convenient for the banks, and that was all that mattered. This is one of the critically important areas which is going to require re-regulation, since the financial system badly needs the degree of control and supervision which could be brought by trading CDSs through a regulated exchange. Note that the 2000 bill – which also included a clause exempting Enron's energy-derivatives business from legislation, the 'Enron loophole' as it's known – passed through both the Senate and the House of Representatives without debate.

This, and the issue of derivatives more generally, is one of the points where the funny smells build up to such an extent that they create a counterfactual. We are led to ask about a road not taken, an alternative path which did not lead to the present we've just been living through. Why should derivatives be traded over the counter at all? Even a lay person can immediately see the risks in having contracts of such immense value knocking around the system, unregulated and indeed not even counted by any central authority. How on earth did we get to such a place of total free-for-all? We could start with the 1982 Garn–St Germain Depository Institutions Act, a bill signed into law by Ronald Reagan with the pronouncement that it was 'the most important legislation for financial institutions in the last 50 years. It provides a long-term solution for troubled thrift institutions.' President Reagan concluded: 'All in all, I think we hit the jackpot.' In fact what happened was that the bill, by creating insurance for mortgage lenders, increased their recklessness and led directly to the Savings and Loan crash of the early 1980s, with a cost to the taxpayer of $124.6 billion. It was this bill which stood at the beginning of two-and-a-half decades of consistent deregulation and loosening regulatory supervision – and all the subsequent legislation moved in the same direction.

The general tide of deregulation and unregulation was brilliantly summed up in the aforementioned article 'The Quiet Coup', by Simon Johnson, a professor at MIT who was formerly the chief economist of the International Monetary Fund. In that role, his day job involved going into crisis-struck countries and banging heads together to get them to accept reforms as a price of IMF aid. He acquired an extensive experience of countries which had effectively been captured by a ruling elite who governed entirely in their own interests. His startling conclusion about the current crisis is that the US has become one of those countries. As the banking sector got richer, its power and influence over US government policy increased – power and influence which the bankers weren't at all afraid to use. So the current crisis was caused by the banking sector's excessive influence on US government policy – what he calls in the title of the piece 'the quiet coup'. This is his summary of what the bankers asked for and got:

From this confluence of campaign finance, personal connections, and ideology there flowed, in just the past decade, a river of deregulatory policies that is, in hindsight, astonishing:

- insistence on free movement of capital across borders
- the repeal of Depression-era regulations separating commercial and investment banking

- a congressional ban on the regulation of credit-default swaps
- major increases in the amount of leverage allowed to investment banks
- a light (dare I say invisible?) hand at the Securities and Exchange Commission in its regulatory enforcement
- an international agreement to allow banks to measure their own riskiness
- and an intentional failure to update regulations so as to keep up with the tremendous pace of financial innovation.[43]

The undoing of the Depression-era banking legislation was a critical component in this. In the aftermath of the Depression, the populist anger at banks and the financial system led to a series of laws designed to ensure that nothing like the crash ever happened again. That is a generally applicable historical pattern: societies tend to regulate their financial systems only in the aftermath of a scary failure. Conversely, when markets are booming, legislation tends to loosen, and so does enforcement of the existing legislation. The centrepiece of the Depression-era legislation was the Glass–Steagall Act of 1933, separating investment banking (the casino, where the bank makes bets on its own behalf) and commercial banking (the piggybank, where ordinary Joes deposit their savings, and the bank lends the money to other ordinary Joes to buy houses and cars and invest in their businesses). The idea was to let investment banks do their thing and blow themselves up without impacting on the general public. This hampered the freedom of the banks, not as a byproduct of the Act but as part of its central intention, and not surprisingly it was never loved by bankers. When the long boom began in 1982, the Act came under pressure from lobbyists, who exerted particular pressure over the point that it was unfair to banks, because they were now competing with a plethora of other, non-bank financial institutions which weren't subject to the same rules.

They were making a valid point, but they were making it the wrong way round. It was certainly true that the banks were now operating in a crowded financial marketplace in which many of the most important institutions weren't old-school banks. The bankers looked at this and drew the conclusion that what was needed was less legislation, so that the banks – the banks proper – were competing on a level playing field with all the other financial intermediaries. In retrospect this was precisely wrong: what was needed was for a much more active and intrusive legislative regime to check risk and leverage within all financial intermediaries (which from now on I'm going to go back to calling 'banks'). But the bankers and their pet legislators drew the opposite conclusion. So Glass–Steagall was abolished in 1999, thanks to a bill sponsored by three Republicans and backed by Treasury Secretary Larry Summers. Only eight senators voted against the bill, one of them Byron Dorgan, who said, 'this bill will in my judgement raise the likelihood of future massive taxpayer bailouts.' Looking back on the amazing correctness of this prediction from a decade later, Dorgan observed, 'The culture is that Wall Street knows best.' The proliferation of non-bank banks grew and grew. As Tim Geithner, President Obama's Treasury Secretary, pointed out, by 2007 more than half of America's banking was being handled by a 'parallel financial system' of largely unregulated institutions. These institutions were, in Geithner's words, 'vulnerable to a classic type of run, but without the protections such as deposit insurance that the banking system has in place to reduce such risks'.[44]

The culture which led to this point was not the exclusive property of one party or one section of the political elite: it was simply the received wisdom of the people in charge. It's for this reason that, although Alan Greenspan can be blamed for specific mistakes, he can't take the rap for the financial crisis overall. The entire climate of opinion, in the world of power, was in favour of laissez-faire and deregulation and 'innovation', so if it hadn't been Greenspan advocating this ideology and pushing through the policies which enacted it, and in turn earning the love and trust of the markets and loving and trusting them back, it would have been someone else. This was the system.

A big part of the problem was also that existing laws which might have been brought to bear, weren't. There are two aspects to financial regulation, the laws themselves and how they are used: call them the framework and the regime. In the US, the framework was undermined by decades of deregulation and had become a dementedly fragmented and patchworky thing. US banks, for instance, are regulated by the Office of Thrift Supervision, the state banking regulators, the Office of the Comptroller of the Currency, the Federal Reserve, the Federal Deposit Insurance Corporation, the National Credit Union Administration and (if the bank is participating in TARP, the Troubled Assets Relief Program) the Treasury; and bearing in mind the broad definition of banks to include other financial intermediaries, they are also likely to have dealings with the other regulatory bodies having a say in the running of financial institutions such as the state insurance regulators, the Commodity Futures Trading Commission, the Financial Industry Regulatory Authority, the state securities regulators (every state has one), the state attorney generals (who sometimes take an interest that the markets would prefer they didn't) and the big daddy of the stock markets, the SEC or US Securities and Exchange Commission.[45] They will also be regulated by the various agencies in the various overseas markets in which they operate. This is a major case of alphabet soup and it reminds me of something I once heard a political scientist say about Italy. That country, he said, makes you understand what an anarchy would in practice look like: it wouldn't be a society with no laws, but one with thousands of laws to which nobody pays any attention.

It is a moot point whether a system as complicated and fragmentary as that can be, to use the jargon, 'fit for purpose'. (President Obama's plans to clean up financial regulation, announced on 16 June 2009, give the Treasury more powers but don't clean up the regulatory tangle. That decision reflects political realities about turf, but might not be the best one in the long term.) Even if it were the best framework in the world, however, there would be a question of the regime which was administering it – and that has, in recent decades, been a problem. Things always get too lax in boom years. That's a fact of psychology. Add to it an ideological belief that markets know best and that government's duty is to shrink itself as small as possible, and you have a recipe for regulators not exactly to look the other way, but to take a shrugging, boys-will-be-boys attitude to actions which look irregular.

Sometimes this involved making new rules to suit the banks. In a meeting on 24 April 2004[46] the SEC agreed to allow the five big banks to cut the amount of capital they had to hold in reserve against potential losses in their investments. The banks involved were Merrill Lynch, Goldman Sachs, Lehman Brothers, Morgan Stanley and Bear Stearns: three of those banks no longer exist and the other two had to end (temporarily, it turned out) their status as investment banks, and *none of that would have happened* if the SEC had not changed the rules that day. The change allowed the banks sharply to increase their leverage – Bear Stearns, for instance, increased its leverage to the point where it had $33 in debt for every $1 in equity.

There was supposed to be a quid pro quo for the change. It was brought in because the European Commission was threatening to regulate the American banks which had brokerage operations – in other words, to extend its legislative remit from the subsidiary stockbroking companies up to the banks which owned them. But the Commission agreed not to do that if the

SEC took the parent companies – not just the brokerages, which it already supervised – under its legislative remit. The SEC agreed and the banks agreed too, the deal being that they were allowed to relax the rules on how much capital they kept in reserve. In return the SEC was allowed access to their books to monitor and assess their risks. By this point, the reader will have no trouble in guessing what happened. The banks took their relaxed capital rules, and the SEC in return did nothing. Its investigations were tentative and when the seven-strong team of investigators did find potential problems – mainly to do with risk, as of course they would be – the concerns were ignored by senior managers. In October 2008, the SEC had not completed a single investigation in the previous eighteen months.[47] In other words, the banks got the rule change they needed to take gigantic risks and in return the SEC got the power it needed to supervise them, and didn't use it.

That was the regime at the body which was supposed to be regulating the banks. Just as President Bush's Environmental Protection Agency and Consumer Product Safety Agency seemed to have been captured by the very interests they were supposed to be regulating, so it was at the SEC. Much of this doctrinaire laissez-faire involved non-enforcement of the rules which already existed. An activist SEC, for instance, would never have allowed Bernard Madoff to run his Ponzi scheme: the very consistency of his returns – the funny smell alluded to above – would have been enough to draw their close attention to his accounts. In 2005, a professional investor called Harry Markopolos, a mild-mannered Boston accountant, wrote a twenty-one-page letter to the SEC, pointing out the high probability that Madoff's fund was a Ponzi scheme. The only alternative explanation Markopolos could come up with wasn't that Madoff was legit: it was that he was doing something called 'front-running' and using private information gleaned from his stockbroking operation to make profits for his other funds. Markopolos had been in touch with the SEC about Madoff off and on since 1999, to precisely no effect.[48] He lived in some fear during the intervening years; he was scared of Madoff and of what might happen if he found out that Markopolos was on to him. As for the SEC, his judgement went beyond scathing: 'My experiences with . . . SEC officials proved to be a systemic disappointment and led me to conclude that the SEC securities' lawyers, if only through their investigative ineptitude and financial illiteracy, colluded to maintain large frauds such as the one to which Madoff later confessed.' That's an extraordinary charge: that the SEC was so rubbish at its job that it in effect colluded with fraud. Add that to a regulatory framework which was full of holes, and a government with an ideological commitment to letting boys be boys in the free market, and you have a perfect formula for not just ignoring funny smells but denying that they are possible.

When we look at who could have done something about this, there are two sets of people who might have raised the alarm: economists and journalists. It's more or less against the law ever to praise the media for anything, but the fact is that print journalists did speak up in public about the risks building up and the vulnerability of the global financial system. Larry Elliott in the *Guardian*, Martin Wolf and Gillian Tett in the *Financial Times*, and even the often overly gung-ho *Economist* all warned about the dangers – and had the satisfaction denied to Cassandra of having everyone realize that they'd been right all along. (Remember, the curse for Cassandra was the fact that no one would believe her.) It may be, as Richard Posner has observed, that journalists have a built-in affinity for narratives of disaster and collapse: the press, as he puts it, 'thrives on drama and therefore conflict and alarms, discord and discontinuities'. (It's also true of course that there were industrial quantities of property-market puffery and hype, a considerable amount of which took place on television.)

I can't claim to have been on to this story early, but once I had started working on it in the late summer of 2007, it was immediately clear to me that the global banking system was facing a structural crisis. If it was clear to me, why wasn't it as obvious to the people in charge of the economy and to the people whose job it is to advise them? It's the kind of question Daniel Kahneman has profitably studied. There is some really interesting work being done in the field of psychology and engineering (where it deeply matters) about 'expert overconfidence': the likelihood of experts in a field to place too much confidence in their own judgements. It may be that the reason why some journalists were more alert to the imminent crunch than their betters was because of expert overconfidence combined with an over-reliance on the idea that because a crisis of this sort hadn't happened, it therefore couldn't happen.

This may be why economists did as poorly as they did in forecasting the crunch. There is a sour joke among financial types, referring to the chronic pessimism and down-speak of 'the dismal science': they say that 'economists have predicted seven of the last three downturns'. Ho ho. But they sure didn't predict this one. Just to repeat the basic point: a 20 per cent drop in US house prices, not on the face of it an extraordinarily unlikely thing, was enough to cause a global banking crisis that nearly destroyed the entire system followed by a global recession, verging on depression. So why didn't more economists seem aware of that possibility? Has the profession really drifted that far away from the real world? The short answer is that with some stellar exceptions – Robert Shiller and Nouriel Roubini and Paul Krugman and John Kay conspicuous among them – yes, it has. The profession's preference for textbook-perfect academic models of phenomena led to it being AWOL during the biggest economic crisis since the 1930s. A profession whose job it is to make sense of economic phenomena collectively failed. In the words of an American university provost, 'I have an entire department of economists who can provide a brilliant ex post facto explanation of what happened – and not a single one of them saw it coming in advance.' Economists no longer have much interest in funny smells. The crisis exposed the profession as being a little like the British army at Singapore, with its guns pointed in the wrong direction.

This failure in turn contributed to the crisis being worse than it needed to be in Britain. The Bank of England and the FSA were sluggish where they needed to be decisive, both in the early days at the time of the collapse of Northern Rock and in the months between that and the next phase of the banking crisis in 2008. Where were the requirements to increase capital reserves, to disclose risky assets, to prepare for the storm which was obviously coming? Or even if they didn't think a storm was coming, why was there so little preparation for the possibility that it might come? In the US, the Bush administration's general laissez-faire torpor and the alphabet soup of regulatory agencies provide part of the explanation. But in the UK we don't have either of those excuses, and indeed by comparison our regulatory division of labour is a model of clarity: the Bank of England is supposed to look after systemic risk, while the FSA attends to the position of specific companies. But a risk which arose in specific companies and spread to the system somehow managed to squeeze between the cracks of a framework which wasn't supposed to have any cracks.

So although things should have been better in the UK, they have turned out to be as bad or worse. The one thing we haven't had is a glaring fraud of the Madoff type – not yet, anyway. But the striking thing about Simon Johnson's financial industry wish-list, cited above, is that once you change the name of the Securities and Exchange Commission to the Financial Services Authority, you can apply all the rest of it word for word. The consequences for our economy are even bigger than in the US, because financial services are a proportionately larger part of our economy. Nobody planned for that to happen; I heard that fact direct from the lips of a senior member of government. But the fact is that, after Mrs Thatcher came to power, the financial sector underwent a three-decades-long expansion, during which it got everything it asked for from the government. The abolition of exchange controls in 1979 and the increasingly international flow of capital, combining with the abolition of restrictions on trading practices which culminated in Big Bang in 1986, have all led to the City's increasing dominance of British economic life. Big Bang in turn caused the 'Wimbledonization' of the City, making it a place where most of the major players were foreign. As for Big Bang, it consisted of a whole series of rule changes which boiled down to one simple thing: the biggest act of deregulation the financial sector had ever seen.

Because financial deregulation has been a primary culprit in the current crisis, there's a temptation to act as if it is inherently a bad thing. You need a short memory to think that. I grew up abroad, and can vividly remember what a pain in the backside things such as currency restrictions were. When Mrs Thatcher came to power, you couldn't take more than £500 out of the country at any one time – a restriction which now seems as distant as that of whale-bone corsetry. The City of London was a club, and a particularly unlovable club at that, exclusively white and male and not just conservative but actively reactionary as a social force. Big Bang changed both the club-like nature of City life and its impact on Britain: global finance was now a radical force, remaking Britain in the image of a laissez-faire free-market economy, tearing up the consensual, all-in-it-together model of governance which both parties had been pursuing since the second world war. Mrs Thatcher seemed to many observers as pure a nineteenth-century Manchester liberal as had ever held office: keen on free trade, keen on the distinction between the deserving and the undeserving poor, and keen to let money take the place of class as the determining principle of British life.

The themes embodied by Mrs Thatcher – free trade and deregulation and the power of finance – were not new ones in British history. What was new was the extent to which financial interests were not just important, but uncontestedly paramount. Much of British economic history concerns the struggle between the financial and industrial interests – between the City and the men from the Midlands – and a good deal of that history boils down to a sense of grievance and misunderstoodness felt by Britain's manufacturers. From the point of view of people who make things, the City always wants to make its money too quickly and too irresponsibly: it wants to take too big a share of the business in return for its capital, is impatient with slow growth, doesn't understand the importance of investment and of relationships, and wants only to achieve a spectacular casino-like payout in the shortest possible time. The reciprocal view, from the City, has been that manufacturers whinge all the time, that they lost the ability to control their workforces and allowed themselves to be held hostage by unions, that they had a farmer-like tendency to complain about trading conditions in all weathers ('The pound's too high! No one can afford our stuff!'; 'The pound's too low! We can't afford raw materials!'), and that they were obtuse about the fact that the final point of all business is to make money, and that everything else is a means to that end.

That was the most important cultural difference. There is a profound anthropological and cultural difference between an industry and a business. An industry is an entity which as its primary purpose makes or does something, and makes money as a byproduct. The car industry makes cars, the television industry makes TV programmes, the publishing industry makes books, and with a bit of luck they all make money too, but for the most part the people engaged in them don't regard money as the ultimate purpose and justification of what they do. Money is a byproduct of the business, rather than its fundamental raison d'être. Who goes to work in the morning thinking that the most important thing they're going to do that day is to maximize shareholder value? Ideologists of capital sometimes seem to think that that's what we should be doing – which only goes to show how out of touch they are. Most human enterprises, especially the most worthwhile and meaningful ones, are in that sense industries, focused primarily on doing what they do: healthcare and education are both, from this anthropological perspective, industries.

Or at least that's what they are from the point of view of the people who work in them. But many of these enterprises are increasingly owned by people who view them not as industries but as businesses: and the purpose of a business is, purely and simply, to make money. The attitudes of a business owner are different from those of people who work in an industry, and from the point of view of business an industry's ways of doing things are often in love with practices inherited from the past, wilfully inefficient, wilfully indifferent to fundamental realities of how the world works. Money doesn't care what industry it is involved in, it just wants to make more money, and the specifics of how it does so are, if not exactly a source of unconcern, then very much a means to an end: the return on capital is the most important fact, and the human or cultural details involved are just that, no more than details. To workers in an industry, the attitudes and thinking of business are often summed up in the shorthand term 'accountants', as in We want to do such-and-such but the accountants won't let us, or Such-and-such used to work well but then the accountants got hold of it. Hollywood, for instance, used to be an industry, primarily involved in making films, in the days when it made many more of them;

now it is a business, whose primary preoccupation is to make money. The films are bigger and stupider and there are fewer of them, but when they do succeed, they make so much money that, in the words of Julia Phillips, the producer of *Jaws*, 'there is no bottom line.'

The City views everything as a business. This has always been true, and it lies at the heart of the fundamental dichotomy between it and industry: because although manufacturers, both historically and in the present, have not been shy about wanting to be rich, they see the City's capital as a means to an end rather than as a master in itself. This has been a theme in British history for about two centuries, but the thing which changed under Mrs Thatcher was that for the first time the City now had unquestioned supremacy. It wasn't a debate any more: what the City wanted, the City got. Manufacturing has declined precipitately in importance in the last three decades. Britain was once famous for its innovative approach to engineering and industry. No longer. The result was that what had once been a more or less balanced economy, with manufacturing and service sectors of comparable importance, now became one in which the financial sector was paramount.

Our banks were already big. Because of Britain's imperial and colonial history, British banks had a broad geographical spread: just as British Airways is 'the world's favourite airline' because of its proliferation of routes and destinations associated with the imperial past, so our banks have long been international in their scope. In addition, we didn't have the wave of bank-taming legislation that America undertook in the 1930s, as a way of preventing a repeat of the Crash of '29 and the ensuing Depression. The Glass–Steagall Act was only the best known of a series of laws designed to limit the size and influence and, especially, the cross-state operation of the American banks. In Britain we never had a comparable set of laws targeting the size and activities of our banks. That was partly because we never had a moment of banker-bashing to rival the one which took place in America during the Depression. The City's place in British life was never at risk from a populist backlash. Laws of this type were on the US statute books well into the 1990s; but Britain had, thanks to Big Bang, fully deregulated the operation of its banks by halfway through the previous decade. Our banks could take part in more or less any type of activity they wanted: investment banking (or 'merchant banking', as it used to be called), securitization, retail banking directed at consumers, derivative trading, you name it. Deregulated and opened to influxes of international capital, our banks grew bigger and bigger, along with the rest of our financial services industry. This was now the biggest and most important sector of our economy and was one of the few areas of British life which had a claim to dominate the world in its sector. (The whole question of what Britain is best at, in global terms, is an interesting one. There are four sectors in which Britain is world-class: finance, arms manufacturing, the creative arts and higher education. Of these, the first receives strong government support, the second lavish investment and strong support, the third is largely left to mind its own business and the fourth has been gradually run down, with three decades of consistent discouragement and underfunding. What would Britain look like today if instead of the arms industry or the City it had been our Russell Group universities which had been the subject of attempts to achieve world supremacy?)

The City of London, with a historical head start, and a head start in terms of the deregulatory boom of the 1980s, became a, or arguably the, global centre of the new financial expansion. The derivatives market about which I've written, for instance, has its global HQ in London: the average turnover of over-the-counter derivatives in London – remember, those are the ones directly traded between two counterparties, with no exchange or regulator in the middle – peaked in 2007 at a value of $2,105,000,000,000 (that's $2.105 trillion) *every day*. That's right: every day. The figure for the total US derivatives market was $959 billion. The AIG unit which wrote all the CDS policies that were eventually to destroy the company was based in London. The head of the unit, Joe Cassano, earned $280 million in eight years running the operation, which despite its UK base seems not to have been regulated by our own FSA, because of a technical issue to do with its being a subsidiary of an American company.[49] Here, again, we have the curse of the non-bank banks: a crucially important piece of global financial architecture which fell between regulatory cracks because the legislation had lagged so far behind the moneymen that the existing rules didn't apply to them. It was like the moment when William Webb Ellis picked up the ball and began to run with it, and in the process invented the game of rugby – except in this instance, the people watching the game stood around scratching their heads for a decade or so, while a multi-trillion-dollar market grew in front of them. That is where the culture of deregulation, and of ignored funny smells, took us: to a single unit of a single company being able to take the global financial system to the edge of destruction, and all without the attention of any regulator at all.

That brings us to the most important funny smell, and the most important counterfactual, of all. The credit crunch was based on a climate (the post-Cold War victory party of free-market capitalism), a problem (the sub-prime mortgages), a mistake (the mathematical models of risk) and a failure, that of the regulators. It was their job to prevent both the collapse of individual companies and the systemic risks which ensued; they failed. But that failure wasn't so much the absence of attention to individual details as it was an entire culture to do with the primacy of business, of money, of deregulation, of putting the interests of the financial sector first. This brought us to a point in which a belief in the free market became a kind of secular religion. The tenets of that religion are familiar, and they have been a central part of the story so far: the primacy of laissez-faire capitalism, the supernaturally self-regulating nature of the market, the superiority of the free market to all other forms of human organization. These are all debatable, contestable positions – but in the Anglo-Saxon world we forgot to contest them. This should be an enduring lesson of the crisis – an understanding that the rules governing the operating of markets were not handed down on stone tablets but are made by people, and are in constant need of revision, supervision and active, imaginative enforcement. We can't afford to forget this point: human beings create markets. A general recognition of that fact, led by the economic profession and taken to heart by politicians, would be a step so important as to be almost worth what it has cost to be reminded of it.

I have people I count as friends who work in the City. We get on in all the ways in which people get on, but there is sometimes a moment in talking to them when you hit a kind of wall. It's usually to do with fundamental assumptions based on the primacy of money, and the non-reality of other schemes of value. You get a glimpse into the world-view when you look at *The Economist*. It is an excellent newspaper (a term they prefer to 'magazine'), in particular full of good first-hand fact-finding. The first 80 per cent of almost every article is full of fresh things. But every single piece, on every single subject, reaches the same conclusion. Whatever you're reading about, it turns out that the solution is the same: more liberalization, more competition, more free markets. However nuanced and original the detail in the bulk of the piece, the answer is always the same; it makes *The Economist* seem full of algebraic formulas in which the answer is always x.

Tom Wolfe's term for the people at the pinnacle of this system was 'masters of the universe'. That was meant to be heavily,

stingingly ironic – but the masters of the universe seemed not
to notice that. They still seem not to. There's a reason for that.
For most adults, the sensation of being proved right is usually
a complex and bittersweet one. You might have said that your
brother-in-law would turn out to be a no-goodnik, or that
the forty-third President would turn out to be the worst in
American history, and you may regard subsequent events as
inarguable proof that you were right – but it's not an especially
happy feeling. It changes nothing about the world outside your
head. You were right. Congratulations. And? One of the pecu-
liar things about the world of finance is that it freely offers the
sensation of being proved right to its participants. Every transaction in the markets has a buyer and a seller, and, in most cases,
one of them is right and the other wrong, because the price
goes either up or down. The cumulative weight of this right-
or-wrongness is one of the things that make financial types
psychologically distinctive. Artists, sportsmen, surgeons,
plumbers and the rest of us have secret voices of doubt, inner
reservations about ourselves, but if you go to work with money,
and make money, you can be proved right in the most inhu-
manly pure way. This is why people who have succeeded in the
world of money tend to have such a high opinion of themselves.
And this is why they seem to regard themselves as paragons of
rationality, while others often regard them as slightly nuts.
Outsiders don't often get a good look at this mindset in its full
pomp, but when we do, it makes an unforgettable impression.
A couple of the best recent examples have come from the
heads of imploded banks. The chairman and CEO of Lehman
Brothers, Richard Fuld, in his no-apologies testimony to a
congressional committee was one example. Another was the
behaviour of Sir Fred Goodwin after the meltdown and public
rescue of RBS, when he claimed a pension of astonishing
amplitude – astonishing not by the standard of banker pensions

but by the standard of a failed company whose liabilities had been taken on by the taxpayer.

These were just lurid examples of the insulating bubble of money, and the comforting security of the cult. It wouldn't matter, if it weren't for the fact that the psychology of the masters of the universe played a vital role in our journey to this point. One of our culture's deepest beliefs is expressed in the question 'If you're so smart why ain't you rich?' But people in finance are rich – so it logically follows that everything they choose to do must be smart. That was the syllogism followed by too many people in the money business. The regulators failed; but they failed because the bankers made them fail. All the rules which existed, about bank capital and reserve requirements, about risk and about cross-border regulatory supervision, were energetically, systematically and determinedly circumvented by some of the banks. They treated the rules as things designed by thick people to slow them down and hamper their rightful profitability. It was self-evident to them that they had a better understanding of the risks they were taking than did anyone else. They behaved like drivers who regard speed limits as things to be obeyed only by muppets. It's as if they saw the 30-mile-an-hour sign, but then realized that the speed cameras wouldn't work if you were doing more than 70 – and took that as their cue to roar through built-up areas at the highest speed possible. The proliferation of non-bank banks, the pervasive use of derivatives to increase rather than to hedge risk, the overwhelming preference for over-the-counter derivatives, the use of off-balance-sheet vehicles – all of these things were critical contributors to the disaster, and all of them had not just as some marginal benefit, but as their central purpose, the determination to get round banking rules. So, yes, the regulators were useless, but their failure wasn't like that of a lifeguard who doesn't notice that some of his swimmers are in trouble; it was that of a lifeguard supervising swimmers who are secretly pouring blood in the water because they think it would be more exciting if the place were livened up by a few sharks. Deregulation was a big part of this, and it should be borne in mind that every single one of the rule-changes which paved the way for the crash was the result of energetic lobbying by the banks. When the banksters couldn't get the degree of deregulation they wanted, they went around the rules anyway. 'Irresponsible': that's a word President Obama has used several times about the actions of the bankers. It's a good word.

It should also be said that it doesn't apply to all bankers. People in the City deeply resent the way they've all been associated with the actions of the (as they see it) relatively small number of people involved in the shenanigans which led to the credit crunch. Most of them don't trade asset-backed securities, or work for off-balance-sheet subsidiaries, and they don't see why they are the target of such generalized anger and recrimination. There is truth in that, but there is also a failure to admit that this was a cultural issue, and not just the result of a set of specific actions. In fact, the bankers have been careful not to show quite how much they've minded being the target of such generalized opprobrium. The damage done by people such as Richard Fuld and Sir Fred Goodwin is caused by the fact that they don't seem atypical: they visibly, manifestly don't feel any sense of responsibility for what's gone wrong, and certainly don't feel that the rewards they earned during the good years were disproportionate. Mervyn King, the Governor of the Bank of England, did not cover himself in kudos during the implosion of Northern Rock, but he now seems to have grasped this fundamental point about where we are. 'The cost of this crisis', he told the audience of City bigwigs at the Mansion House, the definitive annual bankers' shindig, 'is not to be measured simply in terms of its impact on public finances, the destruction of wealth and the number of jobs lost. They are also to be seen in the lost trust in the financial sector in other parts of our economy . . . "My word is my bond" are old words. "My word is my CDO-squared" will never catch on.'

He gets it – belatedly, perhaps, but he does get it. Many of his colleagues in the City seem not to. What bankers will sometimes do, preferably sotto voce and in private, is mutter something along the lines of 'the incentives were wrong.' To civilians, that might seem a way of admitting that bankers paid themselves too much. But that isn't what they're saying. The problem with incentives was not the absolute levels of pay which the masters of the universe awarded themselves, but the fact that their pay emphasized and encouraged the benefits of taking risks, while removing any of the consequences when things went wrong. The result was a system that, with hindsight, was certain to go wrong: if you encourage ever greater levels of risk, you are sooner or later bound to have a blow-up.

Part of this is laughably simple: bankers' pay structures rewarded them when things went up, but did not punish them when things went down. That, added to the fact that so much pay came in the form of bonuses, encouraged a culture of gambling on big returns in good years. The good years were total bonanzas. As for the bad years, they didn't have to pay any money back; the bankers were so well paid that there was in effect no downside.

There was one other, hugely important, additional factor. The banks had a reason for thinking there was no downside to their risks. I've already said that the banks were TBTF, Too Big To Fail, and that this will have enormous consequences for all of us over the next decade or decades. But TBTF also helped us to arrive in the place we're in now, by creating a further lopsided-ness in the incentive structure of the banking industry. The banks knew that however bad and big a hole they got into, it would be impossible for governments not to help them out of it; which meant that they could carry on taking big bets, safely knowing that if the bets went bad their respective governments – which means us, the taxpayers – would pick up the tab. Imagine if you go to a casino and play roulette, and every time you won you keep all the money. It doesn't matter what your system of betting is, whether you bet on red or black or patterns or specific numbers: the point is, you keep all the winnings. Whenever the wheel lands on zero, you lose a sum amounting to ten times all the money you have won to date – but the good news is, you don't have to pay it: the government steps in and picks up the tab, and you keep your previous winnings. How cool is that? In this system, your only incentive is to keep making bigger and bigger bets, and making more and more money.

So 'incentive' sounds like nerd-speak and banker-speak, but it in fact described a critically important funny smell. Misaligned incentives were so much part of the culture that even the most glaring, blatant, reeking examples seemed normal to all partici-pants. The biggest of them, and the one with the worst consequences, concerned the ratings agencies. I've already mentioned these bodies. They award the ratings which have a determining effect on the way all sorts of institutions and debts are regarded; they affect both specific bonds and the companies and governments which issue them. In the words of the *New York Times* columnist Thomas Friedman, 'There are two super-powers in the world today in my opinion. There's the United States and there's Moody's Bond rating service. The United States can destroy you by dropping bombs, and Moody's can destroy you by downgrading your bonds. And believe me, it's not clear sometimes who's more powerful.'[50]

The highest grade of debt, AAA, is supposed to be as safe as US government T-bills; in other words it's the safest debt in the world, and represents the rate of return an investor can expect for zero risk. It's even safer than houses, because house prices go up and down; it's safer than sticking your money under the mattress, because you might get burgled or your house might burn down. The status of AAA-grade debt is written into various statutes; many publicly regulated bodies aren't allowed to invest in anything of lower grade than AAA. In other cases, institutions are legally prevented from investing in anything below BBB-grade debt, so-called junk bonds. The ratings agencies' verdicts are so taken as holy writ that they are incorporated into the Basel rules on bank reserves.

When governments lose AAA status for their debt, it is both an embarrassment and a potential disaster, because that means it's going to be more expensive for them to raise money in the future. For instance, Britain in 2009–2010 is borrowing £175 billion from the markets; if we were to lose our AAA rating – and we've already been on the 'watch list' of the ratings agency S and P's, giving us a yellow-card warning – future borrowing would cost us a lot more, because we would have to pay higher interest rates to attract lenders. There have even been early, tentative mutterings about the AAA status of American government debt. For the US to lose its AAA rating would be an event so unprecedented that no one can even guess what the consequences would be, but it's safe to say it would resemble the alien in *The Thing*: 'I don't know what it is, but it's big, it's weird, and it's mighty pissed off.'

Given how important the ratings agencies are, with the power quite literally to shape the destiny of entire nations, one might expect there to have been strict rules circumscribing their behaviour, their rulings and any influences which could be brought to bear on them. But in fact the ratings agencies had the world's worst case of misaligned incentives. Their main clients – the people who most depended on them for their ratings – were the banks and other investors who traded and bought bonds based on the ratings agencies' assessments. Once upon a time, these investors had access to the agencies' ratings by way of a subscription service, but by the mid-1970s the SEC changed its view of how the business should work, having apparently decided that the ratings were too important to be a restricted, subscriptions-based service, and instead were something that the broader community had a right to know. The ratings still needed to be paid for, of course, so the SEC decreed that from now on the company issuing the bond should pay the ratings agency for its assessment, which would then be a matter of public knowledge. This immediately created a conflict of interest. The SEC, acting from unimpeachable motives, had accidentally set up a situation in which the people who were being marked by the ratings agencies were simultaneously the ratings agencies' main paymasters. The process of assessing bonds and debt instruments is a very, very big business.

Historically, the ratings agencies had mostly been involved in the business of assessing corporate bonds. That changed. From about 2001, when the housing market, and then the mortgage-backed securities market, and then the sub-prime-mortgage-backed securities market, all took off, the ratings agencies were increasingly in the business of assessing mortgage-backed securities. These were very lucrative. A bog-standard package of mortgage-backed securities paid the ratings agencies three times more to assess than a bog-standard corporate bond.[51] Talk about misaligned incentives! The ratings agencies were paid according to volume, so the more business they did, the more they got paid; they were yet another component of the sub-prime chain which basically didn't care whether or not people could actually afford to repay their loans. And they were yet another component of the sub-prime chain whose business boomed. Between 2002 and 2006, Moody's revenue doubled, and its share price tripled.[52] What the companies issuing the securities wanted was AAA ratings, and with the assistance of the ratings agencies – not just in terms of published models, but sometimes with actual hands-on help in designing the debt – that's what they got. The end result was that almost 90 per cent of the mortgage-backed CDOs were assessed as AAA grade. Very little corporate debt is rated AAA, but the entire industry had now gone through the looking glass and persuaded itself of the magically secure status of the new CDO instruments; so we arrived in the bizarre position in which poor people struggling to pay back their mortgages had miraculously produced the world's most secure financial instruments. This was a fortunate conclusion to reach for both the banks which made money issuing the CDOs and the ratings agencies which made money assessing them. The banks were not shy about saying that if an agency would not give them the rating they wanted, they would go shopping elsewhere. All this added up to create a situation in which the ratings agencies had no incentive to point out the weaknesses of CDOs, and every incentive to shut up and rubber-stamp them.

All of this – all the funny smells, the missed warning signals, the misaligned incentives, the distorted attitudes to risk, the arrogance of the masters of the universe, the complicity of regulators, the doziness of legislators – symptomized a culture, and also constituted one. It was the culture of the financial industry. It didn't have to turn out like this. There are occasional frustrating glimpses of how things could have been different in Britain and America. The common good and the interests of the financial industry are not identical – a fact that for the previous three decades has conveniently been forgotten. The financial culture could have been similar, but the outcome different, if it had not been for those failures of regulation and legislation; they were critical to allowing the culture to go too far and produce the credit crunch. We can know that for sure, because of the counterfactual example of a country which had a broadly similar Anglo-Saxon attitude to business, and yet did not go down the

path of doctrinaire liberalization and laissez-faire when it came
to legislating the financial industry: Canada. The Organization
for Economic Co-operation and Development rates Canada's
banks as the safest in the world – the US comes fortieth, two
places behind Botswana, and the UK comes forty-fourth. Canada
is the only one of the G8 countries not to have bailed out its
banks.* The reason is that Canada didn't join in the party. Its
banks had higher capital requirements than elsewhere, the legacy
in part of a scare about bank liquidity in the early 1990s which
left Canada nurturing a realistic sense of the systemic risks, just
at the point when other economies were yelling 'Woo-hoo!' and
tearing their regulatory clothes off. Other features of the Canadian banking system included lower levels of securitization, and
the use of securitization mainly as a way of increasing liquidity
rather than as a tool for spreading risky CDS- and CDO-type
instruments; very low levels of involvement in mortgage-backed
securities; a law insisting that, if anyone was borrowing more
than 80 per cent of the value of the home, they had to take out
insurance on the debt; and no tax relief on mortgage interest.
Most of all, it was a reluctance to join in the fiesta of laissez-faire,
which no doubt owed a good deal to Canada's national appetite
for distinguishing itself from its hyper-capitalist neighbour to
the south. And this, incidentally, did not come at the cost of
falling behind in other areas: since 2004, Canadian average
incomes have grown at 11 per cent a year, compared with 5 per
cent in the USA. A country doesn't have to have a frenetically
overactive financial sector in order to have a thriving economy.

---

* The G8 is a group formed by the UK, the USA, Germany, Italy, France,
Japan, Canada and Russia.

7. The Bill

The last question is the one which, looking forward, is the most important: now what?

I've already mentioned my belief that the western liberal democracies are the best societies that have ever existed – which isn't the same thing as saying that they are perfect. Citizens of those societies are, on aggregate, the most fortunate people who have ever lived. Almost everyone in the west lives a quality and length of life which would have been the envy of a pharaoh or a Roman emperor, and which most of our ancestors, and most of the populations of the rest of the world, would swap for their own prospects in an eye-blink. It's an amazing state of affairs – and it's one which, broadly speaking, was predicted by the greatest economist who ever lived, John Maynard Keynes, in an essay he wrote in 1930, 'Economic Possibilities for our Grandchildren'. He was writing in the immediate aftermath of the Great Crash (which, incidentally, in his capacity as an investor, cost him a packet), but he wasn't pessimistic; indeed, he thought the general contemporary climate of pessimism was overdone. Britain had got steadily richer for decades, and was going to continue to get richer. Keynes, entertainingly, pinpointed the initial cause of British prosperity as Sir Francis Drake's theft of gold from the Spanish in 1580. From her piece of that action, Queen Elizabeth was able to pay off all the country's foreign debts, balance the budget and end up with about £40,000 left over: an amount which, at 3 per cent compounded, added up in 1930 to the £4 billion which was Britain's foreign reserves. In terms of GDP per capita, Britain was four times richer than it had been when

Drake stole the gold. In a century's time, by 2030, Keynes esti-
mated that the country would be between four and eight times
richer again, and that this would mean that, in effect, mankind's
greatest problem, the struggle for bare economic survival, had
been solved.

His prediction is on track – at least, it's on track economically.
With two decades to go to the deadline, we're already 4.6 times
richer than we were in Keynes's day. But Keynes was deeply
wrong about how that would affect us. He thought that we
would realize how lucky we were. 'When the accumulation of
wealth is no longer of high social importance, there will be great
changes in the code of morals. We shall be able to rid ourselves
of many of the pseudo-moral principles which have hag-ridden
us for two hundred years, by which we have exalted some of the
most distasteful of human qualities into the position of the highest virtues.' He was talking about greed and acquisitiveness.

We shall be able to afford to dare to assess the money-motive at its true
value. The love of money as a possession – as distinguished from the
love of money as a means to the enjoyments and realities of life – will
be recognised for what it is, a somewhat disgusting morbidity, one of
those semicriminal, semi-pathological propensities which one hands
over with a shudder to the specialists in mental disorder. All kinds of
social customs and economic practices, affecting the distribution of
wealth and economic rewards and penalties, which we now maintain
at all costs, however distasteful and unjust they may be in themselves,
because they are tremendously useful in promoting the accumulation
of capital, we shall then be free, at last, to discard.

He thought that the overridingly important issue in this world
would be how to live, and how to learn from 'the delightful
people who are capable of taking direct enjoyment of things, the
lilies of the field who toil not, neither do they spin'.

Keynes sure was wrong about all that. The great increase in our prosperity over the last decades has caused no general sense that we should now slow down and reflect on where we are, who we are and what we want from life. That is particularly apparent at the time of writing, after the great economic implosion. Sometimes, when you're on a journey, your arrival at a particular destination completely changes your sense of what happened to you on the way. Looking back, you realize that some of the time you were lost, and didn't know it, and some of the time you were on the right track, and didn't know it, and perhaps you also think that the journey wasn't worth while, or that you would have done the whole thing differently if you had known then what you know now.

That's the point we've now arrived at, at the end of the new millennium's first decade, in the aftermath of the credit crunch. This is the spot from which we look back and realize where we've been and decide what to make of it. Looking back, it turns out that we've just lived through an economic golden age. It turned out to be a fake golden age, one based on debt and on an unsustainable credit bubble and underpinned by a financial system which was, it turned out, taking crazily miscalculated risks – but we didn't know that at the time. In fact, most of us had no idea it was a golden age; we didn't know that we were living through what for many of us will turn out to be the best economic times of our lives. I wish someone had told us: I wish someone had had the nerve to do what Harold Macmillan was roundly denounced for doing in 1957, and gone on TV to tell us that we'd never had it so good. At least we'd have had a reference point, something to disagree with and force us to think about the boom we were living through. Would we have spent quite so much time pigging out on cheap credit? Would we have been quite so unreflecting, so spendthrift, so greedy? This is one of the many ways in which Iceland is an example or forerunner for other countries caught up in the crisis. The Icelandic cab driver who told me that 'it was thirty or forty people who did this, and the rest of us who are having to pay,' was telling the truth: it was indeed, in Iceland and elsewhere, a tiny minority of people directly responsible for the financial shenanigans behind the crash. And it is indeed everyone else who is having to pick up the bill. But there is a missing component there, and it is the fact that so many of us were caught up in the good times when they were rolling.

Credit bubbles and asset bubbles don't just happen without people joining in them, borrowing and spending more, betting on asset prices going upwards and the suspension of the never-untrue, never-popular rule that what goes up must come down. One thing which has been lacking in public discourse about the crisis is someone to point out the extent to which we helped do this to ourselves, because we allowed our governments to do it, and because we were greedy and stupid. It's not just bankers who have been indulging in greed, short-termism and fantasy economics. In addition to our stretched mortgage borrowing, Britain has half of the total European credit-card debt. The industry did everything it could to egg us on, but that is still a horrible fact – and although it's nice to reserve the blame for banks which made lending too easy, the great British public is just as much to blame. We grew obsessed with the price of our houses, felt richer than we should, borrowed money we didn't have, spent it on tat, and now that the downturn has happened – as it was bound to do – we want someone else to blame. Well boo-hoo. Bankers are to blame, but we're to blame too. That's just as well, because we're the ones who are going to have to pay.

Mrs Thatcher began, and Labour continued, a switch towards an economy which was reliant on financial services, at the expense of other areas of society. One can disagree (and I would disagree) with that policy, but what was equally damaging for Britain was the hegemony of economic, or quasi-economic, thinking. The economic metaphor came to be applied to every aspect of modern life, especially the areas where it simply didn't belong. In fields such as education, equality of opportunity, health, employees' rights, the social contract and culture, the first conversation to happen should be about values and principles; then you have the conversation about costs, and what you as a society can afford. In Britain in the last twenty to thirty years that has all been the wrong way round. There was a kind of reverse takeover, in which City values came to dominate the whole of British life. There needs to be a general acceptance that the model has failed. The brakes-off, deregulate or die, privatize or stagnate, lunch is for wimps, greed is good, what's good for the financial sector is good for the economy model; the sack the bottom 10 per cent, bonus-driven, if you can't measure it it isn't real model; the model which spread from the City to government and from there through the whole culture, in which the idea of value has gradually faded to be replaced by the idea of price.

When the credit crunch first began – after the initial waves of panic, and the moment when 'this sucker could go down' – I thought that there might be a general re-evaluation of where we all were. We would notice and reflect not just on the past decade of good times, but on the whole question of what our societies had as their goals, where capitalism had brought us and whether we wanted to keep working quite as hard as we had, in the direction of an always receding vision of contentment. The 'hedonic treadmill' is what this is called: as you have more and more, your idea of what it would be to be happy keeps receding just out of reach. It's always the next pay rise, the next purchase, the next place you move to or where you go on holiday, which will make you happy. The credit crunch could have been a moment to reflect on that. We in the west can do something that no people in history have done: we can show the world that we know when we have enough. As the planet runs out of resources, due mainly to the fact that everyone on it wants to live an equivalent lifestyle to those of us in the west, this lesson would have the potential to save the world.

I now don't think this moment of realization is going to happen. That's mainly because although we might be rich, by global and historical standards, we don't feel it; and even when our livelihoods aren't at risk from the recession and the general slowdown, we are all about to feel significantly poorer. That's because we're about to get the bill. In the course of this book I have a few times laid out things which are bleeding obvious to people in the world of finance, and virtually unknown to those outside. Here's one of them: that the recovery everyone is longing for is the point when we get the bill. It's when we recover that we start to pay back the cost of what happened. Governments can't begin to fix the holes in their own balance sheets – holes which get rapidly worse as tax revenues collapse and spending vrooms upwards – until the economy is growing again. Up until then, the economy is too delicate for the state to get out its trowel and begin to extract the increased taxes it's going to need. The appearance of the famous 'green shoots', and the return to economic growth which follows them, is merely the moment at which we catch the waiter's eye and make the waggling mime to indicate it's time to pay.

And it's one hell of a bill. For the sheer size of the Figures of Doom, nothing can beat the world's biggest economy, which has had a property bubble, a credit bubble and years of growing deficit thanks to George W. Bush's high-spirited experiment in big-spending conservatism. The projected deficit – this is based on the government's own figures – comes to $7.14 trillion over the ten years to 2019. As for the bailouts, there are various ways of calculating their cost so far, with Neil Barofsky, the inspector general in charge of administering the programme, putting the cost so far on 31 March 2009 at $2.98 trillion.[53] By adding to that the imminent bailout of the gigantic financial corporation Citi-

group, the market commentator Barry Ritholtz came up with a
total cost of the bailout as $4.6165 trillion.[54] (He also makes the
point that some estimates of the cost are even higher, and quotes
a Bloomberg News Service figure of $7.76 trillion.) He then put
the figure in historical perspective. That number is bigger than
the cost of the Marshall Plan, the Louisiana Purchase, the 1980s
Savings and Loan crisis, the Korean war, the New Deal, the inva-
sion of Iraq, the Vietnam war and the total cost of Nasa including
the moon landings, all added together – repeat, *added together* (and
yes, the old figures are adjusted upwards for inflation).

Not that we in the UK are any better off. The 30 per cent decline
in the value of sterling is unlikely to go away as quickly as it arrived.
The reason sterling has crashed is simple: the markets are pricing
in the fact that we the taxpayer are on the hook for the losses made
by our banks. The markets assume that we can't or won't default
on our government debts – that would mean we simply can't afford
to pay back the amount we're currently borrowing. They're probably right about that. But Alistair Darling's desperately grim Budget
of 2009 made it clear just how deep in the mire we are. As for how
bad it is, and how quickly it's gone bad, well: in April 2008, at the
time of the Budget, the projected deficit for 2009–10 was £38
billion. By 24 November, the projected deficit was £118 billion. At
the budget on 22 April 2009, Alistair Darling admitted that the real
figure is going to be £175 billion. The total projected borrowing
for the next four years is £606 billion. National debt will hit 79 per
cent of GDP – the highest peacetime figure ever. The economy is
going to have its worst year since 1945. The debt is going to cost
from £35 to £47 billion a year to service – that's just the debt alone.
We'll be spending more on debt than we are on the entire transport
budget. All this means tax rises, a near-total freeze on government
spending, swingeing public-sector job cuts, companies laying off
every worker they can to save costs, and in turn a dramatic upward
spike in unemployment. The one easy thing the government might

be able to do to help itself is to make inflation go up – that helps, because it decreases the real cost of the debt. An inflation rate of 5 per cent means that the debt goes down in cost by 5 per cent every year, effortlessly and just by itself. From the point of view of a heavily indebted government, that's good news; for other parts of the economy, for borrowers and for anyone holding sterling, not so much. Then, to try and bring the inflation under control, the government will raise interest rates, which will slow the economy and cost jobs, and we'll be back where we were in the early 1980s, with high interest rates, high inflation, high unemployment, a government wielding an axe on public expenditure, and a bitterly divided polity, one in which the interests of everybody on the state's payroll (both those on benefits and in state-derived employment) are in direct conflict with those of everybody else.

To compound this already desperate picture, we also have huge levels of personal debt, directly arising from our credit bubble. The average British household went into the crunch owing 160 per cent of its annual income. That makes us, individually and collectively, a lot like the cartoon character who's run off the end of a cliff and hasn't realized it yet. In January 2009 the investor-pundit Jim Rogers advised anyone listening to 'sell any sterling you might have. It's finished. I hate to say it, but I would not put any money in the UK.' That wasn't nice or polite, but it brought into the public domain what a lot of international money-men are saying in private. More to the point, it's a policy on which they have already acted. So roads and schools and hospitals will go unbuilt and unrepaired, medical treatments will go unbought, nurses and policemen and council workers will be laid off. Six hundred thousand jobs have been created in local government in the last few years. Many or most of them will go. And then we'll have the really gigantic argument, over the public service pensions which are paid for out of current tax receipts. I don't know anyone who has studied this problem who thinks that the government will be able to afford them. Can you imagine the fights that are going to happen? The political polarization between public and private sector employees, the savagery of the cuts, the bitterness of the arguments, the furious sense of righteousness on both sides? It'll be Thatcher all over again, and the current period of managerial non-politics will seem as distant as Attlee's creation of the welfare state.

That's because we in Britain are, to use a technical economic term, screwed. Economies across the whole world are struggling. Because nobody is spending money, even relatively blameless countries such as Germany, with low levels of debt and workforces which actually make things, are having a difficult time. Germany's economy is predicted to contract by 5.4 per cent in 2009. A banker explained it like this: 'When your country's economy depends on people buying a car every three years, and they decide that they'll only buy a car every five years, you're finished. Off a cliff.' Something similar goes for Spain, where the end of the property boom has caused a spike in unemployment to 17.4 per cent, almost doubling in a year, or Ireland, which has contracted by a truly horrendous 8 per cent and where people have gone from owning private helicopters to losing their homes in six months flat. All of these countries are in trouble. But there are four things you don't want to have, going into the current crisis. 1. You don't want to have had a boom based on a property bubble. 2. You don't want to have a consumer credit bubble. 3. You don't want to have an economy based on financial services. 4. You don't want your government to have just gone on a massive spending spree. We in the UK have all four of those things that you don't want.

What this will lead to, I think, is more anger. Again, Iceland is the forerunner: there, the incumbent government's obliviousness to the consequences of its own policies eventually triggered the 'pots and pans revolution', in which people banged kitchenware outside the Parliament building until the government quit and called an election. As the bill is paid, and especially as taxes go up

while services and jobs go away, people are going to get steadily
and inexorably more furious. I'm not sure at whom: I hope it's at
the responsible bodies, but I wouldn't bet on it. Public rage is like
lightning, and tends to discharge its energies at anyone who has
the bad luck to be prominent in the wrong way at the wrong time.

As for where the anger would go if it were properly directed,
that's easy to answer: at the banks, and at the governments which
let the banks do what they did. The evidence on this count isn't
yet in, because the all-important question isn't what legislation is
debated and white-papered, but what gets put on the statute book,
and also how the laws are enforced – since, as I've argued, the
regime is as important as the framework. At the moment the
atmosphere is thick with floating proposals, many of them ingenious and timely: for instance, the Obama administration's plan to
force securitizers to retain a proportion of the risks on their own
books, rather than to sell all of it on – now that's an excellent idea,
even if the touted share of the risk to be retained is probably set
too low at 5 per cent. Laws on forcing the banks to have 'counter-
cyclical' reserve levels are a good idea too: the idea is that banks
will have to put aside more cash in boom times, to be prepared
for the subsequent busts. Measures bringing the non-bank banks
and financial intermediaries into the legislative net aren't just obviously necessary, they're twenty years overdue. Laws targeting
mistaken bonuses and incentives, and allowing for the possibility
of 'clawback' if bonuses are paid for actions which are later
exposed as mistaken, are also a good idea. The Tories, who have
taken full benefit for being out of office during the bust (even
though it's 100 per cent certain that they wouldn't have done
anything different if they had been in power), have been much
firmer than the government in advocating policies designed to
separate commercial from retail banking – splitting up the casino
from the piggybank. The idea is that customer-oriented deposit-
holding banks should be guaranteed by the state and tightly

regulated, whereas the boys-will-be-boys willy-wagging masters of the universe should be free to play their games in investment banks which can freely implode at no cost to the taxpayer.

There are two schools of thought about that idea. School 1: It is an indispensable step to restoring the financial sector, and the wider economy, to health. School 2: It wouldn't work. I subscribe to School 1, but School 2 has some strong arguments, among them that modern financial operations are so tightly inter-linked that it simply isn't possible to keep it clean and clear in the manner envisioned. Also, School 2 points to the failure of some 'narrow banks', as they're called, in the current crisis. The answer to that point is that the banks weren't as narrow as all that, and that the systemic crisis was already so far advanced that all bets were off. School 2, however, has another, even stronger argument, which is that the idea that huge investment banks would be allowed to fail is not, in practice, true. In the event of a crisis for someone such as, say, Goldman Sachs, a government bailout would be arranged, whatever the rhetoric had been, because the lesson of Lehmans' collapse was that Too Big To Fail is a reality. It would be lovely if that weren't true, but the unfortunate fact is that when one of these big banks went down, it nearly took the global financial system with it; so we won't be trying that again, thanks. 'No bank should be allowed to become so big that it can blackmail governments,' is how the German Chancellor Angela Merkel put it in September 2009, after a meeting with the French President Nicolas Sarkozy. That's true. But the melancholy reality is that it's too late: they already are, they already can and they already do. Nobody wants to dwell on this fact, because it is such an uncomfortable one for bankers and politicians alike – not to mention for the electorates who paid for the last set of bailouts and will have to pay for the next lot too, if and when the banks blow up again. We are nowhere near what is desperately needed, a set of arrangements whereby banks can fail in an orderly way. The banks must be forced to make 'living wills', arrangements by which they can bring their own businesses to an orderly close, the next time they get their sums horribly wrong. We need to create a system by which banks can fail without bringing each other down; by which they can go into administration and have their affairs unwound in the same way that ordinary businesses do. I have yet to see anybody come up with credible proposals to do that.

I accept School 2's argument that these institutions will not be allowed to fail in current circumstances, but I think this point can be substantially fixed, with another change to the law. The change should be that, if a bank (broadly defined) receives any taxpayers' money, the existing shareholders are (broadly speaking) wiped out. That's what happens to investors in other institutions: if the firm you've bought a share in goes broke, you lose your money. At the moment, that doesn't happen with banks, because of the TBTF problem; which means that shareholders, and their representatives on bank boards, need only to talk the talk about managing risk. This simple and brutal change in the law would make it incumbent on them to ensure that the companies they own stay comfortably on the safe side of the street when it comes to managing their risks, and if that means smaller profits, well, that's better than being completely wiped out. Go and ask the Enron employees who had all their pension pots invested in the company's stock. Without a change along these lines, there is no reason to think that something very like the credit crunch couldn't happen again.

That's because the only thing the laws can address is what's legal. They can't stretch deep into banking and change its culture; but the problem is that that's what most needs to be changed. The power and complexity of modern financial instruments combined with the will-to-profit and the reality of TBTF to create a situation in which, as soon as the rules are made, people will be looking for

ways around them. Not all bankers, obviously – not even a majority of them, nowhere near. But there will always be someone who
wants to try cheating the 30-mile-an-hour speed camera by driving at more than 70. In this case, much of the rule-evading will
involve differences between national legislation about banks. Some
countries will always try to seek a competitive advantage by having
looser banking laws; some banks will always try to exploit the fact.
This story has made it clear, I hope, that finance is completely
transnational in nature: national frontiers are there purely as things
to be exploited, via their differing legislation.

This, again, is to do with culture. The counter-examples to
banking can be found in industries such as healthcare: doctors
don't, for the most part, pride themselves on saying, 'What the
hell, nobody's looking, so I'm just going to reuse this dirty needle.'
An even stronger counter-example is aviation. I am terrified of
flying, but I have to admit that airlines have been extraordinarily
effective at generating a culture of safety, in which that value is
unquestionedly paramount. This is allied to an impressive degree
of transparency – impressive, verging on outright scary, in the
case of America, where anyone can look up the service record of
any aircraft, from a laptop at the airport, just before getting on
board. That is partly because the industry has learnt, in the words
of Easyjet's founder Stelios Haji-Ioannou (who learnt this lesson
in the oil-tanker business): 'If you think safety is expensive, try
having an accident.' But the culture of modern banking is not like
that; in fact it's close to the opposite of that. The bankers' slogan
is something closer to 'We're not that fussed about safety, because
if we have an accident, it's you who pays.' There are already clear
signs that for some banks the party is back on. From the *FT* in
July 2009, at a time when some banks such as RBS, Merrill Lynch
and Citigroup were still deep in the mire: 'thriving rivals – JP
Morgan, Goldman Sachs, Morgan Stanley, Barclays, Deutsche
Bank and Credit Suisse – are talking privately of a record second

quarter. They have benefited from lively markets for commodity and foreign exchange trading, at profit margins that are between two and eight times higher than before the height of the financial crisis last autumn . . . "There used to be fifteen banks competing. Now there are six," says one investment banker. "This is a phenomenal environment. I've never seen anything like this in 20 years in the business."' In other words, the credit crunch has created never better trading conditions – for the banks. Goldman Sachs is the most spectacular example of this. That bank went from having to end its status as an investment bank and take federal support, in September 2008, to declaring all-time record profits – with bonuses to match – in July 2009. The bank which would have gone under without government help, and had to borrow $10 billion from the taxpayer, was less than a year later setting aside $16.8 billion in pay, bonuses and benefits for itself. That is obscene. The incentives, and disincentives, need to be fixed, and in short order. The big club of potential nationalization needs to be taken out and warningly brandished.

Will this happen? I shouldn't think so. The UK and US plans are different, but at their heart they both show the governments going to almost unbelievable lengths in order to avoid taking the troubled banks into public ownership or fully to transfer their risks to where they belong: with the shareholders. Our governments are prepared to pay for them, but not to force the owners to bear the burdens of their risks.

There are four reasons for the reluctance to use nationalization as a threat, of which the first isn't a real reason but a piece of political guff.

1. Because the government would be bad at it. This is the only reason governments are willing to give in public, and it fails the most elementary test of all: only a professional politician can say it with a straight face. Bad at running the banks, compared to the bankers who broke capitalism? Please. But this is the closest they

can get to admitting the first real reason, which is:

2. Because if the banks were taken over, then every decision they take would come at a potential political cost to the government. Your state-owned mortgage lender is threatening to repossess your house, after you fell behind on the payments? Blame the government. Your firm is laying off half its workforce because the bank won't roll over its loan? Blame the government. This, of course, is in addition to all the other economic things for which people are already blaming the government. People are already grumbling but to nowhere like the extent they would if the banks were directly owned by the state. Politicians simply aren't willing to take on the responsibility for the banks' actions.

3. They also don't want to admit the extent to which we are all now liable for the losses made by the banks. Guess what, though: it's too late.

And the fourth and deepest reason why the government won't nationalize the banks is:

4. Because it would be so embarrassing. Some of the embarrassment is superficial: on the not-remembering-somebody's-name-at-a-social-occasion level. The Anglo-Saxon economies have had decades of boom mixed with what now seem, in retrospect, smallish periods of downturn. During that time they/we have shamelessly lectured the rest of the world on how they should be running their economies. We've gloated at the French fear of debt, laughed at the Germans' nineteenth-century emphasis on manufacturing, told the Japanese that they can't expect to get over their 'lost decade' until they kill their zombie banks, and so on. It's embarrassing to be in worse condition than all of them.

There is, however, a deeper embarrassment, one which verges on a form of psychological or ideological crisis. The huge bailouts of major financial institutions mean that the Anglo-Saxon model of capitalism has failed. The amount of state intervention in the US and UK at this moment is at a level comparable to that of wartime. We have in effect had to declare war to get us out of the hole created by our economic system. We have been left with these grotesque hybrids, privately owned banks which are able to generate boggling profits because all the risk is underwritten by the taxpayer. It is a 100 per cent pure form of socialism for the rich. There is no model or precedent for this, and no way to argue that it's all right really, because under such-and-such a model of capitalism . . . there is no such model. It just isn't supposed to work like this, and there is no road-map for what's happened. That is why the thing the governments least want to do – take over the banks – is something that needs to be prepared for, not just for economic reasons, but for ethical ones too.

So: a huge unregulated boom in which almost all the upside went directly into private hands, followed by a gigantic bust in which the losses were socialized. That is literally nobody's idea of how the world is supposed to work. It is just as much an abomination to the free-marketeer as it is to the social democrat or outright leftist. But the models and alternatives don't seem to be forthcoming: there is an ideological and theoretical vacuum where the challenge from the left used to be. Capitalism no longer has a global antagonist, just at the moment when it has never needed one more. Or rather, capitalism has found a deadly opponent; but the problem is that the opponent is capitalism itself. The last eleven years have seen the Long-Term Capital Management debacle, an unprecedented system-threatening implosion generated by flawed mathematical models; the Enron collapse, an unpre-cedented exposure of a huge and hugely respected company as being, in its very essence, an accounting fraud; and now the credit crunch, an unprecedented self-generated financial implosion. The evidence has to be that these scares are getting bigger and faster and happen closer together – and that must be a logical conclusion, given that it describes a simple reality about the bigger, faster global movement of capital. Why wouldn't the nasty turns have got bigger? Everything else has. The trouble is that the western world, and the world at large, cannot afford another bust like the current one – not now, and probably not for a generation to come.

About twenty years ago, the visionary climate scientist James Lovelock said that what the earth needed was the equivalent of a small heart attack. He said that the effect of such an episode is, in an individual's life, often beneficial, because it forces them to face the facts about themselves and to adopt a more healthy lifestyle. The planet needed something like that, to get humanity's attention for what we have been doing to it. The earth didn't get its small heart attack, but the credit crunch is capitalism's equivalent. It's the point at which we all have a chance to take a look at ourselves, and at our banking systems and our politicians, and make some changes. On the political level, we have the chance to insist that our governments change the rules to make sure that this truly can't happen again – because if there is even the sliver of a chance that it can, it will; that's the nature of modern markets. Otherwise, we'll be doing the equivalent of discharging ourselves from hospital after that small heart attack, and going straight out to celebrate with a carton of Rothmans, a bottle of tequila and a supersized Big Mac with jumbo fries. Free-market capitalism's victory party lasted for two decades: now it's time to slow down, calm down and decide how to make the finance industry back into something which serves the rest of society, rather than predating on it. And the level of our individual response is just as important. On that level, we have to start thinking about when we have sufficient – sufficient money, sufficient stuff – and whether we really need the things we think we do, beyond what we already have. In a world running out of resources, the most important ethical and political and ecological idea can be summed up in one simple word: 'enough'.

Epilogue

August 2010

When I was writing this book in the summer of 2009, I felt that I had to be careful about what I said in the area of legislation to prevent a repeat of the crash. It wasn't that I had to be careful in the sense of worrying about upsetting the banksters; I had to be careful because I was concerned that what I wrote might be out of date by the time readers had their hands on the book. If I banged on too much about the changes that were needed to control the banks, all it would take would be the passing of one significant law and the entire discussion would be irretrievably out of date. Hank Paulson, Bush's last Treasury Secretary, put it well:

To address the perception that some banks are too big to fail, we must improve the tools at our disposal for facilitating the orderly failure of a large, complex financial institution . . . The real issue is not that an institution is too big or too interconnected to fail, but that it is too big or too interconnected to liquidate quickly. Today our tools are limited.

It is now two years since the moment when the banks nearly took themselves and the rest of the global economic system over the edge of a cliff. The following paragraph undertakes a survey

of all the legislation in the developed world, and summarizes the
laws which have been passed to prevent a repetition of the crash.

That's right. Nothing. I needn't have been careful; I needn't
have given a second's thought to the question of what legislation
would already have hit the statute books. That quotation from
Hank Paulson comes from June 2008 – and as of right now the
world's governments have none of the new tools of which he
spoke. The question of what is to be done about that central
problem of Too Big To Fail banks is still being addressed in
mainly rhetorical terms. My fear, from over here in the cheap
seats, has been that the level of action has a precise inverse
correlation to the talk. This view has yet to be proved wrong;
no meaningful proposals to effect change have been enacted.
That doesn't mean they never will, but the time for lawmakers
to get on with it is upon us. Governments took bold, decisive
and ultimately successful action to prevent the crash from turning
into a global depression – and one of the ways they did it was
by ignoring their ideology and going ahead with de facto
nationalization. The next step, systematic reform, called for
equal boldness and equal decisiveness, but there was one big
difference: this time the banks were lobbying against it. The
predictable result has been that none of the important changes
have been put into effect.

This doesn't mean that nothing is being done, thanks in no small part to the Democrats' defeat in the Senate contest for Ted Kennedy's former seat in Massachusetts. The day after the defeat, President Obama appeared in public with Paul Volcker. (Volcker is one of the central characters in modern American economic history. He was President Carter's appointment to be head of the Federal Reserve, with a mandate to defeat inflation. He did that by hoicking interest rates, with unpopular short-term consequences which helped eject Carter from office, but with long-term success. Volcker's actions paved the way for the boom in the US economy which began under President Reagan, who reappointed him to the Fed once and then declined to do so again, largely because he wasn't enough of a zealot for deregulation. How the wheel turns.) Standing beside Volcker, Obama floated proposals which for the first time genuinely upset the banks. His plan was for a levy on the size of a bank's assets, a fairly pure tax on bigness, combined with a ban on 'proprietary trading', which is the gambling that the banks do with their own money.

These two proposals fought their way though Congress under heavy jostling from all sides, with populist calls for more action from Democrats vying with Republican attempts to blame Freddie and Fannie for everything that had happened. (That's code for: don't blame the banks, blame the poor and blame the bureaucrats.) The bill which emerged had the mood-music of big change, but the substance of an administrative tweak. The tax on bigness was replaced with a one-off levy intended to fund the cost of a new supervisory regime, which among other things gives a new body the responsibility of addressing the question of systemic risk. That plan for a levy was immediately withdrawn in the face of opposition from the Senate. In addition, the government has new powers to liquidate financial firms that it thinks are going under. There will be a new consumer financial protection bureau. Some

of the banks' activities in trading derivatives will be curbed.*
That's it.

How much did this announcement spook the financial sector?
Well, financial shares rose 2.7 per cent in the rest of the day after
the announcement, and the big banks rose most of all. This means
that Wall Street, which had been worried and saw the moment
of legislation as a big risk for the banks, sees the proposals which
emerged as a big victory. A lot of wrangling is still to happen,
to turn the principles which emerge from the bill into concrete
rules, and there will be plenty of room for hard lobbying to make
every possible nuance of the laws pro-bank and pro-status quo.
The crucial central question of the systemic risks seems to me to
be left exactly the way it was at the start of the credit crunch.

In the UK and the EU we have had just as much talk, just as
little action. One idea which has been gaining some momentum
is for a levy on the banks, raising funds to pay for any future
bailouts. It would effectively be a form of insurance. This seems
to me a fairly thin idea. It's a little like being in a small town
which is plagued by youths roaring around the place on unsafe,
unsilenced motorbikes. At the best of times they are a nuisance,
and at the worst they have a habit of killing other people when
they crash. The European scheme proposes to raise a levy on the
bikers to pay for the damage they cause when they have accidents.
So the nuisance and the smash-ups are still there – it's just that

---

* About derivatives: when this book first came out I was asked a few times if the story
of Keynes forgetting he'd made a bet on wheat futures was true, and had to answer that
I didn't know. The matter has since been cleared up by a wonderfully helpful email from
Dr Tom Banfield, who was a student at King's College, Cambridge, in the 1960s. 'As a
King's undergraduate I heard the tale of Keynes and the wheat futures in about 1962 directly from the lips of Sir John Sheppard, the former Provost and a contemporary of
Keynes. Sheppard was allegedly the lover of both Rupert Brooke and Keynes (though not
at the same time). As he told it, the telegram asking where the wheat should be delivered
arrived at the Porter's Lodge, whereupon Keynes marched into the Front Court and realized that if he could merely(!) requisition the side chapels of King's College Chapel (only
the finest Gothic building in the world), rather than the cellars as mentioned in the book,
then he would have all the space he needed. Sheppard's conclusion to the story, however,
was that the price then rose and Keynes was able to sell without taking delivery!'

the bikers contribute financially when things go wrong. To me this doesn't seem like any sort of fix.

This isn't to say that the politicians don't realize there is a problem. The trouble is they aren't sure what to do about it, in the face of the sheer difficulty of fixing the banks combined with the ferocity of their lobbying. Some of the ideas being kicked around – though I say again, none of them has hit the statute books as yet – are good. The EU is threatening to bring in a regime fixing a tight limit on the cash component of bonuses, and adding a delay mechanism whereby the bonus can't be paid for three to five years. These are interesting notions, though actually turning them into law is not straightforward, especially given how hard all the relevant parties will work at circumventing the rules. The simplest work-around for the banks would be just to increase their own pay – which, let's face it, isn't quite the outcome the legislators have in mind. Here in the UK we have a commission looking into the question of banking reform, under the chairmanship of Sir John Vickers, who is nobody's idea of a fool or stooge. Other members of the commission include Martin Wolf, the *Financial Times* columnist who has been one of the banking sector's best-informed and longest-standing critics. The government's stated programme is to 'take steps to reduce systemic risk in the banking system', and to 'investigate the complex issue of separating retail and investment banking in a sustainable way'. Also: 'We want the banking system to serve business, not the other way round.' Ten out of ten for intent. Unfortunately, in this area good intentions count for nothing. There is also a large irony looming. Any proposals to reform the banks will make them less profitable – that, indeed, is a central part of what the proposals are supposed to do. But at the moment, thanks to the bailout nationalizations, the British state is sitting on a huge shareholding in two megabanks, Lloyds/HBOS and RBS. One of the few potential windfalls to come the way of the government will arrive when those shares are sold, ideally for shedloads of cash. Oh – so what happens if the bank legislation makes the banks worth less? Our share in the nationalized banks will go down in value, and the windfall will go away. The temptation not to reform the banks will be strong, especially as the sum raised by a sale could be in the vicinity of £160 billion. That would cheer up the public finances no end. Any proposals for reform have this formidable obstacle in their path.

At the moment, the politicians are happy to bash the banks with rhetoric but are finding it hard to effect structural change. That looks likely to stay true, and the bank-bashing will remain popular while bonuses are the way they are. Anyone prone to thinking that investment bankers are geniuses should look at their catastrophically maladroit handling of the bonus issue this year. Goldman Sachs clearly thought they were exercising heroic self-denial by awarding themselves a compensation pool amounting to a mere $16.2 billion. Haiti's total GDP is $11.6 billion, and even before the earthquake one Haitian child in eight dies before its fifth birthday; imagine Goldman turning over half its trough to Haiti in an attempt to change those numbers. Instead they praised their own 'restraint' in only awarding themselves 36 per cent of the bank's revenues in pay, down from the usual figure of 50 per cent. News of the new restrained bonuses came out the same day as Obama's new bank proposals, and must have left some of the Goldmaners wishing they hadn't bothered.

Bank bonuses are a moral and political problem at the best of times. Over the last year, the levels of bonuses across the industry were unconscionable. There are three reasons for that. First, thanks to the special measures currently in place the banks can borrow from their governments at, effectively, zero per cent rates of interest. They can then invest the money at higher rates of interest, 5 to 7 per cent, say. This is a direct transfer of wealth from the taxpayer to the banks, and the only difference between it and an actual, physical licence to print money is that the banks don't have a piece of paper with the words 'Official Licence To Print Money' written across the top. Second, the banks' balance sheets are still clogged with the famous toxic assets. Last year, these assets could not be sold, so they were worth nothing; thanks to the accountancy practice called 'mark-to-market', which insists on assets being recorded at their current value, this left big holes on the banks' balance sheets where the assets should be. The US and UK government launched lavishly expensive schemes designed to restore confidence to the market in these assets (in the US, the scheme offered investors a dollar of value in return for 15 cents of their own money), and the market gradually recovered. So the assets got their value back, and the bank's balance sheets rocketed upwards – again, thanks to the taxpayer. Under these conditions, your deceased Aunt Mavis could have generated record returns, simply by not doing anything. Third, the collapse of competitors has created unprecedentedly favourable conditions for the remaining banks. Hard times are good times for banks that are still in business: winding up, fire sales, mergers, bankruptcies, emergency debt issues, debt-for-equity swaps, are all sources of lucrative fees. The banks' activities in this area have always been cartel-like – their fees are known for being suspiciously similar – but with so little competition around now, it really is a fiesta. All of this is underwritten by the taxpayer's guarantee to keep the banks in business if they rack up another set of huge losses. Under these circumstances, the recent bonuses really are, I use the word again, unconscionable.

All the current proposals are at heart an attempt to make the banks less profitable, and make them seem to be paying back the cost of the bailout. No bank would have survived a systemic collapse; the banks are in business thanks to the taxpayer, and their behaviour must change to reflect that. The banks are going to extravagant lengths to not get this point, which in truth is a fairly simple one. The culture of banking is going to be a difficult thing to change, even after the legislative framework has been altered to reflect new realities. The extent of the cultural change needed can be summed up by a name we haven't been hearing much about, in the aftermath of the credit crunch: Sarbanes–Oxley. That was the US Congress's response to the collapse of Enron. It was a piece of legislation intended to be the biggest crackdown ever on dodgy corporate accounting. The law was enacted in 2002, was loudly complained about by Wall Street and, as we can clearly see from the crash, did nothing of value except make financial institutions pay formal obeisance to certain rules they thought were a waste of time. When it came to protecting the wider public, the world's biggest crackdown on lax accounting had exactly zero effect. That was because it's easier to change the laws around investment banking than the culture inside it.

Although there were glimpses into that banking culture before the crash, the rolling-over-of-the-rock has given a much clearer view of the nasties lurking beneath. Even close observers of Wall Street have been shocked by some of the revelations. The scandals keep coming. It is nearly two years since Lehman Brothers, the US investment bank, imploded, almost taking down the rest of the global financial system. You would have thought that there wasn't much more bad news which could possibly come out of the bank. You would have thought wrong.

A new report by Andrew Valukas, a senior lawyer appointed to examine Lehmans bankruptcy by the US government, astonished the world of money through the detail it revealed about what was going in inside the bank. Valukas and his team examined hundreds of millions of documents, and produced a 2,200-page report which shows the astounding lengths Lehmans went to in hiding its problems.

Going into the crunch, Lehmans wanted to disguise how highly they were leveraged, and how exposed to certain types of assets.

They did this by hiding assets from the balance sheet. Imagine that you want to do the same. You want to shield from your creditors just how deep in hock you are. So what you do is lend some assets – say, £100,000 worth – to a neighbour, in return for the equivalent amount of cash, with a promise that you will buy them back days after your creditors have finished looking over your books. That would be ideal, because your books, pumped with all that cash, would suddenly look a lot healthier. Your creditors (or their accountants) would look at your books, and see that everything's OK. The next day, you'd give back the cash and get back the assets. That would be super-cool, except that, obviously, the loaned stuff still belongs to you and will still appear on your accounts as your assets, so the idea is a non-starter. But wait! What if you lend your assets for slightly less than they are worth – say, you lend $105,000 of assets in return for $100,000 cash. Oh, well that's completely different! That's a 'Repo 105', named after the 105 per cent assets swapped for 100 per cent cash. You can now book the deal as a 'true sale' and make the assets disappear from your books. Your accounts are inspected and appear full of cash. Then you take back the assets again a few days later, return the cash, and everything is peachy. That is what Lehmans did, to make $50 billion disappear from its books. Fifty billion!

Does that sound like a good idea? No? That's what US law firms thought, too. So Lehmans came to the UK and got a favourable opinion from Linklaters, one of the City's biggest and best-respected law firms. Linklaters' response to this news being made public was this: 'the examiner [i.e. Valukas] does not criticize those opinions or suggest that they were wrong or improper. We have reviewed the opinions and are not aware of any facts or circumstances which would justify any criticism.' The really shocking, scandalous, unforgivable thing is that that's true. There is nothing wrong with what happened, by prevailing standards. Lehmans' accountants,

Ernst and Young, also signed off on the deal. It was all according to the rules.

This new Lehmans scandal sums up two of the biggest problems that we – the voting, taxpaying general public – still have with the banks, almost two years after they blew up and we bailed them out. First, the operation of capital markets is international, but the legislative regimes which try to control it are local. Financial institutions are constantly on the alert for ways in which they can exploit differences between jurisdictions – the Repo 105 is merely a glaring public example of something which goes on all the time. Even Sarbanes–Oxley, the all-time monster crackdown on tricky accounting by the world's dominant economic power, turned out to be wholly ineffective. Any action on the banks has to be coordinated and international, or it is worthless. Unfortunately, that coordination is much easier to call for than to achieve. This is one of the main reasons why we have as yet had no effective action to restrain the banks.

The second thing we can learn from Repo 105 is that the culture of investment banking is out of control. This doesn't apply to all bankers; it should be stressed that most bankers are responsible people who do not deliberately take reckless risks. The trouble is that there is a culture in which some bankers not only do take those risks but are incentivised to do so, and that there are just enough of these people to be a real danger to the wider polity. When people are bent on doing things as ingeniously reckless as Repo 105, it's always going to be difficult to draw up rules to save them from themselves. We don't routinely drop dead from eating broken glass in supermarket food, or drop dead from mislabelled medication, or die in plane crashes, because the supermarkets and drug companies and airlines have all internalized the need for safety. They are not ethical titans, but they get it: accidents are bad, because accidents can put them out of business. The banks don't get it: they've had their disastrous accident, and it's worked out very nicely for them, so where is the incentive to change?

The unfortunate fact is becoming unmissably clear: the consequences of the credit crunch are going to fall far more heavily on the innocent than on the guilty. In the medium term, those consequences can be boiled down to a single word: cuts. In the years buliding up to the crash, the government had accumulated a structural deficit, in other words a permanent gap between the money it was raising in tax and the money it was spending. That was going to have to be fixed at some point. The ideal thing would have been for the government to allow the economy to grow without taking a bigger proportion of it, so the proportion of public spending would gradually, and as it were naturally, shrink. Instead what happened was the credit crunch, causing a brutal contraction in the UK economy of 6.9 per cent, the worst and longest decline since the great crash of the 1930s. The upshot of that is that the government's finances did the splits: the tax take collapsed just as welfare spending shot upwards. This meant that instead of a gradual rebalancing, the government is setting out on a brutal process of cutting to restore the public finances.

That means that a lot of people who did nothing wrong and who are entirely blameless in the credit crunch are going to lose their jobs. The current estimate for public-sector job losses to come is 600,000, in addition to the 750,000 (mainly) private-sector workers who have lost their jobs already. The bankers whose behaviour lead to the crash have, by contrast, got away unscathed. I predicted anger; I think the process of expressing that anger has barely begun.

The new coalition government's way of dealing with this was initially surprising. They announced cuts of 25 per cent in all 'unprotected' departments, i.e. all departments other than health and overseas aid. Cuts of these levels are unprecedented and far, far exceed anything Mrs Thatcher ever achieved. Labour had already announced £52 billion of cuts to come by 2013–14; the new coalition added another £30 billion on top. No government has ever achieved anything like that reduction in public spending, and it seems to me clearly impossible that the new one will. To put it in perspective, there have since 1950 been only two periods during which public spending was cut for two years in a row. The coalition is proposing to cut it for six consecutive years. This, it seems to me, beggars belief, and I at first struggled to understand why any government would so publicly set out to do something so plainly impossible. The stated target of shrinking the state below 40 per cent of GDP is yet another point on which the coalition is planning to go far beyond the Thatcher government. Why? Who voted for that?

The explanation, I think, is that the coalition – which in practice means the Tory party – is attempting to create what political wonks call an 'inflection point'. They want to make a fundamental change of direction in British politics. There have been two of these in the last decades, the first of them Margaret Thatcher's election in 1979 and the second Tony Blair's in 1997. The election of 2010 wasn't an inflection point, not least because it didn't produce a majority government. So the Tories put into effect what was obviously a plan to create their own inflection point through George Osborne's emergency Budget. The idea, I think, is to change the British political ecology. Public-sector workers, in particular, are supposed to be scared into malleability. The idea is that instead of being grumpy that some of them have lost their jobs, everybody who is still in work will be grateful, relieved, and suitably cowed. It will be a change in direction for the British state and will give a clear way forward for the Conservative Party, as it returns to its traditional identity as the party of the smaller state. 'If they can't do it now,' a Tory friend of mine said, 'when can they do it?' In other words, there will never be a more opportune moment for the party to set out its stall to cut spending. Hence the tearing-off-the-arm eagerness to seize the opportunity.

So the politics of this makes a depressing kind of sense, from a right-wing perspective. What is much less clear is whether the economics of the cutting makes as much sense. Cuts were coming whoever won the election, and the £52 billion of Labour cuts would have been agonizingly painful. But the extra cuts seem to raise to dangerous levels the possibility that the contraction will trigger another round of recession. Bear in mind that at the June meeting in Canada of the G20 – that's the world's twenty biggest economies – a general commitment was made to halve all deficits by 2013, and to 'stabilize' debt by 2016.* That means that every government in the world is simultaneously trying to tighten their belts. So where is the demand going to come from to restart growth in these big economies? If everyone is cutting up their credit cards, how will growth occur? It's supposed to be a 'production-led' recovery, not like the consumer-led boom we've just lived through. Fair enough, as an idea, but production-led recoveries still need someone to buy the stuff you produce. In this vision of a global war on debt and deficit, it's not clear who the prospective buyers are.

Some observers have said that the prospect of a global austerity drive reminds them of the mistakes which turned the Great Crash of 1929 into the Great Depression of the 1930s. Governments, instead of stimulating their economies with spending designed to create employment – the policies advocated by Keynes – instead tried to

---

* A word about the distinction between deficit and debt. The best description of a deficit is the one given by Dickens's character Mr Micawber. 'Annual income twenty pounds, annual expenditure nineteen nineteen six, result happiness. Annual income twenty pounds, annual expenditure twenty pounds ought and six, result misery.' When your annual income is less than your expenditure, you have an annual deficit. Some commentators on the right have argued that the word deficit should be replaced by the more politically charged word 'overspend'. The principle is the same for ordinary households as it is for governments. In the case of Micawber's example, the deficit is sixpence; in the case of the UK, it is £159.2 billion – but the principle is the same. As for the debt, it's nothing more than the sum total of all the deficits accumulated over time. In household terms it's like an overdraft that you've spent years and years building up by not living within your means.

belt-tighten their way out of trouble, by behaving as if they were households with a cash-flow problem. But the analogy between household and whole economies is imperfect, as subsequent events clearly showed. A coordinated global slowdown in government spending might turn out to be exactly the last thing we all need.

Even if we do, slowly and painfully, begin to inch out of the crisis – which is probably the likeliest outcome – there are still hard times ahead. It's difficult to believe this, given what we've been through and what we know about what went wrong, but the biggest risks are still those presented by the banks.

Put all these factors together, and it looks as if governments are not going to be able to fix the banks. That doesn't mean that nothing is going to be done. There is a glimmer of, if not quite hope, then of the prospect of action which might help to reduce the risks posed by banks to the wider polity. The hope does not come in the form of glamorous or decisive stand-taking. Instead it comes in the form of a group of (mainly) middle-aged white men sitting in a committee room in Switzerland. They are meeting in Basel, and they are the Bank of International Settlement (BIS), working on the regulations for what is known as Basel III.

The BIS has already played a part in this story, and so has the town where it meets. The BIS is in effect the central bank of central banks, the body which sets the rules by which the world's banks are allowed to operate. Basel I was the first set of such international rules. Because new forms of financial instruments kept being invented, Basel II came along to control and legislate the trade in derivatives, with such success that the global financial system blew up. The Basel II rules were pure of heart, but they were written with the assumption that derivatives are an effective way of dispersing, and therefore managing, risk; they didn't allow for the kinds of systematic misuse that caused the credit crunch. It's tough to blame rule-makers for the behaviour of people who are certain they know better than the rules, and go to great, ingenious lengths to circumvent them. Basel III will have to write regulations which make more allowance than ever before for the subset of bankers who spend their energies on trying to get round the regulations. That's an easy thing to wish for and a hard thing to do. It is also critical that the action be coordinated and international, because otherwise the banks will blackmail governments with the threat of taking their tax-generating activities elsewhere, and seek to negotiate safe havens where they can carry on business in the old unregulated way.

In the absence of coordinated international action, and the presence of the global banks and the global risks, Basel III is going to have to do to the banks what the Lilliputians did to Gulliver: tie them down with lots of little ropes. Much of this is deeply unerotic stuff about things such as capital reserves, liquidity, and leverage ratios, all of them converging on the theme of (simply put) making the banks have more cash in hand to help them in a crisis. There is a model for this: Canada. The 'friendly giant to the north' (that was the winning entry in a competition to decide the world's least-interesting magazine coverline) was the only one of the G8 countries not to have a bank bailout, and not to go into recession. That was in large part because of its much tighter banking laws, in particular its demands for higher levels of capital reserves. In essence, the Canadian example saw the bankers being protected from themselves by the regulators' reluctance to deregulate. This has been something of a pattern in Canadian history. Canada's banks were notoriously rocky through the latter part of the nineteenth century and in the early part of the twentieth, and it was that very instability which lead to a stricter legislative regime and, therefore, to much sounder banks. Since 1923, there have been only two bank failures in Canada. In the US, there have been 17,000. Sometimes, you do the right thing because you tried the wrong thing, had a nasty shock, and changed tack. During the great leverage fiesta of the boom, only Canada didn't join the leverage party: while the other leverage ratios were in the 30 to 1 range and often much higher, Canada's banks have an average leverage ratio of 18 to 1. That in essence is the reason why they didn't blow up and take the rest of the economy with them.

All these technical rules add up to the first set of Lilliputian ropes. We need more – we need things we are unlikely to get. In the US, the Glass–Steagall act, separating investment banking (the casino where the banks bet against each other, and against us) from retail banking (the piggybank where we keep our money), was only abolished in 1999. Banking was manifestly safer before abolition – manifestly less profitable too, which from the point of view of the wider polity is a good thing. It is hard to re-regulate, and to make fish out of fish soup. But that is what we should be trying to do. The break-up of our huge banks into separate components is not a panacea, and, as critics are quick to point out, several 'narrow banks' (i.e. narrowly defined banks of the desirable type) have failed, both historically and in the current crisis. However, the recent narrow-bank failures, such as that of the Dunfermline Building Society, took place in a context of systemic collapse caused by the status quo; that kind of systemic collapse, deriving most of its momentum from a general crisis of confidence, would be less likely if consumer deposits were less at risk.

Alistair Darling, the Chancellor in the UK during the crisis, has an interesting line on this. He argues that the problem with the banks is not size per se, but interconnectedness – the way in which the banks are so deeply interwoven in each other's business, and in their own different strands of business too. He's right about the interconnectedness, but this is an 'and' rather than a 'but': the banks are both too big and too interconnected. I would love to have a snake-oil-type solution to the question of inter-connectedness, but I don't. If somebody else does, I haven't heard about it. Big, big problem.

The political reality, however, is that the banks will not be broken up and the questions of Too Big To Fail and Too Interconnected To Fail, TBTF and TITF, will not be solved. That means that while Basel III and the proposals enacted by Congress and Parliament and the EU will do something to help, certain crucial fundamental problems will remain. The banks are a juggernaut. The schemes being floated at the moment propose to add a really good new set of brakes to the juggernaut, and also to fix a device which sets a maximum speed limit on the juggernaut, and maybe also new rules about drug and alcohol testing for the driver of the juggernaut. But the juggernaut is still a juggernaut. The safety measures are all good things, but the central point about this huge mechanism is that when something goes sufficiently wrong, it will crush everything in its path.

The sad truth is that the real fix is going to have to wait until after the next crash. As the economist Paul Romer once said, 'a crisis is a terrible thing to waste' – but the opportunity brought by this crisis has been wasted. The risks posed by the financial sector remain intact, and in my view are likely to lead to another systemic crisis at some point within the next few years. I won't pretend to know whether that means five years or ten, and I won't pretend to know the likely cause. (Though, because I've been asked a few times, I will name three possible ones: a panic in the Eurozone, caused by defaults and/or a country dropping out of the currency; a meltdown caused by automated stock trading, which now accounts for over 60 per cent of all activity on the markets; a bubble bursting in China.) When that happens, there will be a period of extraordinary danger, greatly exceeding the crash of 2008, because next time it will be close to impossible for the politicians to help the banks stay solvent. The general ill-will towards the bankers will bring a very high cost the next time the global system needs rescuing, and it may be only then that the stupidity of the banks, in allowing themselves to become so unpopular, will be made fully apparent. Without the nationalizations of 2008, the crash would have become not a recession but a full-blown depression. Next time, if it is politically impossible to nationalize, a depression could well be what we get.

It is then that the work which should be happening now will finally take place. That work involves starting with a blank state and asking what banks are for, and what social purpose they serve. The casino aspect of the banks could have been separated off and allowed to continue if real reform had taken place after the credit crunch, but I would imagine that after the next crash, the mood against them will be so strong that they will be abolished and a lot of their activities made illegal. Banks are necessary to take deposits and lend money and create liquidity for individuals and businesses, and that is not just useful but essential work in a modern society, and it's good and honourable work too – but it's a long way away from a lot of what is happening today. After the crash, we finally get round to designing legislation which ensures that they stick to that purpose, and serve us. So I'm confident that we'll get to where we need to be, even if I also think we aren't going to enjoy the process of getting there. The credit crunch will go down in history as one of the biggest missed opportunities the developed world has ever known.

Acknowledgements

Mary-Kay Wilmers was the onlie begetter of this book. It was her idea for me to write about banks in the *London Review of Books* which got me started, and her subsequent suggestions for follow-up pieces which kept me going. This book wouldn't exist without her and the *LRB*. I'm grateful to her and her colleagues for all their editorial work.

Henry Finder at the *New Yorker* has been his usual distinctive mixture of brilliance and calm. I have been helped immeasurably by his commissioning and his editorial advice.

I am grateful to Lidija Hass for her invaluable sleuthing help.

I would particularly like to thank Sara Stefánsdottír for her assistance in Reykjavik. In Iceland I would also like to thank Rakel Stefánsdottír, Valgarður Bragason, Snorri Jónnson, Kári Sturluson, Helga Vala and Daði Ingólfsson.

In Baltimore, I'd especially like to thank Steve Hunter and Jean Marbella for their hospitality and advice. I'd also like to thank Ann LoLordo, Fern Shen, Lisa Evans, Mary Waldrow, Tony Damazio and Philip Robinson.

At Penguin, I would like to thank Helen Conford, Richard Duguid and Peter James; at Simon and Schuster, I would like to thank Sarah Hochman; at A. P. Watt, I would like to thank Caradoc King and his colleagues.

I would also like to thank Fram Dinshaw, Rhomaios Ram, Nicholas Doisy and Richard Smith.

Earlier versions of passages in this book appeared in the *London Review of Books*, the *New Yorker* and the *Guardian*.

I would like to thank *Atlantic* for permission to quote from Simon Johnson's article 'The Quiet Coup' and the Nobel Foundation for permission to quote Daniel Kahneman's autobiography.

Sources

This is a list both of sources and of suggestions for further reading. These are all books from which I have learnt a great deal.

Liaquat Ahamed, *Lords of Finance: The Bankers Who Broke the World*, New York, 2009

George Akerlof and Robert Shiller, *Animal Spirits: How Human Psychology Drives the Economy, and Why It Matters for Global Capitalism*, Princeton, 2009

Peter Bernstein, *Against the Gods: The Remarkable Story of Risk*, New York, 1998

Richard Bitner, *Confessions of a Subprime Lender: An Insider's Tale of Greed, Fraud and Ignorance*, New York, 2008

James Buchan, *Frozen Desire*, London, 1996

Warren Buffett, *The Essays of Warren Buffett: Lessons for Corporate America*, ed. Lawrence A. Cunningham, 1998

Philip Coggan, *The Money Machine: How the City Works*, London, 2002

William D. Cohan, *House of Cards: How Wall Street's Gamblers Broke Capitalism*, London, 2009

David Einhorn, *Fooling Some of the People All of the Time*, Hoboken, 2008

Niall Ferguson, *The Ascent of Money: A Financial History of the World*, London, 2008

John Maynard Keynes, *The General Theory of Employment, Interest, and Money*, Cambridge, 2008

Charles P. Kindleberger and Robert Z. Aliber, *Manias, Panics and Crashes: A History of Financial Crises*, 5th edn, New York, 2005

David Kynaston, *The City of London*, vol. 4: *A Club No More, 1945–2000*, London, 2001

Michael Lewis, *Liar's Poker*, London, 1990.

Roger Lowenstein, *When Genius Failed: The Rise and Fall of Long-Term Capital Management*, London, 2000

Charles R. Morris, *The Trillion Dollar Meltdown: Easy Money, High Rollers, and the Great Credit Crash*, New York, 2008

Frank Partnoy, *F.I.A.S.C.O.: Blood in the Water on Wall Street*, London, 2009

John Allen Paulos, *Innumeracy: Mathematical Illiteracy and its Consequences*, London, 1990

Richard A. Posner, *A Failure of Capitalism*, Cambridge, Mass., 2009

Adam Smith, *The Money Game*, New York, 1977

Nassim Nicholas Taleb, *Fooled by Randomness: The Hidden Role of Chance in Life and the Markets*, London, 2004

Gillian Tett, *Fool's Gold: How the Bold Dream of a Small Tribe at J. P. Morgan was Corrupted by Wall Street Greed and Unleashed a Catastrophe*, London, 2009

I have also been helped by the work of a number of journalists and commentators. I'd say, as an outsider to economics, that the standard of reporting and writing and commentary in this milieu is bracingly high. I have learnt an enormous amount from the work of Evan Davis, Stephanie Flanders and Robert Peston at the BBC – Flanders and Peston have high-quality blogs, in addition to their old-media work; Philip Coggan, John Kay, Gillian Tett and Martin Wolf at the *Financial Times*; Larry Elliott at the *Guardian*; and although as a Nobel prize-winner he is too grand to count, Paul Krugman at the *New York Times* is also a superb journalist and commentator.

There is a great deal of lively economic commentary on the internet, and the best clearing house for the debates is the superb blog run by Tyler Cowen and Alex Tabarrok, Marginal Revolution, at http://www.marginalrevolution.com/.

Notes

1 You can follow progress towards the goals at http://ddp-ext.world bank.org/ext/GMIS/home.do?siteId=2. The news is less bad than one might expect, providing you can swallow the fact that nothing is improving in sub-Saharan Africa.

2 Paulos, *Innumeracy*, p. x.

3 Ben Funnel, *Financial Times*, 1 July 2009, quoting research by Société Générale.

4 See http://www.economics.harvard.edu/pub/hier/2005/HIER 2068.pdf.

5 Paul Krugman, 'All the President's Zombies', *New York Times*, 23 August 2009.

6 http://www.theatlantic.com/doc/200905/imf-advice.

7 Kynaston, *The City of London*, vol. 4: *A Club No More*, p. 791.

8 For the gory detail, see John Kay at http://www.johnkay.com/ politics/614.

9 From a research paper by Daniel Gros and Stefano Micosi at www. vox.org, an outstanding resource for economic research and debate: http://www.voxeu.org/index.php?q=node/1669.

10 Robert Peston, www.bbc.co.uk/blogs/thereporters/robertpeston/ 2009/07/why_bankers_arent_worth_it.html.

11 Morris, *Trillion Dollar Meltdown*, p. xii

12 http://www.ft.com/cms/s/2/6ac06592-6ce0-11de-af56-00144feabdc0. html.

13 The best version of this story is told in Peter Bernstein's *Against the Gods*.

14 Taleb, *Fooled by Randomness*, p. 29.

15 My account here and in the next chapter draws heavily on Gillian

Tett's superb book *Fool's Gold*. It needs a little basic financial knowledge to follow her account, but if you have that, *Fool's Gold* reads like a thriller – written by someone who not only was following the story, but predicted its outcome.

16 I'm indebted to a piece by Steven Malanga in City Journal: http://www.city-journal.org/2009/19_2_homeownership.html.

17 There is an excellent discussion of Enron and the impact of frauds in George Akerlof and Robert Shiller's *Animal Spirits*.

18 Again, I'm deeply indebted to Gillian Tett's account of the CDO industry in *Fool's Gold*.

19 *A Failure of Capitalism*, 2009. I don't agree with all of Posner's analysis but it is superbly clear and his book is well worth reading as an account of the financial crisis being based on what one might call rational mistakes.

20 Tett, *Fool's Gold*, p. 182.

21 Bitner, *Confessions of a Subprime Lender* has been a great help to me in understanding the bad lending which underlay the crisis.

22 'Bank accused of pushing mortgage deals on Blacks', *New York Times*, 6 June 2009.

23 'US seeks culprits for sub-prime', *Financial Times*, 8 August 2007.

24 Text copyright © The Nobel Foundation 2002.

25 This example is from the best account of the subject, Nassim Nicholas Taleb's *Fooled by Randomness*. I have drawn on Taleb's ideas in this chapter.

26 From 'The Objectivist Ethics' in Rand's *The Virtue of Selfishness*, New York, 1964, p. 37.

27 Greenspan's testimony can be read in full at http://oversight.house.gov/documents/20081023100438.pdf.

28 Again, I'm indebted to Peter Bernstein's *Against the Gods*.

29 The speech can be read at http://www.terry.uga.edu/sanford/speeches/life_value.html.

30 This and the following exchange with Philippe Jorion are taken

from http://www.derivativesstrategy.com/magazine/archive/1997/ 1296qa.asp. and www.derivativesstrategy.com/magazine/archive/ 1997/0497/fea2.asp.

31 I am indebted to Felix Salmon's superb article 'Recipe for Disaster: The Formula that Killed Wall Street', *Wired*, 23 February 2009.

32 Lowenstein, *When Genius Failed*, p. 72

33 See Kevin Dowd, John Cotter, Chris Humphrey and Margaret Woods, 'How unlucky is 25-sigma?' at http://www.ucd.ie/bank ingfinance/docs/wp/WP-08-04.pdf.

34 From Greenspan's testimony to the House committee on oversight and reform, op. cit. (see above, note 2).

35 See www.gmwealthadvisors.com/files/2007%20Fall%20Newsletter. pdf.

36 From Bernstein, *Against the Gods*, p. 290.

37 Posner, *A Failure of Capitalism*, p. 281.

38 I'm indebted to Charles R. Morris's *Trillion Dollar Meltdown*.

39 There's a chilling account of it in his book *The Ascent of Money*, Chapter 6.

40 http://www.fsa.gov.uk/pubs/other/turner_review.pdf.

41 Posner, *A Failure of Capitalism*, p. xii.

42 Quoted by Tett in *Fool's Gold*, p. 97.

43 Simon Johnson, 'The Quiet Coup', *Atlantic*, May 2009.

44 Paul Krugman, 'Out of the Shadows', *New York Times*, 18 June 2009.

45 *Financial Times*, 12 June 2009.

46 You can, amazingly, actually listen to this meeting in its entirety, at the *New York Times* website.

47 'The Reckoning', *New York Times*, 3 October 2008.

48 Michael Lewis and David Einhorn, 'The End of the Financial World as We Know It', *New York Times*, 4 January 2009.

49 'AIG trail leads to London casino', *Daily Telegraph*, 18 October 2008.

50 Quoted by Bitner, in *Confessions of a Subprime Lender*, p. 117.

51 Ibid., p. 112.

52 Morris, *Trillion Dollar Meltdown*, p. 77.
53 *Wall Street Journal*, 31 March 2009.
54 http://www.ritholtz.com/blog/2008/11/big-bailouts-bigger-bucks/.

Index